CREATING A
SUCCESS ENVIRONMENT

CREATING A

SUCCESS

$$SE = (I \times O$$

KEITH

ENVIRONMENT

x H x W) Y

DeGREEN

Library of Congress Catalog Card Number: 79-64210

ISBN 0-934174-02-4

First U.S. Printing: 1979
Second U.S. Printing: July, 1979

Manufactured in the United States of America

Summit Enterprises Inc.
3928 East Corrine Drive
Phoenix, Arizona 85032

Distributed by
Hawthorn Books, Inc.

Keith Paul,

This one's for you.

Love,

Dad

Acknowledgments

Rita Bartolomeo was more than the secretary of this project. She was its commander-in-chief. Without her, this book would not have been done on time or as well.

Stan Smith, professor of Editing at Arizona State University, did more than merely edit. Because of his talented research, many references and statistics were refined and the overall professionalism of the book was greatly enhanced.

Gloria Autrey worked around the clock to do an excellent job designing and composing the book.

Dick Varney is the talented young artist who designed the jacket and who created the outstanding drawings inside the book. You may contact him through Summit Enterprises Inc.

Hundreds of authors and speakers have profoundly influenced the content of these pages. Some of them are mentioned in the text; however, they are but a few of the many to whom I am deeply indebted for their encouragement and ideas.

But it is my wife, Ann, who deserves special thanks. For more than a year she steadfastly believed that the writing and publishing of this book was possible.

And because of her, it was.

Contents

SE

I

O

H

W

Y

Foreword

Just imagine:

A simple mathematical formula that measures success. A system that helps us determine how much of our potential we are using.

Success:

It has been defined as the progressive realization of a worthy ideal. The full utilization of our talent is such an ideal.

How are we doing?

The Success Environment Formula tells us.

Not a final answer. Not a panacea. But a tool — an important device that helps us use the gifts we have, whatever they may be.

Success mentally. Success physically. Success at home. Success at work.

Creating a *total* success environment. Hundreds of ideas. Useful. Practical. Understandable. Distilled to manageable units.

That's what this book is about.

More importantly, it's about you. Your talent. Your gifts. Your potential. Your life.

A simple mathematical formula that measures success.

Just imagine . . . .

May ye always be chasing rainbows.

May your mind be sharp as the stars.

May the hope of the future shine brightly,

And ye truly become what ye are.

SE

I

Wandering Through The "How To Succeed" Jungle

If we can logically discern the different approaches of those who would chart our course to success, and if we can logically separate the shortcomings and benefits of each approach, then it is just as possible to logically combine the best aspects of all.

Calvin Cautious was on safari in Botswana.

Too cheap to invest in an English-speaking guide, he decided to rely upon the directions of the villagers each day as he left the capital city of Gaborone. Calvin soon discovered that the natives in each village spoke a different language. Undaunted, he determined that he could sort out the conflicting languages and obtain the directions he desired.

By the end of the first day, after stopping at several villages for help, he found himself back on the outskirts of Gaborone, where he had started. Each day Calvin would leave the capital city and head into the jungle, always in a slightly different direction. Each day he would encounter several villages, in each of which the natives spoke a different language. And by each day's end, he would find himself back at the outskirts of Gaborone.

Finally, after Calvin spent several days traveling in circles, an English-speaking resident of the city approached him and asked, "What have you learned thus far from your safari?"

Calvin, without hesitation, responded, "I have learned that all the natives surrounding the city are lost."

Those of us who have entered the "how to succeed" jungle from

3

the capital city of our ego have often repeated the sentiments expressed by Calvin. It seems there is an abundance of advice out there: advice that frequently leads us back to where we began. While wandering through the "how to succeed" jungle, we, like Calvin, frequently encounter different languages. As we find ourselves back where we started, we frequently tend to blame the substance of the advice we received, rather than our interpretation of it.

There are at least three separate languages in the "how to succeed" jungle—languages which on their face seem to conflict. But is it the advice that is wrong, or is it our interpretation of it?

Where Is All This Advice Coming From?

There are books on how to live alone. There are books on how to live together. There are books on happy marriages. There are books on happy divorces. There are books on how to communicate with our words. There are books on how to communicate with our bodies. There are books that tell us we can succeed by helping others, and there are other books that tell us we can succeed through intimidation.

Some books tell us it's how we look inside that will make us successful. Other books tell us it's how we look outside that counts. And then there are those books in which no one is too sure what they're saying, including the people who wrote them.

Is it any wonder that we frequently find ourselves wandering in circles through the jungle of this advice? And who are these self-appointed experts on success? Some seem barely qualified to manage their own lives, let alone the lives of others. Others seem eminently well equipped to lend advice, while others who seem academically qualified speak in tongues that no one can understand.

The "Dudley-Do-Rights"

The Dudley-Do-Rights speak the language of Positive. Their message is as old as the Bible and as simple as the Golden Rule. For years they have propounded the simple message that if we wish to have more of the good things of life, then we must treat ourselves and others with more kindness and love than in the past.

The language of Positive revolves around such words and phrases as *self-esteem, self-determination, respect, purposefulness, kindness, hard work,* and *love.*

Some of the books written in Positive have been nothing short of masterful. Dr. Norman Vincent Peale, in his *The Power of Positive Thinking,* and Dale Carnegie, in his *How to Win Friends and Influence People,* established years ago a standard of positiveness and style that others since have only been able to attempt to imitate.

Still other books written in the language of Positive have bordered on the absurd in their simplistic and utopian approach. Somewhere between these two extremes falls the great mass of self-help volumes. But whether simplistic or masterful, the language of Positive emphasizes every man's ability to achieve what he wants if he simply helps enough other people achieve what they want.

The "Hard Chargers"

The Hard Chargers speak the language of Negative. While such books have fallen into vogue only in recent years, probably as a reaction to the more simplistic books written in the language of Positive, their message is at least as old as Machiavelli. It is based upon the premise that through certain affirmative acts we can manipulate others into thinking, feeling, and doing as we wish. Thus we can catapult ourselves to the level of success we desire.

Two of the more successful language of Negative authors are Michael Korda, who wrote *Power: How to Get It, How to Use It,* and *Success: How Every Man and Woman Can Achieve It;* and Robert Ringer, who wrote *Winning Through Intimidation,* and *Looking Out for Number One.*

Others, perhaps less Machiavellian but no less pragmatic, have emphasized that success may be attained through the clothes we wear or the way we position our bodies during negotiations. As might be expected, the language of Negative focuses less upon the rightness or wrongness of any particular approach than upon the pragmatic results thereof. It deals in such words and phrases as *intimidation, power struggle, gamesmanship, one-up-manship, authority, status,* and *control.* But whatever its combination of words, the language of Negative approach remains the same: pragmatism and manipulation.

The "Experts"

The Experts speak the language of Academic. This language has been with us since man first felt the need to over-complicate something. The language employs such terms as are necessary to re-define concepts that were once already perfectly clear.

Its emphasis is upon translating new ideas (and, for that matter, many old ideas as well) into terms that no one can understand. The language of Academic presumes that if one can present his opinion with enough multi-syllabic words,then he will be presumed to know what he is talking about. The words themselves act as a defensive barrier between the persons to whom they are directed and a close scrutiny of the substantive ideas they are intended to express.

The language of Academic is founded upon a words-gamesmanship which permits words themselves rather than the ideas that underlie them to become the primary focus of attention. Academic is to language what rabbits are to reproduction: prolific. Thus, when one book is written in Academic, it frequently spawns several other books by other authors who spend their time discussing not the substantive ideas of the first, but rather questioning the words used therein.

Academic is the language of accumulated data: the selective use of mountainous statistics to confirm already preconceived notions. No doubt the most noteworthy writer of Academic was Freud. His books are generally a monument to man's talent for verbosity. It is only in recent years that enough of his self-imposed language barrier has been stripped away so that other Experts have been able to seriously challenge the substance of what he said.

Refreshing hybrids of the language of Academic in the field of self-help are the works of Maxwell Maltz, most noted for his book, *Psycho-Cybernetics,* and Eric Berne, with his work in Transactional Analysis and his book, *I'm O.K., You're O.K.* . Both men represent a classic attempt by those previously embroiled in the language of Academic to cross the language barrier into the real world.

Behind them, though, within the language of Academic, lurk scores of technicians who have yet to realize that the purpose of a book is not to serve as an inch-thick insulator of an author's ego, but rather to convey ideas in such a manner that they are meaningful to the reader.

They're All Wrong — Right?

You don't have to be much of a cynic to find the obvious shortcomings in all three languages. It's understandable that we acquire a healthy skepticism of the entire "how to succeed" jungle while pointing to the obvious inconsistency of the languages that we find within it.

But knowing vaguely that something is wrong is not nearly as helpful as understanding *specifically* what is wrong. For only by exploring the specifics can we analyze and isolate the shortcomings of each language and discover what is left within each that may be of value to us.

You are sitting in an office on the 15th floor of a large building. You smell smoke. You have a right to be worried, because you have just discovered that something is generally wrong. But it's not until you have obtained more specific information on exactly where the fire is that you can do anything about it. Indeed, your very ability to escape is dependent upon your ability to: isolate the problem, avoid it in order to effect your escape and (hopefully), ultimately to extinguish it.

Walking through the "how to succeed" jungle, many of us have smelled smoke. But it's not until we can isolate the flames that we can begin to solve our problems and protect ourselves. Let's look at each of the three languages of success so that we can find — and extinguish — the fires within each.

Positive Thinking As A Health Hazard

There is an old, old story about the optimist who fell off the top of a tall building. As he passed each floor on the way down, the people inside could hear him say, "I'm O.K. so far!"

The optimist is typical of the many people who have OD'd on positive thinking: people who believe that just by smiling a lot they'll get rich.

There's a difference between being positive and being unrealistically positive. The positive person who is earning $16,000 per year may finance the purchase of a new Chevrolet because he is confident enough that he'll be able to afford the payments. An unrealistically positive person earning the same amount of money may run out to purchase a new Cadillac and live to regret it. I have nothing against Cadillacs, but I have everything against bankruptcy.

The trouble with having just a positive attitude is that it doesn't really prepare us for the setbacks we will inevitably encounter as we strive to reach our goals. Instead, we get all hyped up, ready to roll, believing we're invincible, and WHAMO, we suffer a setback.

Take the case of the young recruit who was going through basic training in the Marines. Of course, the Marines convince recruits that they are invincible. On this particular occasion they were playing war games. Instead of issuing the recruit an M-16 with blank ammunition, they told him to use his finger and say, "Bang-bang! Bang-bang!"

The recruit went into the field. Suddenly he was attacked by a whole platoon. They charged right at him. He was a good recruit so he pointed his finger and shouted, "Bang-bang! Bang-bang!" And the men attacking him started dropping like flies!

He fired again, "Bang-bang! Bang-bang!" and a couple more of them went down! By now the recruit had started believing he really was invincible. In fact, he converted his fingers into an automatic: "Pow-pow-pow-pow!" he shouted.

Then he saw the drill instructor from the other platoon coming at him. He fired at him: "Pow-pow-pow-pow!" Nothing happened. The D.I. kept coming toward him. He fired again: "Pow-pow-pow-pow!" Still nothing happened. By this time the D.I. was nearly on top of him!

The recruit let loose with one more great burst from his fingers: "Pow - pow - pow - pow - pow - pow - pow - POW!" No help! The D.I. walked up and with one punch — WHAMO — leveled him and kept right on walking.

And as the recruit lay there he could hear the D.I. saying over and over again, "Tankity-tankity-tank! Tankity-tankity-tank!"

This planet would be a very depressing place if deep down inside we all didn't genuinely believe that we are capable of accomplishing just about anything we decide to accomplish. But, as in the case of the Marine recruit, it can be hazardous — indeed fatal — to permit that belief to cause us to react in a hasty, irrational, or immature fashion; expecting results to fall into our lap, rather than earning them each step of the way.

The greatest hazard associated with the language of Positive is that it too frequently becomes a catalyst for immature and unrealistic expectations.

Just as there is nothing as empty as an unhappy individual who has acquired all the accoutrements of success, so too is there nothing more shallow than a smiling under-achiever who believes it's only a question of time before the world beats a path to his door.

Success Is Not A Tie

The fundamental objection most of us have to concepts such as those expressed in *Winning Through Intimidation* is that none of us enjoys being the "intimidatee."

"We can succeed through the proper application of intimidation, power and deception."

What's wrong with the above statement? First, it's internally inconsistent. While entire books could be devoted exclusively to the definition of success, certainly any reasonable definition of that word must include self-esteem, peace of mind, and the security that comes from the genuine affection of others. While many people have—and will no doubt continue—to earn large sums of money through the misapplication of intimidation, power and deception, to say that those individuals are therefore successful is to deny the more important elements of the word "success."

Furthermore, it's naive to believe that once great wealth is acquired, a person can then turn his attention toward rebuilding his self-image. Moreover, if we convince ourselves that it's permissible on a day-to-day basis to be selfish, calculating and greedy, then we must necessarily view those with whom we come in contact as being similarly inclined, simply in order to protect our perverted sense of direction.

Our daily existence becomes a contest of imaginative decep-
tions: us against the world. To "win" at such a game, we would
have to lose all the elements of love, honesty and concern that
make the game worth playing in the first place. What begins as a
game becomes a life-style; what becomes a life-style becomes a
thought process; and what once we used only to cause others to
take us more seriously, we now take seriously. If you honestly
believe that you can get promoted just because of the tie you
wear, then you might as well worship a pair of Florsheim shoes.

If, as is frequently the case, it is possible to close that big deal
through the use of intimidation and deception, then such devices
may seem all the more attractive to us. The irony is that getting
the "intimidatee" of that transaction to do business with us a second time will be about as easy as swimming the English Channel
in a pair of lead boots. What have we gained if, in the name of the
quick kill, we alienate the very people upon whom we must rely to
earn an existence over the long run?

Then there is the issue of "pay-back." There is an old saying
that advises, "Don't get mad, get even." That "chump" who was
easily deceived the first time around may have a few ideas of his
own the next time you encounter each other. And this time it may
be his turn.

The Negative approach will cause us to spend a good portion of
the rest of our lives looking over our shoulder.

Academia Strikes Again

It's ironic that an entire book could be devoted to what's wrong
with the language of Academic. It's ironic because what's wrong
is that academics write too many books about nothing to begin
with.

I went to school for 19 years to earn my law degree, and
wouldn't trade that experience for all the tea in China. But during
that period I lost count of the books I read that were about other
books.

Somewhere at the very beginning of the history of the language
of Academic there must have been the original sin: the first book
written which claimed to be a scholarly treatment of a subject of
consequence. From there, other scholarly books came into

existence at a geometrically progressing rate. And when the substantive matter which was the initial subject of discussion lost its appeal, the scholars proceeded undeterred. Since they had all read each others' books, it was only natural that they should start writing in response to what they read. This proceeded at a geometric rate as well with books written about books, theories about theories, treatises about treatises, *ad nauseum*, until reality became an oblique reference, a passing footnote used sparingly and selectively only to support those theories that the author expounded, or to challenge those theories with which he disagreed.

In this environment, the creation of a specialized language was only natural. Through the creation of Academic, the scholars were able to insulate themselves from the ultimate objection to their work: "So what does that have to do with anything?"

The insulating devices used in the language of Academic are fascinating. Perhaps the most interesting is the footnote.[1] Typically, a scholar will be midway through a particularly uninteresting paragraph. While reviewing his material, the author realizes he had better add something to liven up the text. Many writers would have sense enough to insert an anecdote to illustrate their point. But the user of pure Academic instead inserts a footnote.

The footnote serves three purposes: first, it helps to persuade the reader that the author has read at least one other book during his career. Second, it helps avoid cries of plagiarism from the author upon whose book the current book is based. Finally, it allows the author to imply that if the reader doesn't understand what the author is writing about, it is only because he hasn't read all the books that the author has read.

The result can be circuitous. The most classic examples of circuity can be found in law. An attorney researching a point of law in what is known as a secondary source of material will find reference to a case in support of the proposition in a footnoted portion of the material. He will then read the footnoted case, only to find that, in support of its conclusions, it recites by footnote the

---

1. See footnote following page.

secondary source which cited it.[2]

A well written book in the language of Academic will be filled with footnotes which refer to prior works. Its primary purpose is to cause the reader — usually an unsuspecting student who regrets signing up for the course in the first place — to fall to his knees in awe of the author's ability to read and remember all the books he cited.

Of course, professors are particularly fond of assigning such books to their students because they, by implication, are assumed to have read the books mentioned in the book assigned. It is worth noting, although it could go without saying, that just because an author lists an extensive bibliography, it doesn't mean that he has read the books in the bibliography. Even if he has read them, it certainly doesn't mean that he understood them.

So on it goes in the language of Academic, with books propagating themselves at an astounding rate, to the point where, in many fields today, it is literally physically impossible for someone just entering a field to read all of the books in that area during his lifetime.

So what's wrong with the language of Academic as it relates to psychology, self-image, and self-help? What's wrong is that no one — and I'm convinced with increasing frequency that this includes even the authors themselves — seems to understand what those who use it are saying.

They're All Right — Wrong?

You are digging for gold, and after weeks of fruitless effort you finally come upon a vein which holds promise. At first you are elated, and begin to fervidly dig at, and examine, your find. You find large quantities of the genuine thing, but in addition you find quantities of pyrite, or "fool's gold," mixed in. Your enthusiasm is dampened, but you quickly realize that despite the existence of the pyrite, there is still an abundance of gold to be found.

The three languages of success seem similar to that vein of gold. While many of the nuggets found therein are worthless, there is still enough real gold to make mining the vein worthwhile.

2. See footnote preceeding page.

Our challenge as prospectors is to sort out the pyrite from the stuff that is of real value to us.

The fact that each of the three languages of success has its own version of pyrite should not keep us from mining the rest. In our search for sound advice, we must be a little like the young boy who went to visit his uncle on the farm. As soon as he got out of the car, he spotted a ten-foot high pile of horse manure near the barn. Gleefully, he ran to the pile, jumped on it and began digging. Amazed, his parents and uncle ran to the pile and shouted, "What are you doing in that smelly mess?"

The boy kept right on digging and shouted back, "With all this manure, there has got to be a pony in here some place!"

Let's look for the ponies in the language of success.

The Power Of Purposeful Positiveness

In every sales organization there is such a thing as the "Instant Success." Usually it's a young man or woman who has just come aboard and knows little about the product or service being sold. But what they lack in experience and knowledge is more than made up for in enthusiasm and sincerity. These are the people who are, frankly, too dumb to know it's supposed to be difficult to sell things. In that blissful state of ignorance, they go out and set sales records, amazing the old timers and causing the sales manager to reassess his entire sales program.

Unfortunately, there is often an end to this stupendous early start. The end begins when the neophyte finally has an opportunity to realize that others far more experienced than he consider what he is doing unlikely, if not impossible, to sustain.

That negative influence is enough to cause the newcomer to begin to gradually reassess his performance, until ultimately he rationalizes away his fast start and begins plodding methodically and slowly along with the rest. In such a situation the individual begins with the power of purposeful positiveness and ends by joining others in the world of militant mediocrity.

We all enjoy working with an enthusiastic, sincere individual more than with one who is unexcited about what he or she is doing. The ability to sustain that positiveness over a period of time is where the real value of *positive thinking* lies. More aptly named *positive living,* it is a life-style that demands from each individual the highest standard of enthusiasm, commitment and excellence in whatever he is doing. It is a logical, modern extension of the work ethic upon which this country was founded. It provides that even on days when a lesser person might throw up his hands and quit, the positive liver has enough discipline and good sense to keep plugging along, genuinely convinced of his ultimate ability to succeed.

The language of Positive recognizes success not as a destination, but as a journey. The entire process is an inside job. Fundamental to the concept of positive living is the Free Will school of thought, which has been a favorite subject of philosophers for years. It presumes that man is entirely able to effect his destiny as he wishes. Without this basic assumption, the language of Positive would lose most of its meaning.

The two profound advantages of the language of Positive are: first, by presuming our ability to control our future, it provides a level of hope that no other language provides. Second, by insisting that each individual is totally responsible for his own level of success, it imposes a standard of personal responsibility unsurpassed in the language of success.

The ideas within the language of Positive that are of most value to us are those which provide reasonable and realistic techniques that we may use to sustain a level of enthusiasm and sincerity capable of propelling us to the accomplishment of the goals we seek.

The Nonassertive You — The World's Best Kept Secret

Despite its disadvantages, the language of Negative is, to say the least, practical. It deals with pragmatic problems and pragmatic solutions to those problems. So what if you have a good attitude but can't convey that attitude to others? So what if you are competent but can't convey that competence to others? So what if you are properly ambitious yet allow others to use you as a door mat as they walk over you in pursuit of similar goals?

Insofar as the language of Negative reminds us that the world is not always a fun place in which to live, it provides a valuable service by reminding us to be realistic in our assessment of others and ourselves.

The language of Negative can provide a great service, however, only if those who use it avoid falling into the chronic skepticism which it seems to ooze. Its real value comes from the practical and realistic ideas it offers, and when coupled with more positive philosophies, it can be exceptionally beneficial. Consider the impact of combining both the language of Positive and the more practical ideas contained in the language of Negative. What we wind up with is a very reasonable and realistic philosophy which might be entitled, "Trust all men but cut the cards."

The best practical ideas contained in the language of Negative include those dealing with "dressing for success" and "body language."

Let's face it: the way we dress is important. With clothes, we convey a message. Hopefully, the message is one of confidence, authority and success. For most men and women in the business community, wearing something other than the best clothes we can find would distract from our purpose.

Indeed, we wear clothes to signify our purpose in life. Knowing specifically which clothes say what to others helps us announce our intention to the world. Clothes can work with us toward the accomplishment of our goals, or they can work against us. As calculating or negative as it may seem, it is downright practical to consider the impact of clothes.

Similarly, body language, which can help us analyze our demeanor and the reactions of others on a non-verbal level, is particularly practical in assisting us in pursuit of our goals.

Phony? Perhaps. Possibly unnecessary? In a utopian world, yes. But the language of Negative forces us to consider and deal with the real world as it currently exists. How we may wish to change the world is one thing. How we deal with it now is another.

Maybe The Shrinks Have Something

A cartoon in an old magazine I came across the other day depicted a rat hopelessly lost in an endless maze. The rat had obviously come to the end of yet another terminal tunnel. He was staring at a poster on the wall which said simply, "You are here." A large red arrow on the poster pointed to the ground.

Psychologists who routinely deal in the language of Academic must often feel like the rat caught up in the hopelessly complex maze of the human brain. Although many of them know where they are, they have no idea of how to get out. Yet, despite its bombastic verbosity, the language of Academic cannot be discounted in its value to us.

The key word in the language of Academic is "control." The language focuses upon situations, statistics, environments and groups which are controlled. The importance of this approach can most easily be appreciated by recognizing the complete lack of control in the languages of Positive and Negative.

The difficulty in nonacademic approaches toward subjects as complicated as *success, happiness, love,* and *failure* is that facts recited in support of a proposition tend to be anecdotal rather than statistical or cumulative. The mere existence of the language of Academic forces the other languages to rein in the more outlandish examples they might otherwise use. The language, then, is a steadying influence upon our constant search for success.

While still frequently impossible to understand, its value becomes especially apparent to us laymen when the more controlled and analytical approach of Academic seeps through in works such as Berne's *I'm O.K., You're O.K.,* and Maltz's *Psycho-Cybernetics.*

Written in terms that we can appreciate, such works bridge the gap between the language of Academic and a language the rest of us can understand. They contain the best of two worlds: the force and authority of controlled research, and the reason and logic of good sense. While those embroiled in the language of Academic will probably forever continue to harangue one another over distinctions without a difference, the net result of their verbal barrage remains a steadying influence upon our search for success.

So What?

In the Dale Carnegie courses on public speaking, participants are asked to stand before a group and talk about a subject that interests them. During their presentation, members of the audience shout, "So What!"

The purpose behind the Carnegie exercise is to teach all participants that they must always speak in terms of benefits to the other person. All of us, no matter who we are or what we do, are tuned to radio station WII-FM: "What's In It For Me?"

So what if Calvin Cautious kept traveling in circles while on safari in Botswana? So what if the Dudley-Do-Rights speak the language of Positive, the Hard-Chargers speak the language of Negative, and the Experts speak the language of Academic? So what if there are advantages and disadvantages to each approach? So what if some gold exists among the pyrite?

The "so what" of all this is both intriguing and exciting for us all. If we can logically discern the different approaches of those who would chart our course to success, and if we can logically separate the shortcomings and benefits of each approach, then it is just as possible to logically combine the best aspects of all.

Moreover, armed with what they have been trying to say, it is possible for us to focus our attention upon the four sub-environments of our lives upon which they have been trying to focus. The exciting part about this morass of advice is that, distilled down, it becomes a manageable unit: something that can — and should — become a very positive influence in our lives.

This book is devoted to a distillation of the advice we currently find in the "how to succeed" jungle. It proposes that the sum total of all we have heard thus far can literally be reduced to an equation which can be applied toward success in each of the four separate mini-environments of our lives which comprise our total Success Environment.

If advice is only as good as that portion of it that can be used, then the vast majority of advice on how to succeed is worthless, for it has not been reduced to manageable units.

It would probably be pompous and inaccurate to suggest that the ideas expressed herein are new or unique. It may well be that there is no such thing as a new idea: just old wine in new bottles. The truth probably already exists, and is within each of us.

It is our job — specifically the job of this book — to articulate concepts of success in such a fashion that they can be used by each of us every day. Our personal Success Environment will be no greater, nor one bit less, than we personally decide to make it. Equipped with the concepts discussed above, distilled for application in each of the four mini-environments of our lives, we can create a Success Environment for ourselves worthy of our potential as human beings: one in which we may flourish as never before.

"O.K., DeGreen," you say. "I'll keep an open mind and examine this concept of yours. I'll be open, objective and receptive to your ideas. Now tell me about this hair-brained, cockamamie scheme of yours."

I'm glad you asked.

Welcome to a world filled with: *Militant Mediocres, Wishy-Washy Positives, GeeI'mgladIdids, DarnIwishIhads*, reaction mentalities, clutter catastrophies, mental modes, levels of potential, shin splints, hit men from Poughkeepsie, a teacher named Hazor, assorted other creatures both good and evil, and, of course, even a fellow named Calvin Cautious.

II

Overview:
Our Four Environments

Face it. Admit it. You're in control. You're in charge. You are responsible for your success. You are responsible for your lack of success as well.

Calvin Cautious was lost again: this time in his own home town.

While walking down the sidewalk in the business district, he had been, as was his custom, looking up at the tall buildings. That's why he didn't notice the street lamp pole that he walked into head first.

Badly shaken, Calvin couldn't remember who he was or where he lived. He stopped the first person who passed on the street and asked, "Who am I? Where do I live?"

The man, a psychiatrist, said, "You are whom you choose to be, and you live within the confines of your mind."

Calvin didn't need that type of advice just then. What he needed was an aspirin. But he thanked the man anyway, and asked the next passerby, "Who am I? Where do I live?"

The second person, an athlete, replied, "You are whom you choose to be, and you live within your body."

That still wasn't quite the advice Calvin sought. He crossed the street, hoping to find a more specific response to his question. There he asked the next person, "Who am I, and where do I live?"

19

She was a housewife. She said, "You are whom you choose to be, and you live at home."

"But where is home?" Calvin asked.

"Where you make it," she smiled, and left.

Calvin elected to try his luck one more time. He stopped an affluent-looking man and asked, "Who am I, and where do I live?"

The man, too busy to break stride, shouted over his shoulder, "You are whom you choose to be, and you live where you work."

Calvin finally decided he would have to determine for himself who he was and where he lived. "Perhaps if I retrace my steps prior to the accident I will recall," he thought. He recrossed the street and began walking. "Let's see," he thought, "I was looking at the tall buildings and . . . . ." At that moment Calvin walked into the lamp post again. His memory returned instantly. "Of course! I'm Calvin Cautious and I live at 2525 Oak Street, not far from here," he said.

During the short walk home, Calvin reflected upon the advice he had received during his brief bout with amnesia. "Isn't it strange," he thought. "I feel now as though I knew all along who I was and where I lived. That knowledge was buried inside me, just waiting to return. The other people, in their own way, tried to answer those questions for me. Yet, if what they were trying to say is what I knew all along, then why couldn't someone say it?"

If What They've Been Trying To Say Is What You've Known All Along, Then Why Hasn't Someone Said It?

Calvin knew that the advice he had received was correct. It just wasn't specific enough to fit his needs. The passersby and Calvin all agreed on one thing: that he was whom he decided to be. Yet they all supposed that Calvin lived some place else. Each selected the mini-environment to which he or she most closely related. The psychiatrist claimed we live within our minds. The athlete claimed we live within our bodies. The housewife claimed we live at home. The businessman claimed we live at work.

To the extent that each person properly identified one of the four mini-environments which comprise our total Success

Environment, that individual's response was correct. To the extent that each individual excluded the other three mini-environments, that individual's response was incomplete. Among the languages of success, there is general agreement that the results are up to us. In other words, we are whom we decide to be. But too frequently the languages discount the role each of our four mini-environments has in positively or negatively reinforcing our success in the other mini-environments. We wind up with tunnel vision, concentrating on how to think, or how to dress, how to get along with our spouse, or how to make money, to the exclusion of living successfully in all four mini-environments. Yet, in the long-run we can't succeed in any one mini-environment unless we are reasonably successful in all.

Logic compels us to these conclusions:

1. If you think you can think straight without being reasonably fit, having a good home life, and a career that you enjoy, you're mistaken.

2. If you think you can look good and feel good physically without having a decent attitude, a decent home and a decent career, you're mistaken.

3. If you think you can enjoy your home while maintaining a lousy attitude, poor health, and working at a job you don't enjoy, you're mistaken.

4. If you think you can enjoy your job with a poor attitude, while looking like a slob, and while suffering an unenjoyable home-life, you're mistaken.

The bottom line logically is that each of us lives in four mini-environments. We live inside our heads where we think, where we formulate our attitudes, perceptions, feelings and emotions. That's our *Inside* Mini-Environment. We live inside our bodies, and the way those bodies look and feel is a function of how well we take care of ourselves physically and how well we dress. That's our *Outside* Mini-Environment. We live at home, where we seek comfort, companionship, and security. That's our *Home* Mini-Environment. And we live at work, where we pursue the Almighty Dollar and the gratification of doing something constructive for ourselves or someone else. That's our *Work* Mini-Environment.

So what does it all add up to? The manner in which these mini-environments relate to one another, the manner in which they positively or negatively reinforce one another, creates our total Success Environment.

So where do we live, and who are we? We live Inside, Outside, at Home and at Work. And as Calvin discovered . . . we are what we decide to be.

The Mega-Environment: The Sum Is Greater Than The Parts

"Environment:

1. *Something that surrounds; surroundings.*
2. *The total of circumstances surrounding an organism or group of organisms, specifically:*
   a. *the combination of external or extrinsic physical conditions that affect and influence the growth and development of organisms.*
   b. *the complex of social and cultural conditions affecting the nature of an individual or community.*"[3]

Please re-examine the above definition. Study in particular the sentences 2(a) and 2(b).

To the extent that we are "organisms" like amoebas, artichokes, or apes, our environment is comprised of external or extrinsic physical conditions that influence our growth and development. To the extent that we are "individuals"—human beings and (presumably) the highest form of life—social and cultural conditions also create our environment.

The two environments that affect us most as "organisms" are our *Inside* and *Outside* environments: in other words, the way we think, and the way we take care of and adorn our bodies. As "individuals" or members of a community, our environments are *Home* and *Work*: the way we relate to others domestically and economically.

Now here is the rub: let's say we want to define our total, or mega, environment. We can't do so by merely "adding up" the four mini-environments. Here's why:

All of the mini-environments are interdependent. For example: the way we feel physically frequently affects the way we feel mentally. If we are physically down, it's difficult to be mentally up. So physical fitness becomes a factor affecting our *Inside*

---

3. *The American Heritage Dictionary of the English Language*

Mini-Environment. Similarly, what goes on at home, in our *Home* Mini-Environment, can certainly affect what happens in our *Work* Mini-Environment.

To illustrate, say you are a pharmacist in Des Moines, and it's Monday morning. You're in bed, and you open one eye to look at the alarm clock. Panic! You jump from bed. You are 30 minutes late because your wife forgot to set the alarm last night. You know your customers will be lining up outside the pharmacy waiting for you when you arrive.

You shout at your wife as you run to the bathroom, expressing in no uncertain terms your displeasure with her forgetfulness. She returns your comments in kind, and as you are struggling to throw on your clothes, you find yourself in a shouting match with her.

Your 17-year-old overhears the argument, races into the room, and attempts to mediate. He says, "She wouldn't have forgotten to set the alarm if it hadn't been for the car accident and her worry about how to break the news to you."

This is the first you've heard about the car, but you haven't time now to obtain details. You race downstairs to find something to eat. The bread is stale. The orange juice is sour. You are out of milk. No cereal. "Forget it," you think, "I've got to get to the pharmacy!"

You throw open the door and race outside, forgetting your boots and coat, which was not a smart thing to do, because three feet of snow fell the night before. Instantly you are face down in a snow drift. Your wife and 17-year-old laugh. That doesn't help matters. You crawl back inside to find your boots, but you can't, although you do find a coat. You finally make it to the garage and put your keys in the ignition of the car (the one that hadn't been in the accident), only to discover that it won't start. You try again and again to no avail. You have no choice but to walk to the pharmacy, a mile away, with no boots.

You finally make it there, only to find a dozen disgruntled customers standing in front of the door. You reach for your keys. Your hands are nearly frozen. You forgot your gloves, too. Oh, no! The keys are in the car. You trudge the mile back home through the snow, retrieve the keys from your car and trudge back.

Finally, you get the door to the pharmacy open. Your patrons, increasingly angry, swarm to the pharmacy counter. Back and forth you run, filling prescriptions, taking orders and answering the phone. Your customers are yelling at you now from across the counter. There is one interruption after another. Two small boys are stealing comic books from the magazine stand. You race after them, only to knock over the shampoo display. The phone rings; your customers keep yelling. You answer the phone and can barely hear the voice on the other end over the din of complaints coming at you from within the store. It's the sweet but slightly senile little old lady who bought a thermometer from you yesterday.

In her gentle and unassuming voice, she says, "You know that rectal thermometer I bought from you yesterday?"

"Yes," you shout into the phone, "What is it?!"

"How do you use it?" she asks.

Now what would *you* say?

So let's not focus upon any one mini-environment to the exclusion of the others. Let us instead first devote our attention to discovering how each mini-environment positively or negatively reinforces the others.

Next, we'll devote ourselves to exploring how we may improve our lives in each of our four mini-environments so that we may improve our total Success Environment over all.

Who's In Charge Here?

Fundamental to all self-help philosophy is this simple proposition: You're in charge. You're responsible for the results you achieve. If you fail, you have no one to blame but you.

Perhaps it's a tough pill to swallow, but it's the bottom line. If, at the very threshold, we cannot accept this basic propostion, then most, if not all, of our self-help philosophizing will be to little or no avail.

You're in charge. Admit it. Accept it.

We can do so, without going to extremes. On the one extreme is the obnoxious millionaire who, conveniently forgetting all the help he got along the way, claims to be a self-made-man. When we do succeed, we should have enough sense and diplomacy to credit others as well as ourselves.

On the other extreme is the baseball rookie who, while sitting on the bench game after game, pleaded with his coach to put him in.

"Coach," he would say, "those people are cheering for *me*! They want *me* in the game!"

Finally, in a desperate late inning situation, the coach put him in. The rookie went to the plate and struck out. As he returned to the dug-out, the game lost, he was met with the resounding chorus of boos from the stands.

"You see," the coach said, "you're not so popular with the fans now!"

"Oh no," the rookie said, "they're not booing *me*. They *love* me! They're booing *you* for putting me in!"

Too many of us spend our lives "booing" the coach who put us in the game. We have all met those who essentially claim that they aren't successful because their mothers didn't breast feed them when they were babies. There are others who wear a neglected childhood or traumatic adolescent experience like a badge that says, "I have an excuse for not succeeding."

We may not always be able to control what happens to us, especially when we are young. But we can almost always control how we will react to what happens to us.

Face it. Admit it. You're in control. You're in charge. You are responsible for your success. You are responsible for your lack of success as well.

Yet we all take great pleasure in permitting others to control our mini-environments. Is it any wonder, then, that our total Success Environment is so frequently dependent upon what others say and do? We literally lay our lives and our ambitions at the feet of those who frequently couldn't care less. And when we meet with disaster, we blame them rather than blame ourselves for having given them control in the first place. If, in any of the four mini-environments in which we exist, we are at the mercy of the actions or inactions of some other person, then we are responsible for having abdicated control over the situation in the first place. This basic concept that we are in control, as simple as it sounds, is probably the most formidable obstacle we face. Too often, it is too comforting, too convenient, too easy, to blame others for having failed to do what we should have accepted the responsibility to do long ago. We use others as a crutch, as an excuse, as a cop-out to justify our own failure to assume responsibility for our destiny.

Accepting responsibility for what happens to us and for us requires in many ways that we become our own worst critic; not that we should hate ourselves or expect more than we can deliver. But before we can proceed to create a truly meaningful Success Environment, we must first assume, and then totally accept, the notion that it is us and not Joe down the street, our spouse, our boss, our secretary, our analyst, or our parents who are in control and who are responsible for the results that we attain.

Let's take a closer look at each of the four mini-environments, that we may better appreciate how we permit others to control those environments, and also so that we may better understand how these environments relate to one another.

Inside

"He's got his head on straight." "He's a good head." "His head's in the right place."

Sure, we've all heard these expressions before, and we all know generally what they mean. Depending on the context in which they are used, they may refer to an individual with a good attitude, someone who is especially trustworthy, or a man or woman especially adept at communicating well.

Of course, being a "good head" these days may also mean that one has become particularly adroit at rolling his own.

It has become a cliché to say that one of the few things left on this earth that the human mind has not been able to totally figure out is the human mind. It's a complicated thing, capable, as some now contend, of recording every minute aspect of every experience or thought we ever had or held. And somehow those past recollections no doubt relate to our current perceptions and future judgments.

Too often it is suggested that we can improve our Inside Mini-Environment simply by "improving the way we think." There is much to be said in favor of the concept of programming our subconscious mind, as we will discuss later. But it is just too simplistic an approach to believe that we, like a computer, can be "programmed" without taking into account the trillions of often conflicting impulses that are shooting around inside our cerebrums.

Most of us, for example, talk about maintaining a good attitude without having any idea of what *attitude* means. We tend to confuse it with concepts such as *emotions, feelings, dispositions, temperaments,* and even *logic.* At the risk of remaining simplistic, let us concede that there are at least three categories of thought processes that pass through our minds every second.

We'll call the first set of impulses the Einstein Mode. This mode can best be characterized by the words *reason, logic,* and *intellect.* It is the rational decision making we do on a daily basis. It includes the collection and sifting of data, the weighing of alternative choices, and the selection of action.

The second mode might be called the Judy Garland Mode. It is best characterized by the words, *emotion* and *feeling.* Subjective processes which are virtually impossible to define, such as *joy, sorrow, reverence, hate,* or *love,* are within this category. It includes all the things we *feel,* as opposed to what our logic or reason (Einstein Mode) might tell us.

The final category is the Dale Carnegie Mode. It is best described by the words *attitude* and *disposition.* It is our customary manner of emotional response, our temperament; our manner of thinking, behaving and reacting in a characteristic fashion. It is the manner in which our Einstein Mode has programmed us to react to our Judy Garland Mode.

These three modes can and do positively or negatively reinforce one another within the Inside Mini-Environment, just as our four mini-environments do on a larger scale. Each mode is an external factor that can affect the other two modes. For example, through the Einstein Mode (logic) we can condition our Carnegie Mode (attitudes and dispositions) to function and react in a certain way. Similarly, our Carnegie Mode, (our attitudes) can affect our Judy Garland Mode (emotions and feelings) by providing a characteristic manner in which we deal with, sustain, or reject, our more subjective mental processes.

"Oh, wonderful!" you say. "We aren't even through the second chapter and already we have four mini-environments, one mega environment and three modes within the first mini-environment. And this is supposed to be simple! How many more modes, megas and minis will I have to contend with?"

Just a few, and you'll probably survive the process. And I promise that once you make it through Chapter III, it should all fall into place.

The important point about these three mental modes is that they reinforce one another. Therefore we must recognize that when we talk about improving our attitudes and dispositions as the primary method of improving our Inside Mini-Environment, we are at the same time affecting our logical and emotive states. Moreover, when we focus in later chapters upon using our logic to program our mind, we will be affecting the emotive and attitudinal states as well. Yet when we concentrate on one mode, we only indirectly affect the others. All of this means that it is probably a waste of time to try to control directly all of our mental processes all the time.

Too frequently people regard positive self-image psychology as a syrupy panacea, a cosmetic powder with which we should hide the ugly face of our inward discontent: a method of whitewashing and ignoring our true feelings or logic. Instead, this book is devoted to providing the reader with attitudinal tools with which to positively manage some of our deeper thought modes which, after all, make us human beings. Our approach is much like the moral of the story told by the great speaker, Cavett Robert, about the old Indian who watched the white men build a lighthouse.

Day after day the old Indian sat in silence and watched as white men erected the tower. He observed as they ignited the lamp, and he watched its first night of operation. When he returned to his tribe they asked him, "How successful was the white man's lighthouse?"

"Big failure!" he replied. "White man make big tower, light big bulb, cast light into ocean, but fog come in just the same."

Mentally, our "fog" will continue to roll in, especially in the form of more negative or "sad" emotions and feelings. Our job with the Inside Mini-Environment is to create as helpful and positive a context as possible with which to confront, control and conquer these innermost feelings.

Attitudes: Controllable Children Or Visitors From Outer Space?

Isn't it enough that we are rarely able to exert direct influence over our emotions (our Judy Garland Mode)? Why, then, do so many people insist upon treating their attitudes (Carnegie Mode) in a similar fashion?

We've all heard people say, "I feel good today," or, "I feel lazy today," or, "I feel discouraged today," as though they were talking about visitors from outer space: men from Mars who just dropped in for the day to affect their behavior.

It is perhaps more convenient to regard our attitudes or dispositions (our Carnegie Mode) as occasional and unpredictable visitors from outer space. That, at least, relieves us of the burden of accepting the responsibility for our temperament. Yet just an iota of personal worth, and even the slightest acceptance of responsibility for our individual status, forces us to conclude that our attitudes can and should be totally within our ability to control: much as a parent might regard his responsibility toward —and control over—his children.

It's entirely possible that we can only indirectly affect our emotions (the Garland Mode). It is certainly true that we are not all born with the same logical or reasoning prowess (the Einstein mode). But we don't have to be Einsteins or unemotive rocks to be able to control our temperament (the manner in which we perceive ourselves and the world around us). Some may argue that by affecting our Carnegie Mode (our attitudes) we may *directly* affect our Einstein Mode (logic) or our Garland Mode (emotions). They *may* be right, but let's be as conservative as possible and assume that the attitudes we can control will have at least an indirect—and potentially positive—effect upon the mental modes over which we have less control. An indirect effect is better than no effect at all. One out of three ain't bad, in many cases.

Most would agree, for example, that Pete Rose—Mr. Baseball, Charlie Hustle—is a very successful man at what he does. Indeed, for all but one season of his major league career he has batted over .300. But that means that even Pete Rose gets a hit only one out of every three times at bat. If half a loaf is better than none, then a third of a loaf is better than none as well. We can argue all day over the extent to which the adjustment of our attitudes directly or indirectly affects the rest of our mental processes. But that debate is irrelevant if we can conclude—and logic leads us to this conclusion—that it can have some effect—often a profound effect—upon what goes on in our Inside Mini-Environment. Our focus, then, will be upon the Carnegie (or attitudinal) Mode, with the assumption that by positively building our attitudes we can, to a greater or lesser extent, positively build the rest of our Inside Mini-Environment as well.

An Inside Job

Success is an inside job.

The extent to which you take control of, and accept responsibility for, your attitudes is entirely up to you. We must view our attitudes as tools capable of being molded and shaped to the desired form to fit the desired purpose. They are ours to use as the method by which we build our total Inside Mini-Environment. But the tools must be honed and put to use. We must allow our Einstein Mode—our logic—to accept that basic notion. Once accepted, it can positively reinforce our efforts to learn techniques and methods by which we use attitudes as the tools for shaping our Inside Mini-Environment.

But it *is* an inside job, and it begins with your head and your logic. It is a personal responsibility. The results are up to you. Without that basic commitment, all the rest is pure verbiage, a wasted exercise in semantics.

It is entirely possible that real progress cannot be made in any of the three remaining mini-environments before we make progress in our Inside Mini-Environment. Whether that is true is probably irrelevant, much like the chicken and the egg argument. But suffice it here to say that it must start with you inside: in your head. You may choose not to differentiate between emotions or logic or attitudes. You may choose to accept the notion that the mind simply cannot explain itself, and therefore you won't try. You may choose to regard your attitudes as visitors from outer space over which you have no control; or you may choose, in a fashion consistent with your potential as a human being, and with your purpose for occupying space on this planet:

1. That your attitudes are controllable by you and only by you.

2. That there are methods by which you may adopt positive attitudes to be used as tools for affecting your Inside Mini-Environment positively, and

3. That you and you alone are totally responsible for learning and mastering all the methods available to create positive attitudinal tools for use within your own Inside Mini-Environment.

Success is an inside job. It starts with you.

Outside

Did you ever drive by a house that was run-down and grubby, and instinctively know that you had no desire either to meet or become friends with the people who lived inside? Have you ever met a person who was so physically repulsive because of poor health, grooming, or dressing habits that you felt similarly inclined not to make his acquaintance?

I'm sure we all have. The analogy is simple: In both cases we looked at two homes and rejected the owners of each. It is perhaps a cliché, but no less true because of it, that our body is our home to a very real and direct extent. The manner in which we care for our bodies is as much a reflection of our sense of self-worth, likableness and value to others as the frequency with which we cut our grass and trim our hedges.

Our Outside Mini-Environment deals directly with that "home" in which we spend our time during our tenure on this earth. Our Outside Mini-Environment is a function of three component parts: our general condition of health, our grooming and hygiene, and our attire.

To carry the analogy even farther, consider your general condition of health to be the structure of your house. It is a combination of two-by-fours, support beams, dry wall and insulation. Most of us have too much insulation and too few two-by-fours. But most of us rationalize away our unfitness or ill health by saying, "I'm content. I'm happy." Yet, to the extent that ill health or general lack of fitness negatively influences our other mini-environments, it detracts from our efforts to reach our full potential as human beings.

When we speak of fitness, we don't necessarily speak of being able to run a four-minute mile, or being able to lift the equivalent of our weight in barbells. What we do speak of is a general condition of health that permits us to live life to the fullest without undo fatigue, disease and discomfort. At the very least, being unfit negatively influences our conduct in all the other areas of our life: from our conduct at work and at home and our ability to maintain a coherent mental existence right down to our ability to enjoy our sex life to the fullest.

At the very worst, unfitness kills us. The house comes tumbling down.

Our grooming and hygiene might be likened to the time we spend cutting the grass and taking the garbage out at home. Such acts, however minor, are generally a good indication of the pride we take in ourselves.

Finally, our attire can be likened to the manner in which we maintain the exterior of our house. What type of shingles should we use? What color for the shutters? Shall we paint the old barn, or spiff it up with aluminum siding?

Again, we've all passed homes where the owners had made an obviously sincere attempt to dress the place up, and the attempt was a dismal failure. Houses painted blue are a good example. If the owner selects just the right shade of pale blue and accents it with just the right combination of dark blue shutters and down spouts, the results can be strikingly beautiful. But select just a slightly different shade of blue and the effect can best be described as "early tacky."

Put a man in a three-piece pin-stripe suit with club tie, and he may look like a Wall Street banker. But if the pin stripes are just an eighth of an inch too far apart, or too wide, or if the tie is not quite right, you have converted that Wall Street banker into a hit man from Poughkeepsie. Similarly, put a businesswoman in a well tailored skirted suit with subtle accessories, and she is dressed for the board room. Replace that outfit with a "flattering" dress and a neckline that plunges just a half inch too low, and your female executive is dressed for the bedroom.

It all adds up. The manner in which we care for and present that "house" in which we live will have a profound effect on our success in other areas of life as well.

As with the other mini-environments, we are again totally responsible for the results we obtain in the Outside area of our life. It sounds especially ludicrous to blame someone else because they feed us too much, or buy us the wrong clothes, or forget to buy our deodorant. Most of us within the first few days of our existence learned how much food was necessary to sustain our bodies. By age four or five we were competent at dressing ourselves. By age eight we could part our hair without leaving a cowlick with some consistency. Presumably everyone reading this book is an adult or pretty close to it. As such, excuses that it's someone else's fault that you are too fat, or too skinny, or too dirty, or dressed like a schlock won't find much sympathy here. As always, you're responsible. You're in charge.

If You Had A Choice, Would You Deal With You?

Please pick up this book and walk over to a mirror where you can get a good look at yourself.

Go ahead, I'll wait.

Are you at the mirror? Good. Take a look. Take a *long* look at that person standing there. Admittedly, you may not be dressed for business just now. But what about the rest of you? How's that double chin coming along? Looking good? When was the last time you washed and/or set your hair? How carefully did you shave this morning? Or did you shave at all?

Now, if you're someplace where you won't get arrested for doing so, take off your clothes. Go ahead. I won't look! Got your clothes off? Good. Fellows, go ahead and flex those biceps. Go ahead. Oh, you did? Sorry. Ladies, how are those busts coming along? Pointing a little more toward your toes than they used to, eh? Now let's examine the waist line. Ah, splendid! So that's what happened to those cheese cake desserts! Now turn around and take a look at the real you: the part you sit on. A little wider than you remember it last, eh?

Depressing? Hopefully, at least a little. A little honest discontentment helps promote change. Almost all of us need at least some improvement physically. Now go ahead and get dressed in the clothes you would normally wear to work. Just leave me and the book here by the mirror, and I'll meet you when you get dressed.

Are you back? Good! All dressed? Splendid! Now take another look in that mirror. How are you dressed? Do you look the image you want to project? The E.S.P. of business and sales stands for "Enthusiasm, Sincerity and Professionalism." Does your outfit say, "I'm enthusiastic, sincere and professional?" Does your physical demeanor say those things? Does your grooming say those things? Does anything about you say any one of those things? I hope so.

Now take a last long look at that mirror. Where can you improve? How can you improve? Start the wheels turning now.

We'll spend a lot of time later discussing techniques that will project the real outside you. But in the meantime, ask yourself this question: "Based solely on how I look, based solely on that image in the mirror, and if I were a potential customer or client of mine, would I want to deal with me?"

Shut Up And Talk To Me

We communicate on many different levels, you and I. Certainly we communicate verbally and through the written word, as we are doing now. But most important of all, we communicate silently through our demeanor, our attire and our hygiene. We send thousands of messages every day to the people around us without uttering a word. We do so by presenting a silent image, whether in the form of gestures, or through more inert characteristics, such as grooming and health.

We may not always make that big sale or land that big client with our first impression. But we can almost surely *lose* it or him, before ever uttering a word, simply by silently communicating the signal that we are not the enthusiastic, sincere and professional person with whom that individual wants to deal.

Long before a speaker ever opens his mouth, for example, he makes his first and most profound impression upon the audience as he approaches the rostrum or microphone. He does so silently and, without giving any indication of what he will say verbally, he transmits his non-verbal message to the group. Hopefully, it will be a message of enthusiasm, sincerity and professionalism.

The adage that a picture is worth a thousand words holds true in the vast majority of instances.

We paint pictures of ourselves for the world. We paint the picture. We can decide what strokes to use, what hues and shades we will employ. We can prepare the canvas and ultimately find a suitable frame. We are the artist and the subject in one. We can present our work haphazardly to an uncaring or negatively impressed audience, or we can present a masterpiece of silent communication to be met with an appreciative response. All this only we and we alone can do, for again, we are responsible; *we* control the Outside Mini-Environment in which we live.

Home

So far we have devoted ourselves to examining the two mini-environments which are inherent to our status as "organisms," or living beings. That we have thought patterns and a "house" in which we live does not distinguish us much from any other species which exists on this earth. It is a question of degree, not of kind. But our other two mini-environments, Home and Work, relate to our communal tendency as human beings. Whereas the Inside and Outside Mini-Environments deal with the manner in which we relate to and maintain ourselves, our Home and Work Mini-Environments deal with the manner in which we relate to others. So let's examine the communal us. The best place to start is at home.

Our Home Mini-Environment can be defined a lot of ways. Whether we're married or have children or not, it is where we're, well—home, whether we are physically there or not. It is a sense of origin, of order; a nest where we enjoy being most, surrounded by people we enjoy being with most: our spouse, our children, our parents, our friends. Our Home Mini-Environment is usually a series of warm and caring and loving relationships centered around a physical place: home.

It is, or at least should be, the one environment of our existence that we create exclusively for the purpose of loving others and being loved. We manifest the love we experience in this environment of our lives by displaying in various degrees and at various times six separate qualities: warmth, respect, encouragement, sex, affection and caring. Obviously, not all of these qualities are applicable to all of our Home Mini-Environment relationships. But they are the techniques we use to display the love we feel at home, and they are the six methods by which we maintain a happy domestic existence.

While we don't have to be married to have a Home Mini-Environment, marriage provides the clearest example. Most of us get married because we feel, either instinctively or socially, that it provides the most useful context in which we may express our love for another person. A great human tragedy is that, although we may erect this external environment for the purpose of expressing our love, we too frequently construct internal barriers within it which tend to defeat our purpose for having used the institution at all.

Moreover, if love is, as the philosophers say, non-competitive, then surely it cannot flourish in a competitive or insecure environment. Yet too frequently we permit competition or insecurity to permeate the inner domestic sanctum that we have constructed. We permit others and other factors to destroy our Home Mini-Environment.

To complicate matters, our Home Mini-Environment does not lend itself to the same types of goals that we might easily establish in the other mini-environments of our lives. At work, for example, we might postpone immediate gratification or "happiness" in an effort to accomplish some future, distant, goal. Yet, the goals relating to our Home Mini-Environment are immediate, for no matter how they are put, priorized, or pronounced, Home-related goals always amount to the same thing: *the present enjoyment of love.*

In any Home Mini-Environment involving two people, as in marriage, there are actually three parties involved: *You, Me* and *Us.*

You may feel warm and caring and loving. *Me* may feel warm and caring and loving. But if *You* and *Me* cannot relate those feelings to one another, in the context of the Home Mini-Environment we have attempted to create, then *Us* will be in very bad shape indeed.

We'll establish, then, as a realistic and attainable goal for our Home Mini-Environment, *the present enjoyment of love.*

In later portions of this book we will explore the utilization of the six separate qualities (warmth, respect, encouragement, sex, affection and caring) as tools for the accomplishment of that goal.

Do Not Pass GO, Do Not Collect $200

Too many of us regard life as a Monopoly game with no *Go.* We spend our time trying to get from Boardwalk to Baltic Avenue without stopping to collect our $200 and without resting on the only place on the board where it is completely safe. Our Home Mini-Environment is our *Go.* It's where we pass time between rolls of the dice. It's where we catch our breath safe from all competition and insecurity around us.

Yet too often we get so wrapped up in the game itself that we spend little or no time at our *Go.* Ironically, the purpose of the game, at least in part, is to spend time there safely. In life, we certainly start out hoping that through our efforts at work we will have additional time and additional income to share with those people we love most. In practice, we frequently permit the work related goals that we established (initially as a tool for happiness at home) to intrude upon our relationship with the people we love most. While we can't pretend that business or professional problems don't exist, and while most of us must devote a substantial portion of each day to the solution of those problems, nevertheless, our Home Mini-Environment must be built, preserved and protected against intrusions from all sources.

The Value Of Security

Too many people regard security as a dirty word. I suppose that a search for security is less than admirable when that word entails sacrificing lifetime goals in exchange for, say, a small yet "secure" pension, or sacrificing making a serious contribution within a corporate hierarchy for fear of losing a small but "secure" position.

Yet security at home is another matter entirely. If we had to select one synonym for the phrase Home Mini-Environment, that synonym would be *security*. Home is and should be our inner domestic sanctum, our walled and moated castle; that one environment where we can go and relax and enjoy those we love, unaffected by the world around us. Yet despite the close relationship between security and our Home Mini-Environment, many of us fail to establish the security needed for the maintenance of that environment.

Immature and unrealistic financial expectations are the primary culprit. Someday, somewhere, somebody's going to get smart and insist that every young man and woman in high school in this country be required to take *and pass* a course on personal financial management. In the vast majority of troubled homes, the culprit is money. More specifically, it is the inability of one or both partners to deal maturely with money.

We establish our Home Mini-Environment to provide a secure context in which we may express our love and enjoy our happiness. Then we go out and finance a stereo we can't afford, a TV we can't afford, a car we can't afford, a house we can't afford, and a dozen other items that we persuaded ourselves were complete necessities. Then we sit around and spend the time we should be spending thinking about each other thinking instead about our payments. And we just can't seem to understand why we're not as happy or as secure as we intended to be.

Financial maturity is measured by the ability of a person to distinguish between his ability to finance something and his ability to afford something. Financial maturity, in most instances, equals security. Security in many instances equals a happy Home Mini-Environment. It is one of the greatest ironies and tragedies of our time that individuals who, upon marriage, uniformly contend that the most important thing to them is that they have each other, will, once married, proceed to finance the purchase of anything that's not nailed down, thus frequently destroying the relationship they intended to create in the first place.

Work

Please don't let the above section leave you with the false impression that I have anything against money. I like money. It is, by and large, a whole lot better to have it than not to have it.

No matter who we are or what we do, we all want to be greater than we are and do better than we do. We all dream dreams and hope hopes and desire to grow because we all know that no matter what our age or sex or station in life, when you cease to grow, you start to go.

But it's changing those dreams into reality, that's the hard part. Day after day, we often find ourselves so bogged down in routine activities that we don't seem to have the time to spend on those projects that mean the most to us—on those projects that will help us reach our full potential as human beings. And we wind up letting things happen to us instead of us happening to things.

That's the problem we bring with us to work. We don't just work for money, although it's important—darned important. To a very large extent, I think we work because deep down inside there is a part of us that is a child looking around and saying, "Gosh, it's pretty neat that I can go out there with the rest of the adults and do things that make a difference and help people." There is no denying, as the Judeo-Christian ethic provides, that there is an inherent satisfaction to work: a feeling of constructiveness, of accomplishment. Yet too often we satisfy ourselves with the illusion of accomplishment rather than the reality, and we confuse motion with progress.

Our Work Mini-Environment is best defined as that area of our lives where we spend our time in pursuit of economic and professional goals. While just being able to participate ("Gosh, I'm glad to be here") is, and should be, a matter of great satisfaction for us all, it is rarely enough. Instead, we establish work-related daily goals, weekly goals, monthly goals and career goals, and devote our energies toward their accomplishment. For most of us, the betterment of our Work Mini-Environment involves not just being employed, but also involves being able to use our potential to the fullest, and reap the considerable rewards thereof.

Start Your Engines!

So we show up for work seated at the wheel of that machine we call "ourselves" and wait for a voice to announce, "Ladies and Gentlemen, start your engines!" Frequently, however, especially in the professions and in commissioned sales work, no voice is forthcoming. We sit at the starting line, our ignition not even on, and watch others, who didn't wait for permission to start, lap us. It's as though we frequently wait for a special license to succeed. We assume mediocrity is permissible without someone else's permission, but excellence requires expressed approval. So there we sit at the starting line, waiting for someone to tell us it's O.K. to compete.

Frequently, about half way through the race, say middle-age, many of us realize, "Hey, I don't need permission to compete. I can step on it any time I want!" Whereupon we enter the race at a considerable disadvantage. Yet even with that disadvantage, entering late is far better than not entering at all. We've all met many people who spend their entire lives at work with their engines on, idling at best, who simply never understood that at no time did they ever require someone else's permission to get into the race.

Model T Or Formula One?

When cars were first invented, Model T's were pretty hot stuff. But today one would look quaint, almost sad, sitting next to a Formula One. In our race at work, many of us undeliberately drive Model T's rather than faster, more competitive models.

We do so for a number of reasons. There are, of course, those individuals who never fully acquired the technical skills necessary for excellence at their profession. They balk at the suggestion that they pursue continuing education, knowing deep down inside there may be little value to continuing an education which never really began.

More frequently, however, those of us who drive Model T's at work do so because, while the attitudinal vehicle we started with may have been a racy late model at the time, it's grown obsolete over the years. Techniques change. Products change. Services change. Client and customer demands change; and only those who are willing to change with them will remain even remotely competitive. The result is what we frequently see: old-timers and young-timers alike, who latched on to what were a few good ideas when they began, and who persist in employing those methods today, undeterred by all the progress around them. Our success at work, just as the success of a race car driver, must ultimately depend upon our willingness to adopt later models, or at the very least to tune the engine of the attitudinal vehicle we have selected.

Replacing old equipment with new, or at least fine tuning the equipment we already have, is the major focus of our approach as it relates to our Work Mini-Environment.

In our Work Mini-Environment, it is perhaps more tempting than anywhere else to blame others for our lack of success. But again we are faced with the ultimate realization that if others control our degree of success at work, it is only because at some earlier point we permitted them to do so. Hence the responsibility for our successes and failures circles back to return where it ought to be: with us. It's in our hands.

We have made much of the notion that we cannot concentrate exclusively upon one mini-environment if we are to attain any appreciable measure of ultimate success. We have mentioned, too, that our total Success Environment is larger than its parts, in the sense that each mini-environment positively or negatively reinforces the others. We've emphasized time and again that we are each individually responsible for the results we obtain in all four mini-environments; and we have examined in some detail the basic component parts of each mini-environment.

With all this in mind, we can now *mathematically* evaluate the current status of our personal Success Environment by applying the Success Environment Formula to ourselves. The formula can be lightly regarded as a mere parlor game, or it can be utilized as an important tool for measuring the extent to which you personally have realized your full potential as a human being. I hope for you it will be the latter. We already have enough parlor games in the language of success.

O.K., Whiz Kids, whip out your pocket calculators. Here comes everything you wanted to know and more about that guy in the mirror.

III

The Success Environment Formula: Bursting Through The Mediocrity Barrier

Most of us wallow in the Mediocrity Mode. We border on failure. The irony of this status is that with slight additional effort we can geometrically accelerate our rate of success.

Most people are, by definition, average.

In fact, we all have some average qualities about us: average height, perhaps, average weight, average I.Q., average ambition. On the other hand we all possess some exceptional qualities as well: special talents which are ours and ours alone. The combination of average and exceptional qualities varies wildly among us. But despite the various combinations, most people, by definition, achieve only average results with their lives. We will refer to this later as wallowing in the Mediocrity Mode.

It is ironic and a little sad that while most people enjoy watching another try to succeed, few enjoy witnessing his actual success. There exists, in other words, something known as the Mediocrity Barrier, an obstacle as real and as formidable as a brick wall.

The Mediocrity Barrier represents the resentment others feel toward us as we not only strive for, but actually achieve, the goals we have established. Bursting through that barrier is a difficult task. It is the point at which we must be so completely intent upon what we are doing, so completely reliant upon ourselves and not others as our motivating source, that we can break through the barrier without seeking the approval of—or being deterred by the disapproval of—others. It is, as the adage provides: when we suffer set-backs while striving for our goals, we shouldn't tell other people our problems. Eighty percent of them don't care, and the other twenty percent are actually glad.

So How's Your Success Environment?

This chapter is devoted to a nifty mathematical formula designed to help us evaluate the extent to which we have utilized our individual potential. It is designed as a tool to help us burst through the Mediocrity Barrier, by permitting us to isolate and examine those parts of our existence where we're strong, and those parts of our existence where we need improvement.

The formula is not a technique by which we can or should pass judgement upon the relative success of others. It measures us individually only against our own potential, and more specifically against our own perception of our individual potential.

I recommend that you find a pocket calculator to help you conduct the mathematical exercises contained in this chapter. The calculator is not essential, but you will find it very convenient. When fixing values for the various components of the equation, take time to seriously consider each one.

This is a private exercise for your use and your eyes only. It is a tool, not a final verdict regarding your self worth. Most of us who participate in the exercise discover that there is substantial room for improvement in one or more areas of our lives. Because the areas positively or negatively reinforce each other, a minor adjustment in one mini-environment will cause a substantial increase in our total Success Environment. Our purpose is to evaluate that Success Environment to see how we rate on a numerical scale which extends from 1 to 243.

Remember: Theoretically, a man who sells pencils on the street corner may be a success, while a millionaire may be a failure. The difference is the extent to which each individual has used the potential that he has. All men may have been created equal, but God didn't deal all the cards from the same deck. What may be an enormous accomplishment for one man may require little or no effort by another. The purpose of this formula is to measure our success, not relative to the success of others, but relative only to our own potential as we personally perceive it.

$$SE = (I \times O \times H \times W)Y$$

The Success Environment Formula involves simple multiplication. A value of from 1 to 3 is assigned to each letter on the right side of the equation. These values are then multiplied by each other to determine the ultimate value of SE on the left side of the equation.

Let's define our terms before we go any farther:

SE = *Success Environment.* It is the total picture and the ultimate environment in which we conduct our lives.

I, O, H, and W are the four mini-environments that help comprise our total Success Environment.

I = *Inside Mini-Environment.* It is the way we think, our attitudes, emotions and logic.

O = *Outside Mini-Environment.* It is the way we dress and our physical demeanor. It reflects our general condition of health and fitness and our grooming.

H = *Home Mini-Environment.* It represents our domestic existence and the extent to which we prevent outside pressures from permeating our inner domestic sanctum.

W = *Work Mini-Environment.* It represents the way we pursue our livelihood and the efficiency with which we conduct ourselves. It is the manner in which we relate to others while in pursuit of monetary and professional goals.

Y = *The "Y Factor."* It is the average extent to which we control our conduct in our four mini-environments.

We will work the equation in three steps. First, we will fix the values for I, O, H, and W, and then we will attain our Mini-Environment Product by multiplying those values by each other. Next, we will fix a value for Y and determine our average Y for all four mini-environments. Finally, we will see how our Average Y Factor and our Mini-Environment Product relate to one another in creating our total Success Environment.

Fixing Values For I, O, H, And W

To each of the four mini-environments we assign a value of
from 1 to 3, depending upon how satisfied you are personally with
your existence in each environment. You may use—and in fact I
recommend that you use—decimals to depict, as exactly as you
can, the extent to which you are satisfied with each mini-
environment. In no event, however, should you assign a value of
less than 1 to any mini-environment, and in no event should you
assign a value of more than 3 to any mini-environment.

We evaluate I, O, H, and W as follows:

3 = *A totally acceptable environment.* There is no substantial
room for improvement. To assign a value of 3 to any mini-
environment, you should be totally satisfied with all aspects of
your existence within that environment.

2 = *A moderately acceptable environment.* Here there is
moderate room for improvement, and although you are generally
satisfied with your existence within this environment, you see
room for improvement.

1 = *A totally unacceptable environment.* To assign a 1 rating to
any mini-environment you should be totally dissatisfied with your
existence within this particular environment. Substantial improvement must be needed.

Between the values of 1, 2, and 3 you may utilize decimals to
depict as exactly as possible the current rating you give to any
particular environment. For example, when evaluating your
Home Mini-Environment, you may conclude that it is at least
moderately acceptable, but not entirely perfect. Therefore, you
may assign it a value of 2.5. Similarly, when evaluating your Work
Mini-Environment, you may decide that it is basically unacceptable, but there are at least a few aspects that you find moderately
acceptable, and might therefore assign a rating to your Work
Mini-Environment of 1.2.

Only you can decide what rating each mini-environment
deserves. It is important to note that these are current ratings.
They should not reflect the extent to which you were satisfied
with each environment, say, a month ago; and should not reflect
the extent to which you expect to be satisfied, say, a month from
now. It is the degree to which you are currently satisfied with
each mini-environment that is important.

Let's proceed to assign values to each of your four mini-environments. Remember, this formula is a tool for your personal use. Take the time to be honest with yourself. Proceed now to fill in the blanks in paragraphs A, B, C and D below.

A.   The current rating I give to my Inside (I) Mini-Environment is: ____

B.   The current rating I give to my Outside (O) Mini-Environment is: ____

C.   The current rating I give to my Home (H) Mini-Environment is: ____

D.   The current rating I give to my Work (W) Mini-Environment is: ____

We may therefore thus far express your Success Environment Formula as follows:

$$SE = (\underline{\quad} \times \underline{\quad} \times \underline{\quad} \times \underline{\quad})Y.$$

Fill in the blanks above, inserting the ratings that you gave to each mini-environment within the parentheses.

Next, multiply the ratings by each other to determine your Mini-Environment Product.

Please complete the following line:

My Mini-Environment Product is: ____

Let's take an example to make sure we're on the right track. Assume I am completely average, and that I find all four of my mini-environments to be moderately acceptable. I therefore assign a value of 2 to each mini-environment. Next, I insert each rating into the Success Environment Formula as follows:

$$SE = (2 \times 2 \times 2 \times 2)Y.$$

Therefore my Mini-Environment Product is: **16**.

We may express our Success Environment Formula thus far as follows:

$$SE = (\quad)Y.$$

Simply insert the Mini-Environment Product that you have obtained inside the parentheses, and we are ready for the next step.

The "Y" Factor

Now for some bitter truth: Have you ever had the feeling that others controlled the way you thought without your permission; that you spent your time worrying about other people's problems rather than your own; that you were not in control of all the things upon which you were forced to concentrate?

If so, *why* were other people able to control your Inside Mini-Environment?

Because *you* let them.

Have you ever had the feeling that your Outside Mini-Environment was being controlled by someone else, perhaps because others caused you to eat too much, or smoke too much, or drink too much, or not take the time to maintain some degree of physical fitness?

If so, *why* were others able to control your Outside Mini-Environment?

Because *you* let them.

Have you ever had the feeling that someone else controlled your Home Mini-Environment? I don't mean through the type of control we all abdicate in an effort to maintain a mutual existence with a spouse or family, but through the kind of control that caused you to think and act and feel in a manner inconsistent with your own desires: an overbearing spouse perhaps, or children who are rude and inconsiderate—family members who generally tend to defeat the very purpose of home as a source of security and love.

And if so, *why* were those others able to control your Home Environment?

Because *you* let them.

Have you ever had the feeling that others controlled your destiny at work? Perhaps it has been by holding you back, perhaps by consuming enormous amounts of your time on details better left to someone else, or perhaps through office politics or through a dozen other techniques.

If so, *why* were others able to control your Work Mini-Environment?

Because *you* let them.

It is this series of "why's" that prompts us to call the average extent to which you control your conduct within your four mini-environments the "Y" Factor.

The "Y" Factor represents the average extent to which you take responsibility for, and seize control of, your own destiny in each of the four mini-environments.

We could have gotten fancy and not averaged the Y Factors in each of our four mini-environments to find one average Y that we use in the equation. Instead, we could have conducted a series of complex multiplications to show how each mini-environment is profoundly affected by the extent of control we exert over it. However, we stuck with simplicity (or as near simplicity as possible) by dealing with just one Average Y Factor which represents the *average* extent to which you control your conduct within your four mini-environments.

In the preceeding pages we have repeated time and again the importance of accepting responsibility for our conduct. The Y Factor reflects the importance of such acceptance. It compels us to recognize that if we are not in control of any particular mini-environment, it is only because at some previous point we abdicated control to someone else.

It's also important that we distinguish between deliberate and unintentional abdication of control. In marriage, for example, we deliberately abdicate some measure of control over our existence in order to create the institution. But consider the difference between these two examples:

You're sitting in front of the TV with your spouse late one evening. Your spouse turns to you and says, "Dear, I forgot to pick up bread for breakfast. Let's run down to the store and get some."

Now consider the second scenario:

You're seated in front of the television with your spouse late one evening. Your spouse turns to you and says, "I forgot to pick up bread for breakfast. Go get some."

In the first example, abdication of control is deliberate and shared. There is a sense of team effort, of cooperation, of understanding that the spouses work together toward their mutual advantage. In the second example, there is no deliberate abdication of control. The abdication is implied by the forced authority of one person over the other. Similarly, at work, we may deliberately abdicate control as part and parcel of our obligation to our employer to "join the team." But there is a vast difference between accepting a role as a team player and undeliberately permitting others at work to relegate us to roles we do not want to accept. With all this in mind, let's proceed with our equation and determine a rating for your personal Y Factor.

Fixing Values For "Y"

In each of our four mini-environments, we will fix a value for Y much as we did in evaluating our degree of satisfaction with each mini-environment. Y is assessed on a value of from 1 to 3 as follows:

3. A "Y Rating" of 3 indicates that you are totally in control of this environment. You permit others to substantially affect your behavior only upon your deliberate and express approval.

2. A "Y Rating" of 2 indicates that you usually control your conduct in this environment, but occasionally permit others to control your behavior without your deliberate and express approval.

1. A "Y Rating" of 1 indicates that you do not control your conduct in this environment and always permit others to do so without your deliberate and express approval.

As we did in assessing your degree of satisfaction with each of your four mini-environments, I encourage you to use decimals in fixing your Y Ratings. For example, in determining the extent to which you control your Outside Mini-Environment, you may decide that you do usually control your conduct within the environment, but that there are too many instances where others control it without your deliberate and express approval. You might therefore assign a value of 1.5. Similarly, in evaluating your Home Mini-Environment, you may decide that you are usually in control of the environment and frequently are in total control of the environment and therefore might assess a value of say, 2.7. Please give each Y Rating considerable thought and provide as honest an answer as possible to each.

Now, fill in the blanks in paragraphs A through D below:

A. **The current Y Rating I give to my Inside (I) Mini-Environment is:** ____
B. **The current Y Rating I give to my Outside (O) Mini-Environment is:** ____
C. **The current Y Rating I give to my Home (H) Mini-Environment is:** ____
D. **The current Y Rating I give to my Work (W) Mini-Environment is:** ____

Finding The Average "Y"

We now want to determine the *average* extent to which you control your conduct in each of your four mini-environments. To do so, first total the Y Ratings that you achieved in paragraphs A, B, C and D.

Again, by way of example, if I were completely average, and assigned a Y Rating of 2 to each of my four mini-environments, then the total of those figures would be 8.

Next, to determine your Average Y Factor, divide that total by 4, as indicated in the equation below:

$$\underline{\hspace{3cm}} \div 4 = Y$$
TOTAL

You should now have found your Average Y Factor. For instance, using our "average man" example, I would have divided my total of 8 by 4 to give me an average Y of 2. Now please fill in the blank in the following paragraph.

My Average Y Factor equals: ____

$$SE = (\underline{\hspace{0.5cm}}) \underline{\hspace{1cm}}$$

We may now express our Success Environment Formula by inserting the values we have attained for our Mini-Environment Product and our Average Y Factor. Use the formula below to insert the figures you have attained:

$$SE = (\underline{\hspace{0.5cm}}) \underline{\hspace{1cm}}$$

For example, if, as "Average Man," my Mini-Environment Product were 16 and my Average Y Factor were 2, my Success Environment Formula would appear as follows:

$$SE = (16)2.$$

My total Success Environment, therefore, would be 16 multiplied by 2. Therefore, as "Average Man" my total Success Environment equals 32. Please conduct the remaining math necessary to find your final answer, and complete the following sentence:

My Success Environment (SE) equals: ____

Merely assigning a value as a rough estimator of the extent to which we have reached our individual potential as human beings does not do us much good unless we have a model, or a context, to which we can relate the figure. To provide a useful context, we utilize a model called the Success Environment Progression Chart. The chart is divided into Modes and Levels of Potential. But even before we can utilize the chart, we must first understand and appreciate the very nature of the word "success."

Success As A Geometric Progression

You may remember the horse named Affirmed. Not too long ago, Steve Cauthen rode him to the Triple Crown. Now, I'm no expert on race horses, but I'm told that at that time Affirmed was worth about one million dollars. I'm also told that a really good race horse—one that won more than it lost—might be worth about one hundred thousand dollars. If Affirmed was worth ten times more than a really good race horse, it stands to reason, then, that he was able to run ten times faster.

Right?

Of course not. Affirmed couldn't run ten times faster than his opponents.

Then five times faster. Right?

Still too fast.

Then how about twice as fast?

No way.

How about one percent faster?

One percent.

The difference between a one million dollar race horse and a one hundred thousand dollar race horse is that the million dollar race horse can run just one percent faster. If so, then there is no logical reason for us to believe that the difference between a man who earns, say, one hundred thousand dollars a year and one who earns ten thousand dollars a year is that the man who earns one hundred thousand dollars a year works ten times harder, or is ten times smarter. Indeed, just as with race horses, it is that extra one percent that can make all the difference in the world.

This notion of one percent is no mere cliché. It embodies the fundamental concept that success is a *geometric progression*. Notice on the chart at the end of this chapter (figure 3-1) the difference between a geometric and a linear progression. Linear progressions progress along a straight line, whereas geometric progressions reflect a compounding of value by progressing in an upward curve.

In our case, if success were a linear progression, then massive amounts of improvement in each of our four mini-environments would be required to achieve any substantial advancement along the line. Yet because success is a geometric progression, mere fine tuning in any one of our four mini-environments will cause a substantial increase in our total Success Environment figure.

This result occurs because each of our four mini-environments positively or negatively reinforces the others. We have already examined why this is true, and how, for example, a low rating in our Home Mini-Environment can profoundly affect our effectiveness at work (Remember the pharmacist from Des Moines?). The Success Environment Formula reflects this reinforcing nature of the mini-environments by requiring us to multiply the environments by each other rather than simply "adding them up." If all we did was add the values we had attached to each environment, then our progression would indeed be linear. But because they positively or negatively reinforce each other they must therefore be multiplied by each other, which creates a geometric progression.

Using the values we have assigned of from 1 to 3 for each mini-environment and for each Y Rating within each mini-environment, the highest possible score attainable on the Success Environment Progression Chart is 243. To attain that score, an individual would have to assign a value of 3 to all variables in the formula. If you have done so while working your Success Environment Formula, I recommend that, unless you spend your spare time walking on water, you re-work the figures and make a more honest appraisal.

The average Success Environment score is 32. That reflects a completely average value of assigning a value of 2 to each of the variables in the equation. Most people will find their scores close to the figure 32. A score in the average range does not mean you are "average" as compared to the next guy. It only means that you have decided that you are only making an average effort to use the potential that you have.

The lowest possible Success Environment score is 1. To achieve that score, you would have to assign a 1 rating to all of your mini-environments and to all of your Y Ratings within your mini-environments as well. If, after working the Success Environment Formula, you determine that your total Success Environment equals 1, I recommend that you seek immediate professional help.

It is interesting and important to note that the average Success Environment score of 32 is a whole lot closer to the lowest possible score of 1 than it is to the highest possible score of 243. This result is achieved because of the geometric nature of the formula. By the fine tuning of just a few knobs within each mini-environment, the "average" success can accelerate geometrically into what we will next describe as the Success Mode.

Modes

If all we did was stick to whole numbers, the Success Environment Formula could produce 92 separate results. Nevertheless, these results can be lumped into three categories, called "modes." Please examine the chart entitled "Modes and Levels of Potential" (figure 3-2) at the end of this chapter. It shows that the lowest possible mode extends from 1 through 3. It is called the "Failure Mode." It depicts a total Success Environment that is genuinely unsatisfactory to the individual involved.

The median mode extends from 4 through 48. It is called the "Mediocrity Mode." It is where most of us spend most of our time, and depicts a level of satisfaction that is only marginally satisfactory. Again, it is important to note how mathematically close both the Failure Mode and Mediocrity Mode are located, due to the geometric nature of success.

Finally, the highest possible mode extends from 49 through 243. It is called the "Success Mode." It depicts a genuine satisfaction with most, if not all, aspects of an individual's life. Individuals operating within the Success Mode are utilizing, by their own calculation, more than an average amount of their own potential.

Most of us wallow in the Mediocrity Mode. We border on failure. The irony of this status is that with slight additional effort we can geometrically accelerate our rate of success. Generally speaking, the extent to which we are satisfied with each of our four mini-environments will not change substantially until we change our Average Y Factor by personally seizing control of—and responsibility for—our conduct in each of the four mini-environments. This requires a critical evaluation of our Y Factor and immediate efforts to seize control.

A mode is nothing more than a mathematical guideline: a useful but general tool for assessing the extent to which we are utilizing our full potential. It provides a check-at-a-glance approach to assess our progress. The modes are disproportionate in size because of the geometric nature of the equation. It is ironic that so many of us find ourselves crowded into the smaller Mediocrity (or worse, Failure) Mode when there is literally so much room at the top.

Levels Of Potential

Each of the three Success Modes can be divided into three levels, referred to as Levels of Potential. There are a total of nine Levels of Potential.

While they are mathematically arbitrary, Levels of Potential have the effect of dividing each mode into three equal levels. The result is that we can measure our progress within a particular mode as we fine-tune our lives within each of our four mini-environments.

Examine the "Success Environment Geometric Progression Chart" (figure 3-3) at the end of this chapter. There you will notice horizontal categories depicting the three modes: Failure, Mediocrity and Success. The nine vertical divisions represent the Levels of Potential. Levels 1 through 3 are inherent to the Failure Mode. Levels 4 through 6 are inherent to the Mediocrity Mode; and levels 7 through 9 are inherent to the Success Mode.

Now, using the Success Environment Formula, determine the value of your Success Environment and complete the following sentences:

A. **My SE** = _____

B. **I currently operate in the** _____ **Mode at the** _____ **Level of Potential.**

For example, if my SE equalled 32 (exactly average), I would operate in the Mediocrity Mode at the Fifth Level of Potential.

Remember, these values were fixed by you. They represent your own assessment of the extent to which you are realizing your full potential.

The purpose of this exercise is not to depress you. It is to provide, instead, a useful learning tool that may be used as a system of continuing evaluation as you continue your journey called success.

The Success Environment Geometric Progression Chart lends itself to the realistic establishment of goals. If, for example, upon conducting the exercise for the first time, you found your rating to be within the Mediocrity Mode, at the Sixth Level of Potential, then you might realistically establish a 30-day goal of being in the Success Mode at the Seventh Level of Potential. Periodically, at least monthly, the exercise should be conducted anew, so that your progress can be charted each step of the way.

Please remember that this exercise is just a model, a conceptual tool. If you happen to land in the Failure Mode this time around, it doesn't mean that you are now, and always will be, a "failure." It only means that you personally are not satisfied with the status of your existence at this time. Consistent with our entire approach, the solution to that dissatisfaction rests with you.

Now, please re-examine your ratings in each of your four mini-environments. Determine where you are in special need of improvement. In which mini-environments is your existence not satisfactory? Upon which mini-environments should you concentrate your efforts to improve?

Next, examine your Y Factors. In which mini-environments are you in complete control? In which do you exert only moderate control; and in which are you out of control? Where should you focus your attention to regain the control which it is your right and responsibility to exercise?

The real value of this entire process is that it permits us to isolate those areas of our lives that are not satisfactory. By "fine tuning" our existence in those mini-environments that need help, we can create the geometric progression we discussed earlier. Remember, you don't have to be able to run ten times faster to be ten times more valuable to yourself, to those with whom you work, and to those whom you love.

There you have it: the Success Environment Formula that you can use to evaluate the extent to which you are satisfied with your own existence.

More important, it is a tool to be used for isolating those areas of your life that need improvement. With this tool, you can now focus your attention upon those techniques and methods which will help you increase your rating in those areas which require special attention. The rest of this book is devoted to providing you with "just what the doctor ordered"—good advice on how to lift your personal ratings in each mini-environment. While I recommend you read the entire book first, you may want to concentrate most heavily upon those sections dealing with the mini-environment in which you perceive the need for special action.

In the sections to follow, we will explore methods and techniques that are practical, useful and effective for improving your rating in each of your four mini-environments. Read the book through first, then go back and concentrate on those mini-environments in which your score was particularly low. Apply the advice contained herein, and once each month re-evaluate your progress by reworking the Success Environment Formula.

Our Success Environment approach is a system distilled down to manageable units: a context in which we can relate all the advice we receive and ideas we have to the betterment of our existence in one or more of our four mini-environments. We can proceed now, equipped with an accurate idea of where we, as individuals, require special attention. We can evaluate and implement advice relative to that need, secure in the knowledge that among our own potential is the ability to ignite a personal geometric rate of success equal to, and worthy of, our enormous potential as human beings.

Linear v. Geometric Progressions

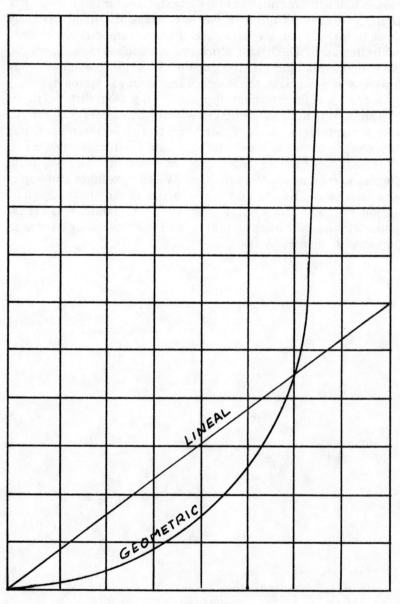

Figure 3-1

Modes and Levels of Potential

MODE	MINI-ENVIRONMENTS (I) (O) (H) (W)		Y FACTOR (Y)		SUCCESS ENVIRONMENT (SE)	LEVEL OF POTENTIAL
FAILURE MODE	(1 × 1 × 1 × 1)	×	1	=	1	1st
	(1 × 1 × 1 × 1)	×	2	=	2	2nd
	(1 × 1 × 1 × 1)	×	3	=	3	3rd
MEDIOCRITY MODE	(2 × 2 × 2 × 2)	×	1	=	16	4th
	(2 × 2 × 2 × 2)	×	2	=	32	5th
	(2 × 2 × 2 × 2)	×	3	=	48	6th
SUCCESS MODE	(3 × 3 × 3 × 3)	×	1	=	81	7th
	(3 × 3 × 3 × 3)	×	2	=	162	8th
	(3 × 3 × 3 × 3)	×	3	=	243	9th

Figure 3-2

SUCCESS ENVIRONMENT
GEOMETRIC PROGRESSION CHART

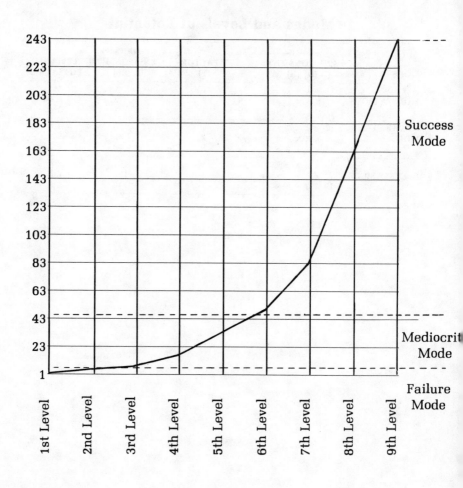

Figure 3-3

IV

Critical Evaluation:
Getting Straight
With Number One

*Our past will control our conduct and thoughts
unless we use all the current rational abilities we
have to program ourselves in another direction.*

This is Calvin's heart at age four.

It is red and robust and strong and growing and filled with excitement as Calvin jumps from bed on a fine summer morning.

It feels no strain as Calvin bustles about his room selecting his clothes in an effort to dress himself.

"This will make Mom and Dad proud of me," Calvin thinks as he puts his shirt on backwards and forgets to zip his trousers. "I'll run downstairs and eat and show Mom and Dad I dressed myself and then go play with Tommy all day down at the creek!"

Calvin runs downstairs through the living room, toward the kitchen and breakfast. But as he does, he brushes against a table and knocks over a lamp.

His father observes, grabs Calvin by the arm and shakes him. "Calvin," he says, "you're the clumsiest boy I've ever seen! Stop running around the house and settle down."

That breaks a little piece of Calvin's heart, but he remembers the clothes and the creek and Tommy, and he bounds into the kitchen to announce, "Mom, look! I dressed myself!"

"Oh Calvin," she says, "you did it all wrong. Your shirt's on backwards and your pants aren't zipped. I don't know what I'm going to do with you! And I bet you left your room a mess, to boot."

Another piece of Calvin's heart breaks off.

"Sit down and eat," his father shouts. "And try not to make a mess."

Calvin tries, but to no avail. His milk winds up on the floor.

"Enough!" his mother shouts. "Calvin, you just can't seem to do anything right. Up to your room with you. You can spend the day there thinking about the mess you made, and clean up that pig sty while you're there."

As Calvin begins to trudge upstairs, his father's voice follows after him: "You're a big disappointment, Calvin. A big disappointment."

This is Calvin's heart at age fourteen.

It's beating wildly today, filled with excitement from the news he is bringing home from school.

"Wait 'til they hear," he thinks. "I got an 'A' on my test, and I made the football team—all in the same day!"

Calvin bursts through the back door with a bang.

Calvin's mother shouts from the kitchen, "Calvin, how many times have I told you not to slam that back door? Quit making such a ruckus."

Calvin races into the kitchen. "Look Mom!" he says, "I got an 'A' on my paper and I made the football team. Here, you want to see my test?"

"Not now, Calvin," his mother says. "I'm busy fixing dinner. Go show your father. I think you're too small for football. You'll get hurt."

"Look at my test, Dad! I got an 'A', and I made the football team!" Calvin says, as he races into the living room.

His father is reading his paper. He doesn't look up. "That's nice," he says. "Go get ready for dinner. And why aren't your chores done? There will be no football unless the grass gets mowed. I'm tired of harping at you, Calvin. Run along now, I'm busy."

As Calvin makes his way to his room, his father's voice follows him:

"You're a big disappointment, Calvin. A big disappointment."

And a little more of Calvin's heart breaks away.

This is Calvin's heart at age twenty-five.

It's filled with love today—and excitement and hope.

"I know she'll say yes," Calvin thinks. "I know she loves me,too. It will be great! The two of us and—maybe—we'll have kids!"

All evening his heart nearly bursts as he wines and dines the girl he loves. Finally, moments before he pops his question, she says, "Calvin, I won't be able to see you again."

"But I . . . but I . . . why?"

"Tommy and I are in love," she says. "But we'll still be friends, won't we?"

"But I . . . but I . . .?"

"Good night, Calvin."

And as Calvin watches her walk away, he hears a little voice from deep inside say:

"You're a big disappointment, Calvin. A big disappointment."

And his heart nearly breaks in two.

This is Calvin's heart at age forty.

It's excited today, and beating a little fast. But it knows that if the boss approves that new marketing idea, it will mean a big boost to Calvin's career.

It flutters slightly as Calvin walks into the boss's office to hear his decision on the idea.

"It's a good plan," the boss says. "I think we'll use it."

Calvin's heart swells with pride.

"But," the boss continues, "I want a younger man to manage it. We need youth and vitality to manage a new program like this. With this much money invested, we can't afford any disappointments. Here's a hundred dollar bonus for the idea. Go back to work now, Calvin. And on the way back to your office tell young Johnson I want to see him."

Calvin obediently delivers the message to Johnson and returns to his desk.

"No disappointments," Calvin thinks. "They can't afford disappointments."

And from somewhere inside, Calvin hears a voice say: "You're a big disappointment, Calvin. A big disappointment."

Another chunk of Calvin's heart falls to the floor.

This is Calvin's heart at age seventy.

It's brittle now and scarred, and filled with regret at what might have been.

"It's not fair," Calvin thinks. "Here I lie on my death bed with just minutes 'til the end, and I will die not knowing why I never accomplished much, or enjoyed much, or loved much. What did I do wrong? Where did I fail? Why were so many others able to do so much while I accomplished so little?"

"I don't know," Calvin thinks. "I just don't know. And I guess I'll die not knowing."

And as Calvin closes his eyes for the last time, the last words he hears come from somewhere deep inside: "You're a big disappointment, Calvin. A big disappointment."

And then his heart broke forever.

That Guy In The Mirror

You are not a disappointment.

Most of us spend our entire lives trying to please someone else; trying to live up to someone else's standard. How ironic that we should spend our time trying to meet a standard that we perceive someone else has imposed upon us, when in fact others have enough dificulty determining what they expect from themselves, let alone what they expect from us.

It is natural enough that in our early years we attempt to live up to someone else's standard. As children, we have no other criteria upon which to base our conduct, other than the standards established for us at home. Eric Berne, in his work on Transactional Analysis, describes this as adopting a "You're O.K., I'm Not O.K." posture. Here a child attempts to emulate the conduct of adults and, of course, in most instances fails miserably. With each failure we are told either outright or by implication that our conduct constitutes a disappointment to others, and the first seeds of self-depreciation are planted in our minds.

As the years progress, we try to meet other standards. As we more often than not fail to achieve those standards, those seeds of self-depreciation are nourished until they become a strong and semi-permanent part of our psyche.

We wind up—quite literally—with a little voice inside which keeps whispering to us: "You're a big disappintment, Calvin. A big disappointment."

Yet, there is only one person on this earth whom we truly have to please. And we cannot please him entirely so long as there remains so much as a whisper within our minds telling us we're a disappointment. That one person is, of course, the guy in the mirror. He is the ultimate arbiter of your self worth. He is the guy with whom you must live. He is the guy with whom you must sleep. He is the guy who must fully and unconditionally support your every idea and effort.

Of all the people you know, he is the only one you'll die with. Indeed, the number of people who attend your funeral will be determined largely by the weather that day. He's the only fellow you know you can count on to be there. The efforts we undertake to improve our rating within our Inside Mini-Environment must begin from this foundation:

The *only* person we are trying to please is that guy in the mirror.

We must begin by asking ourselves, "Who am I now? What am I now? Why do I hold the particular attitudes I hold?" We often tend to sell ourselves short and to hold self-defeating attitudes because of unpleasant past experiences. It is our responsibility to constantly hold those old self-defeating attitudes up to the light of current reality and to measure them against what we honestly can *do* now, what we honestly can *be* now. No one else will do it for us.

> Mirror mirror on the wall,
> Am I short or am I tall?
> Am I old or am I young?
> What is my idea of fun?
> Am I selling myself short
> Just because of some past hort?
> (That's supposed to be "hurt,"
> But I couldn't make it rhyme!)
> What do I really want to be?
> A millionaire, a bum, a tree?
> Surely I should read a book,
> To study life and better look.
> And if that yacht I will own,
> I'll have to do it all alone.
> No one else controls my life.
> I can choose success or strife.
> Yes, mirror mirror on the wall,
> *You* and *I* can earn it all!

How Others See You: Self-Fulfilling
Prophecy As A Y Factor

Here is some logic with which we can all agree:

1. Our ability to succeed depends on our ability to conduct ourselves in a manner consistent with our own highest level of potential.

2. Our ability to conduct ourselves in such a fashion depends on our own self-image, i.e., on our belief in our ability to utilize our full potential.

3. Others can, and frequently do, reduce our self-image by telling us either outright or by implication that we do not possess all the potential that we do in fact possess; and:

4. Their appraisal of us can act as a self-fulfilling prophecy by reducing our own level of self-esteem and therefore our success.

In other words, we frequently play roles in order to fit the image that others have laid out for us. Children are the best example of this phenomenon. Tell a little boy that he's serious minded and a deep thinker and he'll *act* serious minded and like a deep thinker. Tell a little girl that she is frivolous and carefree and she'll act frivolous and carefree. Tell a child that he's no good in math and he'll be no good in math. Tell him he displays a knack for English and he'll display such a knack.

Adults are no less immune to the process. Tell an impressionable young salesman, *"You can't sell that!"* and he probably won't. Tell an impressionable young lawyer, "There's no way you can win that case against old counsellor Smith," and he'll probably lose. Unfortunately for adults, most of these self-fulfilling prophecies are conveyed on a more subtle level.

By implication, the rest of the world may say to you: "An individual with your education and in your age group should only be earning 'X' number of dollars per year." Or, "A woman in your position should be glad to have the job, let alone a salary increase." Or (even more subtly), "Of course there is no reason for you to take that idea of yours seriously, since obviously none of us takes it seriously."

In a nutshell, we let the rest of the world program our potential. We let them tell us what we're capable of doing, when by right and design it should be exactly the other way around.

In sum, the most formidable obstacle most of us face in increasing our Y Rating in our Inside Mini-Environment is the expectations of others. If other people are by definition average, then, by and large, expectations regarding us are probably going to be average as well. Rather than permitting others to assign us to average roles, we must be assertive enough to establish—and then live up to—our own.

If our personal level of competence and conduct does not happen to fit neatly into the image of mediocrity that someone else has comfortably carved out for us, then that irreconcilable difference is their problem and not ours. The chances are excellent that by acting in a manner consistent with our potential we will surprise some people, for such conduct will not neatly fit into the image they have established for us. But better to surprise others—even unpleasantly—and utilize our full potential, than to waste away that potential in an effort to comply with, and conform to, a mediocre mode that others have established.

How You See Yourself:
The Prophetic, Fulfilled Self

How do you see yourself?

It is your image of "you" that is important. Unfortunately, we often receive so much input from others in the form of self-fulfilling prophecies that we find it difficult to reach an objective personal appraisal of our potential. Let's utilize the Einstein (logic) Mode we discussed earlier to achieve a fair and objective evaluation of your true potential.

To get to the bottom of matters, we'll make some lists. Find some paper and a pencil and we'll begin. On the top of one sheet write, "How Others See Me." Using synonyms, list all the ways that others see you. For example, your list might look something like this:

"How Others See Me:

Frequently forgetful

Boring

Sometimes loving

Easy to fool

Good Natured

Fat

Average intelligence

Average ambition."

Now, write at the top of another sheet, "How I See Me." Again, list all the words that describe you. Except, this time, don't worry about how others perceive you. Instead, describe the "real you" as only that fellow in the mirror can do. Your list might look something like this:

"How I See Me:

Never forgetful

Exciting

Loving

Fit

Intelligent

Ambitious

Astute."

Now pull out a third sheet and entitle it: "My Five Strongest Characteristics." Enter on it the five things about you that you like most. Your list might look something like this:

"My Five Strongest Characteristics:

1. I have an exceptionally good humor and I share it with others.

2. I am exceptionally good at managing figures and am therefore extremely competent at my job.

3. I have the ability to make others want to share their innermost thoughts with me.

4. I am a very good parent and work hard at raising my children.

5. I am in very good physical condition."

Now at the top of another sheet write, "My Five Weakest Characteristics." List those five characteristics about you that you like least. Your list might look something like this:

"My Five Weakest Characteristics:

1. I have great difficulty expressing myself honestly to others.

2. I am too frequently intimidated by others.

3. I am frequently selfish and overbearing at home.

4. I smoke too much.

5. I permit myself to become too easily depressed."

Please look again at the lists you have made. Set aside the opinions of others for a moment, and carefully study the three remaining lists. Evaluate each entry on each list. Does each entry honestly reflect your personal appraisal of yourself, or are you simply repeating what others have been "whispering in your ear" all these years? Is your appraisal based upon honest self-analysis, or is it merely the self-fulfilling prophecy of someone else?

Who is that guy in the mirror? Are his characteristics best described on the list entitled, "How Others See Me," or are his characteristics best described on the other lists that you have made? Whose expectations shall that guy in the mirror try to fulfill? Shall he continue adopting attitudes and actions consistent with the descriptions of others, or shall he begin today completely and unequivocally to conform to his self-described potential?

Now take a special look at the list entitled, "My Weakest Characteristics." Do the items on that list accurately reflect those of your characteristics about which you are not pleased? If so, then regardless of what they are, I congratulate you, and I suggest that you add a sixth item to the list entitled, "My Strongest Characteristics." That item should read:

> "I have the ability to honestly analyze myself and to list those characteristics about me with which I am not pleased. I recognize that through this ability I also have the ability to improve my conduct in each of the areas listed, because I know that identifying the problem is the first and most important step in the process of overcoming obstacles."

Accept The Nomination!

Before Secretary of State Henry Kissinger was married, he spent a considerable amount of time pursuing beautiful women. He was once asked by a reporter, "Is it true that there is a special relationship between you and Jill St. John?"

In his inimitable style, Kissinger responded, "Currently there is not. But she has not said that if nominated she would not run, and if elected, she would not serve."

In the space of a single brilliant statement Kissinger made it clear that while he was still in the primaries, so to speak, with Jill St. John, the contest was far from over.

Too many of us spend our entire lives mentally in the primaries, with no real expectation that our name will be on the ballot at the general election. We spend the primary contest, much as politicians do, "showing the voters our stuff," hoping that the voters will give us the opportunity to compete by certifying our name as their candidate. Yet unless we are, in fact, running for office, the only voting public with which we should be concerned is that elector in the mirror. No one else's "vote" is necessary for us to win the nomination.

What are the things you can become? What is the election you can win? On another piece of paper, list these goals, however general they may be. Outline the very limits of your potential as you see it today. In later chapters we will discuss the mechanics of goal setting. But for now, just find the words, the basic formula, the one notion that describes the things you know you can become. Write it down and study it. What have you decided about you? Who is that guy in the mirror? What strengths do you have? What weaknesses? What can that fellow make of his life?

Now look again in the mirror. Go ahead, take a long, long look. Smile at that fellow there. He's a great guy. And shout these words:

"I nominate myself to reach my full potential as a human being!"

Say it again: "I nominate myself to reach my full potential as a human being!"

Smile again at that guy in the mirror. Be nice to him. He's the best friend you'll ever have. He just proved that by nominating you for greatness. Now shout back at him and the rest of the world as loud as your lungs can bear:

"I accept the nomination! I accept the nomination!"

You are *not* a disappointment.

For no matter how many little voices may be buzzing around inside, it is only your voice that counts, it is only your voice that matters. And *your voice* has just told you that you are geared for greatness, designed for accomplishment, and engineered for success.

Start From There

The friction between Sir Winston Churchill and Lady Astor was legendary.

One night they both attended a crowded party. Sir Winston had imbibed a little too much. Lady Astor, who had stationed herself across the crowded room from Sir Winston, suddenly turned to address her nemesis.

A hush fell over the crowd as she addressed Sir Winston, some feet away.

"Sir Winston, you are drunk! What's more, you are *very* drunk!" she snapped.

The crowd remained silent as Sir Winston squared himself to address Lady Astor.

"Lady Astor, you are ugly," he said. "What's more, you are very ugly. What's more, *I'll* be sober in the morning!"

While Lady Astor may have suffered from a terminal case of the uglies, it's nice to know that our personal shortcomings are, if we choose them to be, temporary—regardless of the weaknesses we may have listed above, and regardless of our ratings in each mini-environment when we conducted the Success Environment Formula exercise for the first time. It's comforting to know that we, like Sir Winston, can be "sober in the morning."

The ability to change those characteristics about us which are unsatisfactory rests, first, upon our ability to make a critical evaluation of where we are now, as we have done, and second, upon our ability to start from there in realizing the potential that we possess.

It's All My Mother's Fault

In an effort to relieve ourselves of personal responsiblity for our destiny, many of us grope for excuses. We are eager to blame someone or something else for our lack of success. Almost every one of us at some level is guilty of this form of rationalization.

Our finger-pointing may be blatant, as in the case of the individual who blames his lack of success on the fact that his mother didn't breast feed him when he was a baby. Or it may be more subtle, as in the case of the man who vaguely says, "I never had that chance." In each example, both individuals are blaming someone or something else for their failure to reach their full potential.

It would be naive to contend that others do not have a profound effect upon our lives—especially in the early years. But as we reach adulthood, we should become more and more aware that the influences which were exerted over us in our youth should no longer have a *direct* effect upon our adulthood decision-making processes.

Nevertheless, it's a convenient crutch that we frequently carry with us into adulthood. The excuse, "It's all my mother's fault," is replaced by, "It's all my spouse's fault," or, "It's all my boss's fault," or, "It's all my children's fault."

In our effort to improve the extent to which we realize our full potential, we must not start from a foundation of incidents that occurred years ago. Nor may we start from a foundation of rationalization which recognizes others in our adult years as being the primary moving forces in our lives. We must return again to that guy in the mirror and accept him and love him as he is, intent upon improving him, consistent with his own potential.

Others may take too simplistic an approach and announce boldly that our past experiences and thoughts should have no bearing whatsoever upon our ability to make rational decisions now. Others contend at the other extreme that we are totally locked into a course of conduct and thought which is totally predetermined by our previous experiences.

I suggest a middle ground that proposes that our past will control our conduct and thoughts *unless* we use all the current rational abilities we have to program ourselves in another direction.

There is a huge difference between saying that we are the *products* of our past environment, and saying that we are the *victims* of our past environment. The former implies that there are certain past incidents and thoughts that, when multiplied together, produced the current "us." It does not preclude that other factors may be added to the formula and thereby affect the product. The latter statement implies that as a result of past incidents and thoughts, we are locked into a mode of behavior over which we have no control.

(We can become deeply philosophical at this point and explore the advantages of the Free Will school of thought as opposed to the concept of Determinism. But such talk is [pardon the pun] academic. For even if a system creates merely the illusion of control over one's destiny, that illusion is better than no control at all.)

But enough of this heavy-duty philosophizing. Suffice it to say that if you're a non-productive, self-demeaning chump, it's not your mother's fault. It's your fault.

Fantasy Land: "One Of These Days"

Many of us spend our whole lives waiting for our ship to come in, even though we never sent one out. We regard our future as a diffuse blob with no real boundaries or perimeters: just a vague, distant destination where we'll wind up "one of these days."

We read in the paper or see on TV news of great accomplishments or happenings, and we say, "One of these days that'll happen to me." And then we wait and wait and wait for something to happen.

The sensation that life is passing us by is a very real sensation for most of us. We all, at some time in our lives, have experienced the feeling that the world is proceeding on its merry way without our direct involvement, and that it will probably get along quite well even after we've left. In an effort to throw ourselves back into the mainstream of events, we frequently establish hurried and ill-defined goals: occasionally written, but more often not recorded anywhere. These "goals," as we call them, are more like wishes than concrete and specific decisions regarding our lives.

And still we sit and wait for the world to beat a path to our door. We wait for things to happen to us, rather than us happening to things. We regard our life as carrying us toward some distant destination, rather than us causing our lives to reach that destination. We abdicate control to fate and, despite the lack of any specific image of what it is we want to become, and despite any effort on our part to reach our "goals," we are content to sit back and assume that things will come our way "one of these days."

If it is the clear establishment of our goals, and the acceptance of our responsibility for pursuing those goals, that are the primary ingredients for avoiding the "one of these days" mentality, then why do we so often neglect to set specific goals?

I think it's because we fear failure.

We fear failure.

The greatest defense in the world against failure is to not have a goal. There's no way we can fail if we're not trying for something

in the first place. Failing to set specific goals, then, protects us
from our fear of failure, because if we never quite decide what it
is that we want, then, when we don't get it—and we won't—we
can always say, "Oh, I didn't want that, anyway."

There is a name for that. It's called the "I didn't want to win,
anyway" syndrome, and we see it all around us every day.

We see it in the man who didn't get that promotion: "Oh, I
didn't want to move up in that organization, anyway."

We see it in the family that can't afford that vacation: "We
thought we'd just stay home this year."

We see it in the lawyer who didn't win his case: "Oh, the client
was probably guilty, anyway."

And we see it in the salesperson who didn't make that sale:
"Did you get any orders today?"

"Yeah, two. Get out and stay out."

In short, we see it in all of us every day. Of course, where
we most frequently see the "I didn't want to win, anyway" syndrome is when it comes to money. Sometimes it seems as though
there are only two kinds of people on this earth: those who have a
lot of money and those who say, "I didn't want a lot of money,
anyway."

If your goals don't happen to include having a lot of money,
that's fine. There's nothing wrong with that. But what really
burns that part of me next to which I normally keep my wallet is
when I hear people regard money as something unwholesome,
unhealthy, unclean, something about which those who have it
should be ashamed. Some people will tell you money can't buy you
friends or health or happiness.

Well, they're talking about Confederate money.

It's money that builds our churches and synagogues. It builds
our hospitals, feeds the hungry, houses orphans and gives
families time to spend together. Saying that money is something
less than that is just another way of saying, "I didn't want to win,
anyway."

But whether we're talking about setting specific financial or
Work goals, or Home goals, or Inside goals, or Outside goals, the
fact is most of us don't have any real goals at all: just vague notions of what it is we want to have happen to us instead of what it
is we want to make happen. And day after day we too often plod
along, ignoring that we haven't made anything *good* happen, but

thankful that nothing *bad* has happened to us. And we just keep saying, "It's all going to come my way—one of these days."

"It's All Right Now"

The lyrics of a recently popular song go:

> It's all right now.
> I've learned my lesson well.
> You can't please everyone,
> So you've got to please yourself.

By assuming control of our own destiny, we are bound to get someone angry. Maybe it will be your boss, who currently has you pegged into a neat little role you no longer wish to assume. Maybe it will be your spouse, who will be at least temporarily uncomfortable because you no longer fit the role of the relatively insensitive and uncaring spouse she (or he) has come to know.

But your spouse will probably adjust, and so will your boss. In the meantime, by pursuing your own specific goals, you'll be working to "please yourself" directly.

Your own critical evaluation process must deal with the extent to which you can begin immediately to "please yourself" by establishing your own priorities and seizing control of your own life. It can be, especially at first, a lonely process. Suddenly the only "image" you must live up to is your own. Suddenly the voices from outside which used to either cheer you on or hold you back are irrelevant. Decision making becomes your own responsibility. Results become your own responsibility. Your action or inaction becomes your own responsibility.

But if we have spent the better part of our lives trying to please others, then it is entirely possible that we still lack a firm notion of what will please us. In the next chapter we will discuss the three-step formula for establishing personal priorities. But first we must take another few pages to get as close as we can to "Number One."

"Getting To Know You"

There is another song which goes:

> Getting to know you
> Getting to know all about you . . .

Suddenly there we are: intent upon asserting our own individuality, intent upon managing our own conduct in each of our four mini-environments in such a fashion that we will reach our own full potential as individuals. Yet we may have no clear idea of the direction we genuinely wish our life to take. In fact, our ability to assess the direction that will please us most is inversely proportional to the extent to which we have spent our lives previously trying to please others. We must establish direct and unobscured communication with the innermost soul of that guy in the mirror.

Oh, Oh! Here I Come!

We often hide from ourselves. We dilute that sensitive communication system between our innermost feelings and our outermost actions. We act and think and talk in a manner not entirely consistent with what's going on deep inside.

It was Bill Cosby, I believe, who once suggested that many of us hide from ourselves through the use of alcohol and drugs. Every time we hear that little guy inside trying to catch up with us, we drown him with a shot of bourbon or space him out with a barbiturate so he won't give us any problems or ask us any questions we may have difficulty answering.

A lot of us don't want to meet that guy in there because we're afraid we might not like him, or worse, because we're afraid he might not like us. But he is the real us—our innermost feelings and thoughts.

There are a number of devices such as prayer, contemplation and meditation which can help us get in touch with that little guy, and it's important that we try. For whatever our outermost thoughts might say, it is only the deepest of impulses that can help us conclude what will truly make us happy.

Many Eastern religions are, in particular, noted for their emphasis upon this effort at reaching the innermost self, and they use many methods to reach these higher "levels of consciousness." Without ever having deliberately attempted to do so, many of us have simulated, to a very small extent, these efforts. The devout dieter is a good example. He quite literally fasts, not in an effort to heighten his consciousness, but in an effort to improve his waistline. But frequently the dieter will experience a sense of heightened consciousness simply because his body, with less food in its system, suffers fewer distractions. Under such circumstances, thoughts frequently become more coherent. Lines of reasoning become more complex. And revelations about oneself, however minor, frequently occur.

Once when I was very broke, I decided it was time to go on a diet—mainly because I couldn't afford to buy groceries. I fasted for several days, and then existed for about two weeks on small pieces of lean red meat and eggs. I didn't own a TV, and my only radio was broken. The only two pieces of furniture in my apartment were a chair and a bed. At night I would sit in the chair, sip water, and stare out the window. I lost a lot of weight during those two weeks, but, more important, some of the best writing I've ever done flowed from the thoughts I had during that period. (I *do not* recommend "fasting" as a device to achieve heightened consciousness, except under the supervision of qualified medical professionals.)

That little guy inside—the one we usually drown out through over-eating or over-drinking, or with the sound of a TV—is usually a pretty nice fellow, and he has our best interests at heart. Getting to know him is usually a far more pleasant experience than we would expect.

I recommend that you explore, through qualified and experienced professionals, meditative techniques by which the two of you can become more intimately acquainted.

Total Unconditional Acceptance

Getting to know ourselves is frequently fun. It can result in a heightened level of self-esteem which has been defined as the degree to which we feel warm and loving toward ourselves. Lilburn S. Barksdale, of the Barksdale Foundation, has defined this phenomenon of genuine self love as Total Unconditional Acceptance (T.U.A.) of self. As such, T.U.A. is a natural by-product of getting in touch with, and establishing meaningful rapport and meaningful dialogue with, that little guy inside.

In the book *Stand Up, Speak Out and Win*, William J. McGrane defined T.U.A. as the realization that:

> *You are a unique and worthy individual regardless of your mistakes, defeats and failures, or your human*

frailties and real or fancied shortcomings, despite what others may say, think or feel about you or your behavior, regardless of your great accomplishments or lack thereof.

It stands to reason that T.U.A. is a natural requisite toward effective goal setting and toward turning loose the enormous potential that we as individuals possess. For unless we as individuals can accept the notion that we are worthy of all that we wish to accomplish, we will continue to be our own worst enemy by holding ourselves back.

Your VERY Best Friend

Look again in the mirror. There he is. Your very best friend. There may be others whom you love. Many, I hope. There may be others who love you. But it's that guy you're looking at who always has been, and always will be, your very best friend.

When my son was very small, I frequently asked him, "Who is your very best friend?" He would always respond by providing the name of one of his playing companions. The name would vary, depending upon whom he had seen the most of during the past several weeks.

But then I'd always ask again, "But who's your *very* best friend?"

We repeated the exercise many times, until the answer became apparent to him. Ask him today who his very best friend is, and he'll say, "You're looking at him!" I hope it's a lesson he'll carry with him for the rest of his life, for it's one of the best this father has to offer. "Know thy self," the philosopher said. And he meant it. Show me an individual who is in touch with himself, and who has clearly established priorities in each of the four mini-environments of his life, and I'll show you an individual who is, by any definition of the term, a "success."

That guy in the mirror. Number One. Numero Uno. The Chief Enchilada. The Main Man. The Boss. The Nominator and Nominee all rolled into one. That superb and unique package called "you."

Let the self-fulfilling prophecies of others fall upon other ears. Let others wait for permission to begin. Let someone else blame the rest of the world for the successes they have not achieved. And let others talk of "one of these days."

For you, it's "all right now." You're "getting to know you." You're meeting that little guy inside. And you can accept him totally, unconditionally. And why not? He is the best friend—the very best friend—you'll ever have.

Let's travel now to a place called the Sleepy Time Motel to discover how, with your brains and his help, the two of you can utilize the enormous potential at your disposal.

V

Turning On Your
Success Mechanism:
The Sleepy Time Motel

*The mere ability to choose, standing alone, is
not freedom — it's chaos. True freedom is the
ability to make knowledgeable, meaningful
choices.*

The Sleepy Time Motel is located just outside of Cincinnati.
Rooms were $12 a night. If you stayed for a week, they were $10 a
night. I know this because my best friend stayed there for a week.

The rooms there weren't very clean. In fact, they weren't clean
at all; and if you wanted to shower in the morning, you had to do
so before 7:30, because they ran out of hot water early. I know
that, too, because, as I say, my best friend stayed there for a
week.

He stayed there because he didn't have any place else to stay,
and he couldn't afford a nicer room. He had just lost his family in
a divorce. He had lost his house, almost all his possessions,
business interests and most of his income.

Oh, he had two dimes to rub together, but he wouldn't do it for
fear one of them might wear out. He was broke, all right. Almost
bankrupt. It was a shame to see him that way—my best friend—
because even though he'd made his share of mistakes, he'd worked
hard and come through a lot.

We spent a lot of time together that week in that motel room, my
best friend and I, and we talked a lot. My best friend would look
me in the eye and he'd say, "I know goals are just as important as

83

can be, but how in the world do you really establish effective
goals and make them work?''

And I'd say, "That's easy, friend. You must do three things."

He'd smile at me and say, "What are they, DeGreen?"

And I'd smile right back and say:

"*First we must establish our goals and understand why their
mere establishment, if maintained, will work. Second, we must
adopt a conscious mental process by which to sustain the vivid image of our goals; and third, we must relax and let our built-in success mechanism work for us.*"

My best friend would lean forward, look me in the eye, and say,
"Tell me more."

So I did.

First we talked about why *we must establish our goals and
understand why their mere establishment, if maintained, will
work.*

Establishing Goals

Have you ever taken a trip without first having at least some
idea where you were going? Did you ever play basketball without
a rim, football without a goal line, baseball without home plate, or
tennis without a net? Have you ever left the house to do the weekly shopping without having at least some idea of where you'd stop
for groceries?

Probably not. Yet isn't it strange that while vacations we take
merit goals, while the games we play merit goals, while even the
shopping we do merits a destination or a goal; nevertheless, rarely do we establish goals for the most important journey of
all—life.

The first great key to success begins with us, a piece of paper,
and a pencil. It begins with goals. But just as important as writing
these goals down is believing that *their mere establishment, if
maintained, will work.*

The Complete Person

Man is a purposeful creature. Whether we're selling or courting or praying or exercising, it is when we are seeking a goal, a vision, a destiny, that we are at our best. Without goals, we lose

purpose. Without purpose, we lose meaning. Without meaning, we lose life.

But we can't set goals in just one area of life and expect to be complete. We can't concentrate on, say, just the economic area of our life and lay the others to waste. The trouble is that we are a complete package, you and I. We are walking, solid-state units. We can't adjust only one tube to bring our picture of the future into clearer focus. We must examine the entire circuit and deal with it as an integrated unit.

Commitment

A very successful young friend of mine once told me that if he ever wrote a book, he'd call it "Almost Persuaded," after the hymn.

People, he said, often break down into two categories: those who set their goals with such overwhelming desire and commitment that they cannot help but succeed, and those who set their goals with so little desire and commitment that they cannot help but fail. "Almost Persuaded" describes those people who almost, but not quite, persuade themselves that they are worthy of, and capable of, achieving their goals: those people who create a vision of what they can become, but who fail to sustain the vision in the face of adversity.

Goals are not promises, but commitments; not wishes, but visions. We don't dream them and hope they'll find us. We believe them and search for them, confident that they are there, until we find them.

Goals don't start in the brain. They start in the heart; with a desire so intense, and a commitment so complete, that they can withstand the largest obstacles, the most profound discouragements, the most bitter disappointments.

The sad fact is that we cannot rely upon the rest of the world to help us sustain our goals. We must rely upon ourselves. We cannot look around us for help. We must look within. And if we fail at the outset to etch our goals with the burning fire of desire into the very fiber of our being, then we, too—upon encountering the first obstacle, or the second, or the tenth—will stand, heads hung in despair, with all the rest who were "almost persuaded."

"Oh," but you say, "I don't want to be that pinned down. I want to be spontaneous, free, able to do what I choose, when I choose to do it. I don't want some pre-ordained vision against which I must measure my every thought and motion."

But if freedom is what you really want, then a vision is what you've got to have. The mere ability to choose, standing alone, is not freedom—it's chaos. True freedom is the ability to make knowledgeable, meaningful choices. Freedom comes from having a meaningful standard against which we can evaluate alternatives.

Take steak. I like mine rare. I always thought "rare" meant a red but warm center. Yet I've discovered while traveling around the country that not everyone has the same meaningful standard of "rare." For most, "rare" means whenever the cook remembers to take the meat off the flame, which is usually somewhere between medium-well and incinerated. Still other places go to the other extreme. Some restaurants might just as well give the meat three half-hearted flicks of their Bic, throw it on the table, hand you a gun and tell you to finish it off yourself. But there's no sense complaining, because there's no meaningful standard of "rare." There isn't a known alternative against which raw meat and carbon cinders can be measured. So if there's no pulse, I eat it.

Setting lifetime goals and selecting alternatives is much the same. Write your goals on paper; don't chisel them in stone. As we grow, we may want to change our goals, and that's fine. But the decision to select alternate goals should be a rational, conscious decision, weighed against standards previously etched with desire and preserved with commitment. Only then can our power of rational choice enjoy full—and meaningful— freedom.

Through your goals, fix your sights upon your star. Determine your personal standard of excellence. Find your own promised land and use it—and no other—against which to measure the direction of your every journey upon your map of life.

Deciding Equals Achieving

But can merely deciding upon goals, even if vividly imagined, actually cause us to achieve those goals? Yes it can! Please don't just take my word for it. Great thinkers and scientists throughout the ages have come to this conclusion time and again.

Henry Thoreau said:

"If one advances confidently in the direction of his dreams, and endeavors to live the life which he has imagined, he will meet with a success unexpected in common hours."

Disraeli said:

"The secret of success is consistency of purpose."

Yes, a goal consciously set, honestly arrived at, and to which we are thoroughly committed, will be attained because *we are what we decide to be*—nothing more, nothing less.

In his book, *Psycho-Cybernetics*, Dr. Maxwell Maltz explained that no matter how hard we try or concentrate, we can never feel or behave or achieve in any manner whatsoever that is inconsistent with our own self-image. We cannot succeed if for some reason, any reason, we feel we are not worthy of—or capable of—success.

Yet the self-image can be changed. Dr. Maltz recited example after example of how we can control our own self-image and succeed thereby.

George Carlin may have exposed the "seven dirty words you can't say on TV," but I think there are six others that are equally offensive.

What does your child say when he brings home a bad grade in math? What do we say when we over-eat or over-drink? What do we all say whenever we need a convenient excuse about ourselves?

Look out! Here they come!

(1) That's (2) just (3) the (4) way (5) I (6) am!

Replace those six with these seven:

(1) We (2) are (3) what (4) we (5) decide (6) to (7) be!

Each of us has his own built-in success mechanism similar to the instinct mechanism which controls the preservation of other species. But ours is far more creative and imaginative than the instincts of other species, for only we can create and dream and imagine future accomplishments and conditions which, as yet, don't exist.

But our automatic goal-striving success mechanism, sitting there between our ears on idle, can't get us from where we are to where we're going until we tell it where we're going. It must have a target, or a goal, to work toward. Once it has a clear target at which to shoot, it alone, like a self-adjusting missile, will absorb the necessary data, compensate for negative feedback, duplicate for positive feedback, until it ultimately, invariably and undeniably hits its target.

Yes, *we are what we decide to be.* We need only firmly establish our goals in all the four mini-environments of life. We need only permit each goal to stem from a vivid and burning desire, protected by a persistent commitment against all adversity; and we need only believe that we are equipped with a mind powerful enough and creative enough and imaginative enough to achieve all we seek.

For we are endowed with the seeds of greatness, the tools of accomplishment, and the power of purpose.

And that's pretty much what I told my best friend about why *we must establish our goals and understand why their mere establishment, if maintained, will work.*

He sat in that old motel room and nodded and said, "I think I got the picture. But tell me about why *we must maintain a conscious mental process by which to sustain the vivid image of our goals.*"

I said, "I'd be glad to."

That Rational Mental Process: NIOPs & Negativism

Once upon a time in the land of yore,
A young man said, "Hey, I want more!
Today I'll leave this old shack,
And with my fortune I'll come back!
Across the valley, yes I know,
There awaits a pot of gold.
Like an arrow I will make
Straight to the gold I will take."

But as the boy proceeded down
The valley, there jumped all around
NIOPs from behind each tree.
And each one said, "Listen to me!"
Some said, "Change your course, young man;
The gold's not here, but in the glen!"

Others said, "There is no gold!
You'll search and search 'til you grow old!"

The young man thought, "The NIOPs know,
Because the valley is their home.
If change course they suggest,
I will abide and do my best.
And if they say no gold there is,
Who am I to challenge this?
Besides, with the advice they say,
Now I'm lost, so I'll make my way
Back home again, and there I'll stay.
For the NIOPs behind each tree
Say there'll never be gold for me."

The Key To Character:
Overcoming The NIOPs

It's get-tough time.

It's time to consider just how tough it is to sustain that positive mental image, that vivid dream, that goal, in the face of all the negative influences and people around us.

The world is filled with NIOPs. They're lurking in your home, in your TV set, in your newspaper, at the office, at your church, across the street.

What is a NIOP? It's the speaker Zig Ziglar's phrase for the *Negative Influence of Other People.*

They've got advice to give, and they're dying to give it. Just ask them. They'll tell you why what you're doing can't work. They'll spend all day with you on that happy subject. Or turn on the TV and get some really good news. Find out which ambassador was kidnapped and which plane was hijacked today. Pick up the local newspaper. Read about your neighbor who was just indicted for tax evasion. Read about the shooting down at the local bar.

Yes, the NIOPs are everywhere, and they're just dying for a little corner of your mind, a little piece of your mentality, a fertile niche of warm brain in which to plant their negative seeds; and once planted, they'll watch them grow until eventually you'll become a NIOP, too.

NIOPs aren't born, they're made. And there are new ones being made every day, because every NIOP on the face of this earth seems to feel a moral obligation to bear witness to his negativism. And he will work overtime to find somebody, anybody, upon whom he can dump all the bad news and negative thoughts he can think of.

That's why, in the face of this negativism, *we absolutely must establish a NIOP-proof, conscious mental process by which to sustain the vivid image of our goals.*

We frequently tend to assume that positive attitude or positive motivation is a trait: something you're born with. We've all met people who seem instinctively positive and instinctively motivated, and we assume they were born that way. But we forget that those people face as many, or more, negative obstacles each day as we do. Being a PIOP—or a Positive Person—is not a trait. It is a discipline, an acquired skill. PIOPs aren't born any more than NIOPs are born.

But from the day of our birth forward we begin formulating our attitudes; and ultimately we control—not our mothers, not our fathers, not the world around us—but *we* control what our attitudes will be. We cannot always control what happens to us, but we can always control how we will react to what happens to us.

The Rev. Robert Schuller tells the story about a friend of his who was very ill and very broke. He went to visit him one day and found the man very much at peace with himself and inwardly quite happy. The Rev. Schuller said to him, "You know, it's strange how sickness and hard times can color the personality."

The man looked him in the eye and answered: "Yeah, and I decided to pick the colors!"

Only *we* control our reactions to the world around us. If our attitudes and perceptions are negative, we have only ourselves to blame.

Yet, too often we tend to regard positive thinking as a syrupy panacea; as a cosmetic powder with which we should cover and hide the ugly face of our inward discontent. But the kind of motivation to which I refer is not the shallow and short-lived waters of spasmodic inspiration. It is a deep blue sea which marks a sustained, consistent and disciplined way of life which itself rests upon a rock-hard bed of that thing called "character."

Cavett Robert defines the measure of a person's character as the manner in which he conducts himself *after* the inspiration of the moment has left him.

In the last analysis, there is nothing pleasant or funny about having to work hard, really hard, developing attitudes and perceptions capable of withstanding the many negative influences around us: capable of protecting our fragile visions of the future, our dreams, our goals. And to sustain themselves, these attitudes cannot begin from outside us and work their way in. They must begin from within—from that bedrock called "character"—and work their way out.

When our positive attitude, our motivation, becomes a function of continuing discipline and character, then we will, as the arrow, head straight toward the target of our personal pot of gold.

And let the NIOPs be damned.

The Einstein Mode:
Our Personal Control Knob

Most of us treat our TV set with more respect than we treat ourselves.

For example, when our TV picture is not quite in focus; when the vertical hold won't "vertic" and the horizontal hold won't "horiz," what do we do? We find the right knob and we adjust the set, right? When your horizontal hold goes blip, blip, blip and you find yourself looking at the bottom of the screen to see the top of the picture and the top of the screen to see the bottom of the picture, you adjust the knob, right? You turn the knob so the picture goes blip . . . blip . . . stop. You don't turn the knob the other way so it gets worse and goes blipblipblipblip!

Yet that's exactly what we do with our own brain 90 percent of the time. We turn the knob the wrong way, and we spend our whole lives going blipblipblipblipblipblip!

Our automatic success mechanism, or what the Freudians call the "subconscious," is absolutely impersonal. It operates as a machine. That's not to say you are a machine; it is only to say you *have* a machine which you can use, and which has no "will" of its own. It always tries to react appropriately to our current beliefs and interpretations concerning environment. It always seeks to give us appropriate feelings and to accomplish the goals that we consciously decide upon. It works only upon the data which we feed it in the form of ideas, beliefs, interpretations and opinions.

It is *conscious thinking*, or the Einstein Mode, which is the control knob of our unconscious machine. What we put into our minds in the form of beliefs about ourselves and our world and our future through our conscious mind will come back out of our subconscious in the form of feelings and behavior. Doesn't it stand to reason, then, that our conscious perception of reality and ourselves is awfully important?

If you have ever failed at anything—anything at all—please raise your right hand.(Go ahead. I know you'll feel silly, especially if there are other people around. But look at it this way: in previous chapters we've already had you strip naked, talk to mirrors and scream at the top of your lungs. The people around you already think you're crazy. No sense disappointing them now.) If you didn't raise your hand, please contact me as soon as possible. I have some water I'd like you to turn into wine.

Now please raise your left hand, too, if you have ever had a negative or bad experience—any kind of negative or bad experience at all.

Please keep your hands up. If your hands are up, and if you have ever, as a result of past failures or negative experiences, suffered the slightest tinge of self doubt about your own abilities—however slight—please raise your left leg.

Now, if your arms and left leg are in the air, please lift your right leg, too, if you have ever allowed that tinge of self doubt to affect your behavior in any way.

At this moment, if you're honest, you should have both arms and both legs in the air. And where does that leave us? Where does that vile combination of past failures, negative experiences, self doubt, and tainted behavior leave us?

It's a simple formula: we have one head to think with, and one tail to sit on. Heads you win. Tails you lose.

I hope you can honestly come to the conclusion now, that just because you failed at something in the past you are not a failure today; that just because you had a negative experience in the past does not make the present a negative day; that there are more things in your present condition to support feelings of self confidence than there are things in your past to support feelings of self doubt; and that your actions of today should logically be based upon the reality of today, and not upon the musty, dusty, old data of past failures and bad experiences.

Don't be a walking blip! Don't turn that knob—the conscious mind—in the direction of the past. Tune in on today, and let your actions of tomorrow and the next day be based upon your purposeful, positive perception of *now*.

Important Perceptions

In computer terminology, the acronym "GIGO" stands for "Garbage-In, Garbage-Out."

What it means, of course, is that if you feed a computer all the wrong data, then when you ask it a question, all you'll get is a wrong answer.

What is the weakest link in any computer programming system?

The computer programmer, of course. If the programmer's perception of reality is incorrect, then his or her translation of the data will also be incorrect. Hence, the data fed to the computer will be incorrect, and the feedback obtained from the computer when called upon to solve a problem will be incorrect.

Likewise, if our personal programmer, the conscious mind or Einstein Mode, incorrectly perceives data in the form of illogical or wrongly held beliefs or opinions, then its translation of that data will be incorrect. It will then feed incorrect data into our computer, the subconscious success mechanism, which, in turn, will provide us with certified garbage when it is called upon to solve a problem.

That is why the most crucial element of the conscious mental process by which we sustain the vivid image of our goals must be that element which causes us to constantly evaluate and re-evaluate our opinions and beliefs.

Remember, we cannot sustain a mental image or goal which is inconsistent with some deeply held belief. If we honestly believe we're a schlock, then we cannot sustain a mental image which says we're not a schlock.

Bertrand Russell explained what we must do mentally each day to combat old misconceptions and inaccurate beliefs. He wrote:

> *Do not be content with an alternation between moments of rationality and moments of irrationality. Look into the irrationality closely, with a determination not to respect it, and not to let it dominate you. Whenever it thrusts foolish thoughts or feelings into your consciousness, pull them up by the roots, examine them, and reject them. It is necessary that a person should think and feel deeply about what his reason tells him.*

Our first line of defense against selling ourselves short, and our goals down the river, is that complex coalition of reverberating nerve endings and synapses, juxtaposed geometrically in such a manner as to facilitate the highest laws of physics and the most complicated of chemical and hormonal reactions—otherwise known as "horse sense."

Evaluate, don't vegetate! When from time to time you feel, as we all do, that for some reason what you dream just can't come true, use the good sense that God gave you; find the cause of your conflict within that computer, examine it and conquer it!

If we launch our ship of dreams from the bedrock of character, if we bathe it in the ocean of disciplined motivation, if we steer our craft by the wheel of purposeful, positive perception, and if we chart our path along the course of constant evaluation, we will miss the Port of Men-Who-Might-Have-Been and reach the shore of success.

> The Port of Men-Who-Might-Have-Been
> Lies just off Hasbeenville.
> And all the men-who-might-have-been
> Are shabby, grey and still.
> One missed a punch; one married wrong;
> Ambition died in one.
> One loved the light; the light o' nights
> That blaze behind the sun.
> By Gosh! It gives a man a chill
> To see them, shabby, grey and still—
> So many men-who-might-have-been
> In the port of Hasbeenville.

The Port of Men-Who-Might-Have-Been
Is crowded to the doors.
And all the men-who-might-have-been
Are very dreadful bores.
Their tales are old; their tales are dry—
One trusted in a friend;
One lacked the part; one lacked the heart
To seek the rainbow's end.
By Gosh! it gives a man the mopes
To see them sitting there like dopes—
So many men-who-might-have-been
In the port of Busted Hopes.

The Port of Men-Who-Might-Have-Been
Is east of Used-To-Be
And all the men-who-might-have-been
Are carried passage free.
I've seen it pass, their boats of glass,
And drift along the years
With all the men-who-might-have-been
Past shoals of bitter sneers.
By Gosh! it makes a fellow sigh
To see the good ship, Alibi—
With all those men-who-might-have-been
And cargoes of careers!

— *Author Unknown*

I told my friend that poem, too. It brought a tear to his eye. He said, "That sounds a lot like me."

I said, "No, you're a lot closer to the shore of success than you think. But there is a third ingredient to effective goal setting—the most important of all: *We must relax, and let the success mechanism that God gave us work for us.*"

Relaxing For Success

You may say, "This stuff about an unconscious success mechanism—a computer fed by goals—is a little hard to take.

Besides, I get things done by concentrating with my conscious mind. I can't control my subconscious brain. I just sub-lease that space. It thinks what it wants. I don't know what's down there. I don't want to know. That guy in there might be crazy. Anyhow, the kind of thinking you're talking about, that kind of genius, just applies to writers and poets and scientists who make great discoveries. I run my business and my home and my life with my conscious mind."

I respectfully disagree.

Between your ears there rests at this moment a genius equal to, or greater than, the genius of the greatest minds that ever lived. What's more, you use it everyday—at home, at the office, wherever you go—and what's more, that genius comes to you not from concentrating with your conscious brain, but by allowing your subconscious creative success mechanism to work for you; and the more we relax and allow that success mechanism to do its thing, the more genius we will display and the more goals we will attain.

Ultimately, it is not through concentrated conscious thought that things become a part of us. It is through the effortless functions of our subconscious mechanism, and it is there that our genius begins. We need only relax and let it work for us.

The Subconscious Success Mechanism At Work

One of the most common mistakes we make in this age of stress is to jam our gears by worrying too much. Of course we're going to worry. We all have substantial responsibilities that require serious thought. But we tend to worry too much, especially about our own ability to succeed—our ability to reach our goals.

At some point, we must accept as an article of faith that we were not put on this earth to fail: that we are all, each of us, fully equipped for success, and that success is inevitable.

We are, in short, forced into a position of trust in ourselves.

Conscious rational thought selects the goal, gathers information, concludes, evaluates, estimates and starts the wheels in motion. But it was never engineered to solve problems. That job belongs to our subconscious success mechanism. And the more we worry about whether it will work, the more we jam the gears, and the less able it is to do the job for which it was intended— mainly, to help us reach our goals.

All of the scientific evidence points to the conclusion that in order to receive an inspiration, or a hunch, or that spark of genius, we must first of all be intensely interested in solving a particular problem. We must think about it consciously, gather all the information we can on the subject, consider all the possible courses of action, and above all have a burning desire to find a solution. But after we have defined the problem, after we see in our imagination the desired end result, secured all the information and facts that we can, we've got to stop worrying. Continued worrying at that point does not help, but actually hinders the final resolve.

For example, Thomas Edison used to take short naps when stumped by a problem, and time and again the answers would come to him after a period of rest. Also, after months of unfruitful conscious thought, Charles Darwin, while riding in a carriage, thought of the idea which became the foundation of his book, *The Origin of Species*. Indeed, it has been said that nearly all of the discoveries in research laboratories come as hunches during a period of relaxation following a period of intensive thinking and fact gathering. Yes, the creative success mechanism which will get us where we're going will work if we relax and let it work.

Maltz's Four-Step Relaxing Formula

Relaxing, however, is not a relaxing matter. It's easier said than done. With all the pressures upon us, it's not always easy to push our worries aside and allow our success mechanism to help us reach our goals.

So how do we do it? Try this four-step formula proposed by Dr. Maltz. It may help.

First, as the gamblers say, do your worrying before you place your bet, not after the wheel starts turning.

Once we decide upon a course of conduct, no constructive purpose whatsoever is served by worrying about the outcome. We should have enough faith in our own decision-making processes to follow through on what we decide, and to let the rest take care of itself. In other words, relax.

Second, work on worrying about today and only today. Yesterday is gone, and tomorrow may never come. A worry is a thousand carbon copies of a single possibility. For tomorrow we must plan, but it is today we must enjoy. So concentrate on today and relax.

Third, do one thing at a time. If in the back of our mind we're worried about the dozen projects we know we should be working on, we'll never be able to fully concentrate on the task at hand. There is no need to feel badly, because you can only do one thing at a time. That's all any of us can do. So do it and relax.

Fourth, sleep on it. If you have a troublesome problem, don't go blind trying to solve it all at once. Don't fall asleep worrying about it. Instead, keep a pad of paper and a pencil next to your bed. You'll be amazed at the number of ideas and solutions you'll have the next morning, after your success mechanism has had an uninterrupted night to work on your problem. So sleep on it and relax.

Yes, we all possess great genius. What we think of as genius is nothing more than a natural process by which our mind works to solve any problem. But we mistakenly apply the term "genius" only when that process is used to write a book or paint a picture.

We, each of us, has within us the greatest and most vaulable gift ever presented to any species which ever existed—the human brain.

That brain is a precious tool which we must use to get us from where we are to where we're going, from someday to today, from tomorrow to now.

We need only use that treasure between our ears to *establish our goals and understand why their mere establishment, if maintained, will work. We need only use that gift to establish a conscious mental process by which to sustain our vivid image of our goals; and we need only relax and permit that tool to operate as the automatic success mechanism for which it was intended.*

And if we do these things, the genius within each of us will grow and flourish as never before, and we will reach our goals; and each day will be the brighter for us and for those whom we love and touch.

And that's pretty much what I told my best friend.

I know he is no smarter today than he was when he and I spent that week together in that dingy little room at that motel. But he seems to be using what he has a whole lot more effectively now.

I'm pleased and flattered that he took my advice. He established his goals and understood why their mere establishment, if maintained, will work. He adopted a conscious mental process by which to sustain his goals; and he relaxed and allowed his built-in success mechanism to work for him.

He's made mistakes in the past, and certainly so have I; and I don't presume to have all the answers. I can't even be certain that what I told him will ultimately work.

But it seems to be working now. My best friend no longer stays at that motel. Of course, he's rarely home, either. He's too busy. He seems to get along very well with himself and the people around him. He's rapidly becoming a wealthy man in more ways than one. He's written books, he owns a publishing company, and he travels all over the world giving talks to great people like you about the importance of goals.

I am blessed with many good friends. But, yes, my *best* friend is that fellow I see in the mirror each morning; that fellow I saw in that mirror in that room at that motel. And he and I had a long talk.

Somehow I suspect that every man and woman who will ever read this book—one way or another at some time in their lives—has stayed at the Sleepy Time Motel.

But how long we stay and what we make of it is up to us. A lot of us check in and never leave. But I know you won't. For you have miles to go, people to meet, great goals to accomplish, and great happiness to enjoy.

And you are capable—fully capable—of achieving it all.

VI

Programming Your Computer

. . . We have a right to get angry at those people who, through their words, actions, or attitudes will not permit us to realize our full potential.

Calvin Cautious was on his way to Europe. He called his sister and asked her to watch his pet cat while he was gone. Calvin loved his pet cat.

His sister said, "Sure Calvin, I'll watch your cat."

Calvin went to Europe. As soon as he got there, he called his sister. He said, "Sister, sister, how is my pet cat?"

She said, "The cat's dead."

He said, "Oh my God!" He hung up the phone.

It took him two days to recover.

Two days later he called back and said, "Sister, don't you know I have feelings, too? Don't you know you were too negative? Don't you know you should have broken the news to me much easier? The first time I called you could have said, 'The cat's up on the roof and we can't get it down.' Now *that* I would have understood. The next time I called, you could have said, 'The cat's up in a tree, but the police and fire department are here, and we're trying to get it down.' Now *that* I would have understood. And the third time I called you could have said, 'Well, the cat ran away from all the noise and confusion, and we don't expect to see it again.' Now *that* I would have understood."

And Calvin's sister said, "Calvin, you're right. I'm sorry I didn't think. I was too negative. I wasn't positive. Forgive me."

Calvin said, "It's all right, it's over, it's done, it's through. How's Mom?"

"She's on the roof."

We frequently encounter negative influences even from those people who least desire to be a negative influence. Much like a computer, we are programmed every day. Some of the input we receive is positive, but most of the input we receive is negative. It is not that we *are* computers and simply collect and regurgitate data. But the evidence does indicate that our minds do work in at least a similar fashion.

In the last chapter we discussed the importance of maintaining a rational mental process by which we sustain the vivid image of our goals. In other words, we discussed the need for programming ourselves on a daily basis with input that will help us reach our goals, and the need for attempting to avoid input that will pull us down and deter us from the accomplishment of those goals.

This chapter is devoted to exploring the techniques available for programming that computer, and maintaining that conscious mental process which is so necessary for success. It is, to a very large extent, us against the world: the images, thoughts, and attitudes that our mind can conjure and feed into itself versus the negative input so readily available around us, and so eager to make its way into our subconscious mind.

Here we will explore the use of logic (our Einstein Mode) to affect our attitudes (Carnegie Mode), which in turn will ultimately reach, and exert some control over, our emotions (the Garland Mode). Logic is the key. Conscious thought is the control knob.

Pepsi Cola® Hits The . . .

Complete the following sentences, if you can:
"Pepsi Cola® hits the _____."
"Call for _____ _____."
"Ivory Soap® is _____."
Were you able to complete each sentence? Probably so. Now here's the bad news. None of those commercials have been on TV for many years. Why do we still remember them? Why will we take those slogans with us to the grave?

Surely, when you first heard those commercials you didn't make a deliberate attempt to memorize them. When the commercials came on TV you didn't say, "By God, I'm gonna learn this!" In fact, you did just the opposite. You probably got up from your easy chair and went into the kitchen for a snack. But the sound followed you throughout the house and it sank in. It was repeated to you over and over and over again, until eventually it seeped into your subconscious and became a permanent part of you.

You've been programmed, like it or not. Thousands of times each week we are exposed to slogans and advertisements, until the information the sponsor wants us to remember becomes permanently registered on our mental tapes. Just like a computer, we've been programmed.

The technique used to accomplish this purpose is called "spaced repetition." We'll be exploring that concept in more detail below.

If Physically We Are What We Eat . . .

We've all met the deep thinker who worries about everything. He even worries about why he worries. He wears depression like a badge that says, "Look, I'm obviously intelligent. I know so much about the world around me that I'm worried stiff!"

That individual and others like him exist on a mental diet of concern and consternation. They take great pleasure in worrying about things over which they have absolutely no control. They frequently use that process as an excuse not to worry about things over which they do have control. It's the "What difference does it make, anyway; Russia's bound to attack China any day now" syndrome.

There are other mental diets available as well. The housewife who gets to spend all day conversing with 2-year-old children while ironing her husband's socks and watching soap operas exists on a mental diet of mono-syllabic words, stained diapers, and John-loves-Mary dialogue. Is it any wonder that this type of audience becomes so emotionally involved in day-time programming, when it is the only thing in their world which even closely approximates adult living?

The business executive who spends all day receiving and processing input relating to business can develop a balance sheet mentality devoid of any emotional considerations or social concern.

It's all a product of mental diet. Just as there is much truth to the adage that we are, physically, what we eat, so too is it true that we are, mentally, what we permit our minds to consume. Just as the teenager who exists on a garbage-dump diet of cheeseburgers, french fries and soft drinks can be helped physically by a lean cut of prime rib and some salad, so can those of us who exist on a diet of garbage-dump thinking composed of negative and demeaning thoughts be helped, mentally, by an occasional dose of the good, the pure, and the positive.

But there's no such thing as a free lunch. Just as the rest of the world is not going to supply you with food for your physical diet, neither will it spoon feed you the positive or fulfilling thoughts which must be a part of your mental diet. Just as we must furnish our own food for the table, so we must also furnish our own thoughts for our minds. But we can't go to the store and buy, say, a "motivating meat loaf" or "positive pumpernickel." We must manufacture that mind-food ourselves. But we possess the capability to do just that.

Generating Qualities

You may wonder why so many self-help volumes spend so much time discussing the importance of goals, as we did in the preceding chapter. The reason is that goals seem to generate all the qualities necessary for their accomplishment. Goals are the energy source that we utilize to manufacture the motivating and positive thoughts our mental diet requires.

We've all seen many examples of how goals tend to generate first the thoughts and then the qualities necessary for their accomplishment. You can perhaps think of such an example within your own family.

My older brother, Peter, is a medical doctor; and if you had met him twenty years ago you would have known exactly what he was going to become. Many children make up their minds, as did Peter at a very early age, as to exactly what it is they are going to become. Long before they ultimately reach their goal, they manifest the qualities characteristic to the status to which they aspire. Peter acted and talked and thought like a doctor when he was fourteen. His ultimate attainment of that goal was a foregone conclusion. In the interim, that driving desire generated all the other qualities necessary for its accomplishment. The attitudes were there. The logic was there. The emotions were there. Peter didn't become a doctor when he graduated from medical school. He became a doctor at about age fourteen, when he saw a film on childbirth, came home, and announced simply, "I know what I want to do."

Children provide the clearest example of this phenomenon, probably because they are generally too dumb to know how tough it's going to be. Conversely, adults establish goals and spend a good portion of their time thereafter talking themselves out of the desired end result. Yet, despite the tendency of adults to take "a more realistic view," the clear establishment of goals in which we genuinely believe at the adult level is especially important to the process of generating the thoughts and attitudes that will help us achieve those final destinations.

The effect is circular. On the one hand, a goal will help us generate the thoughts, hopes, and aspirations necessary for its accomplishment. But on the other hand, we cannot expect our goals to be constantly self-fulfilling and self-supporting. We must constantly search for additional positive input to help us sustain that goal. The most useful device available is known as spaced repetition.

Spaced Repetition

The commercial slogans discussed above were examples of spaced repetition. That little voice inside our head that says, "You're a big disappointment, Calvin," is another example of spaced repetition. The expectations of others, although frequently not verbal, are also a form of spaced repetition, in that after years and years of seeing the rest of the world quietly expect from us only mediocre results, we begin to expect the same from ourselves.

We learn through the constant repetition of material into our minds. It is a continuing and subtle process. We can either exert no control over the input that we receive, and continue to permit radio, TV, newspapers and those around us to program our computer; or we can adopt our own program which will, at the very least, help counter-balance the less desirable repetition we receive from others.

It is to a very large extent a battle between positive and negative repetitions. We can rely upon the fact that the rest of the world will not provide us with too many positive repetitions. Those we must manufacture ourselves. Then we must deliberately and logically feed those repetitions into our computer. For every voice that whispers in our ear, "You're not so hot. You can't succeed. You are just average," we must manufacture our own voice, which says, "You are the greatest! You are the greatest! You are the greatest!" A friend of mine actually goes to the extreme of verbally canceling negative input. If, for example, he catches himself putting himself down by saying, "I'm not much of an athlete," he'll instantly respond by saying out loud, "Cancel, cancel, cancel. What I meant to say was, 'I've never spent much time developing my athletic abilities'." When someone approaches him and says, "This is a tough business we're in," he will smile, but say to himself, "Cancel, cancel, cancel. I can make it. I can make it. I can make it."

When the world comes to our door and announces, "Joe, you're fat," or "Mary, you're forgetful," or "John, you'll never amount to much," we must, in our own way (and saying it out loud *is* an effective approach) cancel, cancel, cancel that input with positive input of our own.

It can be a lonely business. But it's our job and our ultimate responsibility to ourselves not to let the rest of the world pull us down to its level of complacency. Rather, we must be so self-sustaining and so self-motivating that ultimately we pull the world up to our level of excitement.

Militant Positiveness

Enough of this Mr. Nice Guy stuff.

Too many people regard positive thinking as something that would cause us, after we were run over by a truck, to check and see that we didn't hurt the tires. Instead, we must bear this basic premise in mind at all times: We have absolutely nothing to apologize for.

Whether or not people like our attitude is their problem, not ours. Whether or not people like our ambition is their problem, not ours. No one has the right to drag us down or hold us back.

When we permit others to do that to us, we permit them to limit our self-actualization as a human being.

Militant Positiveness, then, is a form of discipline. It is an acquired skill: a mental state wherein we remain highly conscious of the extent to which those around us pull us down, and let them know in no uncertain terms that we won't permit it.

Being positive in this context does not mean that we're going to be Mr. Nice Guy at all costs. It means that we can be very un-*nice* to those whose words, actions, or attitudes threaten to deter us from the realization of our goals. Militant Positiveness is not a "success at all costs" philosophy. It simply provides that we have a right to get angry at those people who, through their words, actions, or attitudes will not permit us to realize our full potential.

With all this in mind, let's get down to specific techniques for warding off the NIOPs.

Positive Affirmations

Positive affirmations are as old as the Old Testament and as new as the young fellow writing about *positive mental attitude*. They're as old as Moses and new as Muhammad Ali. Somewhere in the Bible it says, "Whatever passeth thy lips, so too shall ye be." Another way of phrasing it, I suppose, is that we better be careful of what we hope for, because we're likely to get it. When, many years ago, Muhammad Ali stood in front of the television cameras and he said, "I am the greatest!" everyone thought he was blowing smoke. But for nearly two decades he was just that.

There are many ways to express positive affirmations. One of my favorites is the Flip Wilson style. Let's try a positive affirmation in that style right now. Go ahead and stand up wherever you are. If anyone is within shouting distance of you, they are about to think you're crazy. But that's all right. We've already agreed that what they think is their problem, not yours. Now put your left foot forward. Put your right hand on your hip, lean back and shout these words:

"I'm looking *good!*"
"I'm feeling *good!*"
"I am the *greatest!*"

That wasn't loud enough. Try it again. Go ahead. So, maybe you feel a little foolish. You've spent a whole lifetime being programmed with negative input. It stands to reason that receiving positive input may feel slightly out of character for awhile. But go ahead and try it again, anyway. This time shout much louder. Make the rafters ring. Cause the neighbors to call the police. Convince that fellow worker down the hall that it's just a question of time before they carry you away. Go ahead:

"I'm looking *good!*"

"I'm feeling *good!*"

"I am the *greatest!*"

There are other, more conventional, forms of positive affirmation which are no less effective. One of the more popular ways to start each day, suggested by Dr. Norman Vincent Peale, is to recite these words aloud: "This is the day the Lord hath made. I shall rejoice and be happy in it!"

A favorite of mine that I frequently repeat time and again, especially while jogging, is, "I am here to be happy, to enjoy each day, and to use my abilities to the fullest."

There is no requirement that we use someone else's positive affirmations. Finding a combination of words that is meaningful to us and repeating those words to ourselves several times each day is what's important. There may be a saying or slogan that says it all, as far as you're concerned. If so, that should be the positive affirmation you adopt. If nothing immediately comes to mind, then take a moment, a pad of paper, and a pencil, and write your own. Be sure that it is totally positive. Be sure that it reflects your own deep-seated belief in yourself and in your potential. Be sure that it says the one thing that you want to remember each day. Repeat the affirmation at least three times each day and witness its virtually magic affect at lifting your spirits.

Sound silly? Sound corny? Sound unadult? There is nothing silly or corny or unadult about reaching your full potential as a human being. If we can logically accept the notion that we're constantly deluged with negative input, then it should not be difficult to accept the notion that we must provide some positive input of our own.

Positive affirmations that are meaningful to you are critical weapons in your arsenal against negativism. You may choose to change the affirmations you utilize each day, perhaps as frequently as once each month. But I suggest you record an affirmation before retiring it. A year or two down the road it may constitute that combination of words that hits your hot button and meets your needs at the time.

Avoiding Canned Negativism

So there we sit moments before going to bed, listening to the news of the day. Another war is reported in Outer Slobovia. Ten children met a fiery death when their school bus collided with a train. The national debt is increasing. The dollar continues to decline. The Dow Jones average is down three points. A protest ended in a scuffle with police. And it's going to rain tomorrow. The news is over. Time for bed.

Pleasant dreams.

What a wonderful conglomeration of information to be feeding our subconscious mind moments before we turn off our conscious mind and go to sleep! Is it any wonder that we wake up depressed and reluctant to face the coming day?

Some people jump from the bed in the morning and shout, "Good morning, Lord!" Other people lie in bed and say, "Good Lord, it's morning!" Which are you? The canned negativism to which you submit yourself moments before going to bed can have a profound effect upon your attitudes in the morning. It can even profoundly affect the extent to which you get a good night's sleep.

We owe it to ourselves to, at the very least, create a buffer between television's version of canned negativism and our own subconscious state called sleep. After the news and prior to bed, we owe it to ourselves to read a few pages of an inspiring book, to review mentally all the good things that had happened that day, or to review with our spouse all of our positive expectations for tomorrow. At the very least, we should wait a few minutes after the news and listen to a few talk-show jokes before going to bed.

Newspapers can be just as devastating to our positive perceptions. By and large, an item is considered newsworthy if it will help sell newspapers. Good news doesn't help sell newspapers. Bad news does. On the television show *60 Minutes* the producers not long ago yielded to the request that they report some good news in addition to the bad. They spent about seven minutes reporting on a New York to London flight filled with people that didn't crash. They described each stage of the journey, including how the people looked and felt as they walked off the plane. The flight was uneventful and safe, as the vast majority of flights are. The report was concise and factual. It was also overwhelmingly boring.

The fact is, the media report bad news because it is bad news for which we are willing to pay. There have been many attempts to produce "good news" newspapers, "good news" television stations and "good news" radio stations, and the results have all been the same. They all folded because no one read, watched or listened. The media provide us with the information for which we will pay; and, generally speaking, we pay for catastrophe, disaster, pain and suffering, at least on the level of "news."

Yet any reporter would be quick to admit that the news that winds up on our TV, radio, and in our newspapers constitutes less than a *millionth* of the significant events of the day, worldwide. Reported news does, however, represent a relatively fair cross section of the trauma and disasters which are occurring around the globe.

Day after day, week after week, month after month, year after year, we listen to all the bad news on the radio on our way to and from work. We read all the bad news in the newspaper once we get home from work; and then we watch television coverage of the same bad news before going to bed. Is it any wonder that our perception of the state of this world is distorted and depressed? The news media are like any other industry. They're a business. Their product is information. Their most saleable product is depressing information. Thus, they have become a form of canned negativism.

There are those who suggest that we should isolate ourselves from all news regarding current events. I disagree with this approach. As members of a free society, we have a responsibility to remain informed. But we must at all times remember that the vehicle through which news reaches us is an industry that is paid to focus upon the more negative aspects of world and local events. We must, at the very least, provide a buffer between the canned negativism to which we are so frequently exposed, and our own personal, positive, aspirations.

The choice is ours. We can be programmed indefinitely with this canned negativism, not putting it into the proper context to which it belongs, allowing it to taint our perception of ourselves and the world in which we live; or we may recognize that the news that reaches us represents, for very basic economic reasons, the more sensational, traumatic and negative events of the day. We should opt for the latter, secure in the knowledge that for every single piece of bad news that reaches us through the media, there are millions of positive events that occurred that day . . . that went unreported.

The Two Biggest Threats

Beware of the Wishy-Washy Positives and the Militant Mediocres!

Both are a species of NIOP, and either can destroy the positive program you are feeding to your computer.

Indeed, these two species pose a more insidious threat than does canned negativism. Canned negativism can at least be readily recognized. But the Wishy-Washy Positives and the Militant Mediocres are more difficult to spot.

The best way to identify a Wishy-Washy Positive is to compare him to a person who is Militantly Positive. The Militantly Positive person might say something like, "It's a great day, and I feel great!"

The Wishy-Washy Positive might say, "It's a great day . . . considering."

The difference between the two perspectives can make all the difference in the world. The person who is Militantly Positive is constantly programming and reinforcing himself for success. But the Wishy-Washy Positive is constantly canceling out his positive assertions with negative assertions.

There are degrees of Wishy-Washy Positives. One person may say, "I feel great . . . considering." Another person may say, "That's a good idea . . . but let's be realistic." Each in his own way can pull the Militantly Positive person down; and each Militantly Positive person must guard against becoming a Wishy-Washy Positive.

Suppose we scored points on either side of the spectrum. Positive affirmations equal one point. Negative affirmations equal minus one point. By such a system, Wishy-Washy Positives are walking zeros. They keep canceling out whatever positive programming they may, by accident, do upon themselves with counter-balancing negative assertions.

But perhaps an even greater threat is the Militant Mediocre. This is the person who actually gets angry at you for maintaining a positive frame of reference. Worse yet, he may regard you as some sort of flighty bimbo because you refuse to be as depressed and pessimistic as is he.

The Militant Mediocres actually get angry at success— especially someone else's. They are hell-bent on the notion that you should put in your time, collect your pay, go home and not make waves. Ask a Militant Mediocre how long he's been working at his current job, and he's likely to respond by saying, "Ever since they threatened to fire me." To the Militant Mediocre, striving for success is a sign of weakness rather than a sign of strength. To him, it is a patentable form of immaturity; and he remains continually intent upon reminding you that what you're doing can't possibly work.

If you're about to earn a larger income, he'll tell you why money complicates life. If you're about to buy a bigger car, he'll tell you how his compact gets better gas mileage. And if you're about to buy that great home you've worked so hard for, he'll tell you why he prefers his one room apartment: It's easier to clean. In fact, no matter how great the cost they may incur, no matter how great the inconvenience they may suffer, we may unquestionably, absolutely, count upon the Militant Mediocre to try to destroy our confidence.

There is good reason why they should become so angry at our success. Our success and our attempts to reach success are direct contradictions to the perceptions that they find so comfortable. The smiling over-achiever who is intent upon his own projects and undeterred by the criticism of those around him represents to the Militant Mediocre a disconcerting piece of evidence that he has rationalized away his life.

By being on guard for the Wishy-Washy Positives and the Militant Mediocres, we can recognize their presence and intent, and prevent their input from interfering with—or worse, canceling —our own positive input. We can accept them for what they are: individuals who never fully accepted the power of positive purposefulness, and to whom such purposefulness constitutes a genuine threat to their comfortable, although incorrect, perception of the world.

Sustaining That Positive Input

We are placed in the position of having to provide our own programmable material for our personal computer. We must seek out and discover new sources of positive input: input that will help us sustain our goals, and consequently help us achieve the things we desire.

To seek new methods requires that we break old molds. It requires, in many instances, that we adopt new behavior patterns, new friends and new centers of influence. Each of us has at his disposal a variety of tools that he can use to help sustain that positive image of himself and his destiny. But none of the tools that are currently available will, except by accident, come our way without our help. We are required to take affirmative action, seeking out those things that will help us reach our full potential, and that will help counter-balance and indeed conquer the many negative voices around us.

It seems the older we get, the more difficult it becomes to change our life style and our habits. I've heard cynics describe positive motivation as worthless because, in their words, "I tried it for a week, and it didn't work." But if we view our perceptions and attitudes as products of a continuing discipline, then we must take continuing action over the long run to sustain that positive approach. "People," Lincoln said, "are about as happy as they make up their minds to be." Sustaining a high level of enthusiasm and self-esteem, and a deep-seated belief in our ability to accomplish our goals, cannot be accomplished on a Monday–Wednesday– and Friday–only basis. It is a 24-hour per day, 7-day per week task.

It is obvious, based merely upon a cursory inspection of the many negative voices around us, that we must latch on to any device we can discover that is capable of helping us maintain attitudes worthy of our potential as human beings.

It has been said that ten years from today we will be the product of three things: the people we hang out with, the books we read, and the tapes we play. The sum total of the sources of positive input that we can find for ourselves can be lumped into one of these three categories. Let's explore each one to see how it may help.

The People We Hang Out With

If you want to fly like an eagle, you must hang around with eagles.

A man or woman who wants to earn, say, $60,000 per year has little to gain in an economic sense by hanging around with those who struggle to earn $15,000 per year. We must seek out the acquaintance and friendship of those people whom we admire most. We must come to know and understand what makes such people tick. Why do they have the things I don't have? Why do they do the things I don't do? Why do they believe the things I don't believe?

A less than sensitive observer once said, "Poor people ought to take rich people to lunch." The mode of expression may be questionable, but the sentiment is on target insofar as it expresses the notion that we have much to learn from those who are more successful than we.

I do not propose that you become a "hanger-on." We've all met those who wallow about in the presence of more successful people; hanging around with the hope that a "big deal" or "opportunity" will be gratuitously thrown their way. What I propose instead is that you become a student of the people you admire most. Unabashedly announce to them that you have deliberately made their acquaintance so that you may learn and observe and grow. Successful people are by nature busy people, and it is frequently difficult to get to them without unduly imposing on their time. But the belief that such folks are uneager to share their ideas, or that they are inaccessible to all but a few, is simply false.

As a young and inexperienced attorney in Cincinnati, I had the gall to open my own office and attempt to handle any legal problem that walked in the door. It wasn't long before I realized that I needed help in solving such weighty problems as what to charge for a divorce, and where to park down at the court house. I picked up the phone and contacted some of the most prestigious and well-respected attorneys in the city. They were, rather than being inaccessible, eager to share their ideas. I would simply make an appointment to see them, explaining that I was a new attorney and that I needed help. What would always begin as a scheduled thirty-minute discussion would usually last most of the afternoon, with the "old timers" bending my ear with the war stories and ideas that they had accumulated over the years.

Many of my friends in other professions have experienced a similar phenomenon. It is our collective opinion that successful people are generally *eager* to share their ideas with sincere and forthright neophytes. All they ever ask in return is that they be listened to seriously, and that their advice be taken for what it is: the accumulation of a substantial amount of experience and expertise.

It is a heartening and enlightening experience to make the acquaintance of someone whom you have admired from afar, and to discover that he is eager and willing to share his ideas and insights. It is especially heartening upon getting to know such people to discover that they, like you, have their ups and downs, their successes and failures, and that, in the vast majority of instances, they are still growing as are you.

Consider for a moment the people with whom you hang around, and weigh what they have to offer against the goals that you have established. Are these the folks with whom you really should be spending your time? Are they pulling you up, or dragging you down? Is that friend or neighbor really not in a position to understand or appreciate—regardless of how well intentioned he may be—the sincerity with which you have set your goals and the intensity with which you intend to pursue them? If he isn't, I submit that it is not fair to either of you to continue a relationship, however close, that has the effect of pulling one or both of you down.

Make a list today of the people whose opinions you would value. Decide upon the acquaintances you would like to make, and the questions you would ask those people, if you had the chance. Set that list aside for now. Later in this book we will discuss the process for converting goals into actual conduct. At that point, you may want to reflect upon the specific things you can do to meet, and learn from, the people you admire most . . . and to fly with the eagles.

The Books We Read

The value of a book is not so much in the words that it contains, but in the thoughts that it provokes.

The child who reads a book about outer space, for example, benefits in the long run perhaps only marginally from the information contained therein. But more important, he or she benefits by fantasizing about what it would be like to be a voyager in space. That same child who daydreamed over the words in a text that described rocket ships might some day pilot such a ship to the outer reaches of the universe.

As adults, we have an enormous and broad selection of books available to us. Too often we are content to read merely the headlines on the front page of our paper, or to sit mesmerized in front of the Boob Tube. Yet, by merely picking up a book and paging through it, we can open whole new worlds to ourselves. Regardless of the "language" in which the book might be written —positive, negative, or academic—books that deal with basic concepts of self help can be of enormous help to us.

After all, what is a good idea worth? If we read a book, any book, and it provides us with one good idea, and that one good idea helps us, say, close one additional sale, what's it worth? If we read a book and we obtain one good idea, and that one good idea helps us improve communications with our spouse, what's it worth? If we have books sitting around our home where our children can page through them, and if by doing so they get one good idea which provides them with just a little more meaning and direction in this often confusing and always competitive world, what's it worth?

The value of books cannot be measured purely in economic terms, or emotional terms, or intellectual terms. Their effect is too potentially profound and far reaching. But if we are to continue to program our computer, if we are to continue to overcome the abundant negative influences around us, we must wade through the pages, thoughts and ideas of others and build upon those ideas with thoughts of our own.

The Tapes We Play

Years ago, many of us were bookworms. Now many of us are becoming tapeworms.

Pound for pound, penny for penny, motivational and instructional cassette programs offer the finest positive programming technique available.

While the value of a formal education can, of course, not be overstated, I am increasingly convinced that cassette education is the greatest educational advancement since the invention of the Gutenberg press. The trouble with formal education is that it is very time consuming and very expensive. On the other hand, no one will hand you a diploma for listening to a cassette program. But what you will receive are things which are, probably at this point in your life, of a whole lot more value: more income perhaps, better personal management techniques, better business management techniques, effective ideas on communication, and pure, unadulterated inspiration.

Consider that for $29 you can go down to your local radio discount shop and purchase a reasonably decent tape recorder. You can put that tape recorder on the front seat of your automobile, turn *off* the "du-wa-ditty-ditty" station on the car radio, and turn on your instructional and motivational cassette programs. We all literally have a classroom on wheels where we spend many hours per week. We must turn our driving time into learning time.

Cavett Robert, who has pioneered the use of cassette training programs, points out that school is never out for the pro. He emphasizes that through the use of cassette programs we can "grow" through life, not just "go" through life. Constant self-improvement can't be had by trial and error. Experience may be the best teacher, but the tuition is too high. Just about the time we figure out the rules, we're too old to play the game. Instead, cassette education gives us the opportunity to use *O.P.E— Other People's Experience*. Cassette education gives us the opportunity to hang around with eagles by listening to the organized, recorded, ideas of successful individuals.

That inexpensive tape recorder and those cassette programs comprise our own private tutor. He works for pennies a day whenever we want him to, and he gives us the opportunity to constantly program our mind in a positive fashion through spaced repetition.

Finally, with cassette programs we have, whenever we choose, our own positive voice to counteract and conquer the many negative voices around us. While the rest of the world is saying, "No, you can't! No, you can't!" that little voice on the car seat next to us is saying, "Yes, you can! Yes, you can! Yes, you can!" Cassette education gives us the oppurtunity to use our off-peak time: while shaving in the morning, perhaps, over lunch, during a coffee break, while driving in our automobile, and before going to bed.

The use of cassette tapes is especially beneficial just prior to sleep, not only as a buffer against the more negative news you may have received during the day, but also because it permits our subconscious mind to concentrate upon something positive during the night.

Moreover, cassette education is relatively inexpensive. Many of us own hundreds of dollars worth of stereo equipment, and we invest readily in records and eight-track tapes of music. When compared to musical recordings, cassette education is, in fact, less expensive. For example, a cassette program containing six cassette tapes, which will normally contain five to six hours of instructional material, will usually cost substantially less than a comparable amount of music. A single instructional cassette tape is comparably priced to an eight-track tape, and frequently contains up to twice as much recorded material. Music itself can be a form of uplifting and positive input. But words are the fingers that mold the mind of man.

The process of improving our Inside Mini-Environment involves three steps:

First, we must get straight with that guy inside. We must critically evaluate who he is now, and what he can become. We must accept the notion that the way others see us may become a self-fulfilling prophecy, if we let it. We must spend our time not blaming past experiences or other people for our failures, but instead, accepting responsibility for our destiny. And we must totally and unconditionally accept ourselves as the very best friend we'll ever have.

Second, we must turn on our success mechanism by accepting, logically, the three-step process we must undertake to realize our goals and reach our full potential. First, we must establish our goals and understand why their mere establishment, if maintained, will work; second, we must adopt a conscious mental process by which we sustain the vivid image of our goals; and third, we must relax and allow our automatic built-in success mechanism to work for us.

Finally, we must program our computer each day, every day. We must use the logic that we possess to affect our attitudes, which in turn will affect our emotions. It is us against the world in this regard. We are bombarded continuously with negative repetitions which cause us to demean ourselves and lower our goals. We must adopt a stance of Militant Positiveness, fed by positive affirmation, through which we avoid the threats of canned negativism, Wishy-Washy Positiveness and Militant Mediocrity. Finally, we must sustain that positive input by recognizing that in the future we will be the product of three things: the people we associate with, the books we read, and the tapes we play.

It is in many ways a tough business, being a success. It is not easy to reach our full potential. For even before we can begin utilizing the tools we have, we must overcome the obstacles that have been laid before us. This section has been devoted to a discussion of methods that can help us do just that.

But managing our Inside Mini-Environment is only one-fourth the battle. We move next to that machine which houses all of our equipment—our Outside Mini-Environment.

VII

Operating Instructions For The Human Machine: Male And Female Models. No Assembly Required

"Sensory Man" of millenniums ago has become "Mental Man" of today. Somehow in the process he has divorced his mental and physical existences and fallen out of touch with that portion of him, which is most of him, that thinks and feels without conscious thought.

Welcome to Cal's New Body Lot!

Why, for a minimum investment, we'll put you in one of these spiffy new models.

That's right! We have millions of styles to choose from, and colors galore: tan, black, beige, yellow, brown, white, red and just about every shade in-between.

We've been in business for a lot of years, folks. Why, these machines have been in production now for more than a million years. We must be doing something right. Since production began, there have been no major changes in our line. Sure, there have been a few small adjustments. For example, a million years ago, these models operated on all fours. Now they stand upright, freeing the arms for more useful things.

123

Yes, these bodies are a remarkable engineering accomplishment. The frame on this model is composed of 206 bones which are so superbly rigged and balanced that it can run, jump and bend despite its small feet. And just take a look at these shocks! Although bones can break, they are generally so strong that this model can jump high in the air, even pole vault, without shattering its frame. In fact, the tubular thigh bones of an athlete—that's an athletic model over there; we've been fine-tuning it for months —can withstand up to 20,000 pounds of pressure per square inch without breaking.

Sure, models can and do wear out, but they come with a lifetime guarantee: a general warranty not offered by any other equipment manufacturer. If something goes wrong with your machine, chances are you won't even have to take it into the shop. It will fix itself! That's right! Unless something serious occurs, which requires the attention of a trained mechanic (you call them doctors), your machine will adjust itself.

Yes, you get quite a deal with this little baby! Did I mention the power system? There are more than 600 muscles that act as cables to pull the body. The muscles work in pairs, one contracting to pull a bone forward, the other to pull it back. By so doing, the muscles provide the machine with a huge versatility and variety of movement.

When these models arrive from the factory, they average only 7.3 pounds in weight. Yet by the time they reach maturity, the male models will weigh between 112 and 204 pounds, and the female models between 92 and 173 pounds, on the average. The engine will maintain a constant average temperature between 97 and 99 degrees Fahrenheit. The heart will beat at an average of 70 beats per minute; and most models even come with approximately 120,000 hairs on the head!

How much does it cost, you wonder? It would seem to cost a fortune. Why, even the manufacturers of a Rolls Royce would freely admit that their engineering and craftsmanship hardly compares to ours. As beautiful as their machine is, it generally will not last as long, won't run as far, hasn't as many versatile uses, and requires substantially greater maintenance (not to mention the gallons more fuel it consumes). Yet a Rolls may cost well over $60,000.

Heavens, you must think, these models must be worth more than a million dollars! Indeed, they're worth at least that much. I heard not long ago of a young gal who lost a leg in an auto accident. She sued the other driver, and the jury awarded her a million dollars! Why, these days, in some circles, people are paying a million dollars or more just for the spare parts to our machine. You can imagine what it must be worth fully assembled and operable.

But folks, at Cal's New Body Lot, we're in business to serve you. That's right! We don't care about making money. We just love to sell bodies. In fact, we lose money on every deal. How do we make it up? Volume!

You might expect to pay more than a million dollars for any of these models, and indeed you might say that any of these models is priceless. But at Cal's you can walk off the lot in one of these beauties for free! That's right! Free! No money down, no payments; and the machines still come with a lifetime guarantee!

All we ask is that you learn as much about them as you can, and treat them right. By understanding the standard performance features of your machine, by learning what to expect from your investment, by mastering the proper warranty maintenance, and by understanding that there are certain abuses not covered by your warranty, you can get a lot more use out of your machine—a lot better mileage. It won't let you down nearly as often, and you can keep it out of the shop.

That's right, folks! Here at Cal's New Body Lot the bodies are free! All we ask is that you take good care of them, and treat them right. And if you do, they'll provide you with a long lifetime of faithful service.

Standard Performance Features: What To Expect From Your Investment

Although you have no money invested, certainly the time and effort you spend attempting to maintain your machine is worth something. It's worth knowing, therefore, what to expect from an average body. What are the standard performance features, and how well does your model measure up?

Certainly, three of the more important equipment groups within our body are the cardiovascular system, the respiratory system and the nervous system. Let's take a brief look at each, to explore how they perform.

Initial evaluation is as important with respect to our Outside Mini-Environment as it was with respect to our Inside Mini-Environment. But whereas we can't specifically define the "normal" functioning characteristics of our attitudes, emotions or logic, such measurements can be taken with respect to our bodies. We are at an advantage, therefore, in evaluating our Outside Mini-Environment, because what is normal here is far more clearly established.

Pumps And Hoses: The Cardiovascular System

The heart is an incredible muscle. About half the size of a man's fist, it weighs in men about eleven ounces, in women about nine. It beats 100,000 times a day, resting half the time between beats. It thus beats about 2.5 million times in a lifetime. It sends 5,000 to 6,000 quarts of blood through 60,000 miles of arteries, veins and capillaries per day. The heart beats on the average of between 60 and 80 times per minute in adults. An infant's heart will beat about 120 times per minute.

The cardiovascular system has a computer-like ability to direct a heavier flow of blood to areas that require it, and to detour around organs not needing it. This enhances circulatory efficiency, and is the basis upon which man may exert himself.

The importance of a sound cardiovascular system cannot be overstated. In 1975, for example, cancer killed 365,000 Americans. That same year, diseases of the heart and blood vessels killed 994,000 Americans. Cardiovascular ailments are the leading cause of death in America today.

According to the American Heart Association, cardiovascular disease cost Americans about 28.5 billion dollars in 1978. Almost 30 million Americans have some form of heart and blood vessel disease. Of that number, 24 million suffer from hypertension (that's one in every six adults). More than four million suffer from coronary heart disease. Almost two million suffer from rheumatic heart disease, and almost two million suffer from stroke. One fourth of all the people killed by cardiovascular disease are under the age of 65. Arteriosclerosis (hardening of the arteries) is the leading contributor to heart attack and stroke deaths. The three primary causes of cardiovascular disease are high blood pressure, high cholesterol levels and cigarette smoking. A man with a systolic blood pressure of over 150 has more than twice the risk of heart attack and nearly four times the risk of stroke than a man with a systolic pressure of under 120.

A man with a blood cholesterol count of 250 or more has about three times the risk of heart attack and stroke than a man with a cholesterol level of below 194. Finally, a man who smokes more than a pack of cigarettes per day has nearly twice the risk of heart attack than a non-smoker.

It is clear that the cardiovascular system has enough to do without needless interference from us in the form of increased risks caused by cigarette smoking, heightened cholesterol levels as a result of poor diets, or heightened blood pressure levels as the result of little or no exercise.

Intake, Compression & Exhaust: The Respiratory System

The lungs, too, are incredible devices. The body's trillions of cells require so much oxygen that we need about thirty times as much surface for its intake as our entire skin area covers. Even though our lungs weigh only 2½ pounds, and even though they fit neatly within our chest cavity, they provide this surface area. They do so through membranes that fold over and over on themselves in pockets so thin that a sheet of the finest paper seems thick by comparison.

Moreover, the lungs are fussy. Even in what we might consider to be the purest of air conditions, they're constantly rejecting particles and substances contained within that air. The air must pass the nose, the trachea or windpipe, the bronchi and bronchioles before it is accepted by the lungs. Twisting passages, mucus and cilia (tiny hairs) filter out all but the most persistent of viruses and bacteria.

At least that's the way it is supposed to work. The smoker, for example, simply destroys most of this filtering system. (Like so many other parts of the body, the respiratory system has enormous regenerative abilities. Stop smoking and the system will rebuild itself.)

The adverse effect of many environmental factors and smoking is highly visible. The lungs of an infant are bright pink. An adult city dweller who smokes will likely possess lungs that are dull grey and spotted with black. This difference in coloration provides dramatic visual evidence of why smokers are so much more susceptible to respiratory disorder and disease than are non-smokers.

In fairness and in honesty, I should note that until several months ago I smoked two packs of cigarettes a day. It's true, however, that the convert is often the greatest zealot. Smoking is, in fact, a vile, stupid, expensive habit. That I once smoked makes it no less so. That it was not so considered when you began smoking and became addicted to tobacco makes it no less so.

Now I, as do many non-smokers, insist that those who do smoke not do so under circumstances that will force me to inhale the deadly fumes that they insist upon exhaling. It amazes me that some people still think it is rude for a non-smoker to insist upon his right to fresh air.

If a pedestrian has the right to be angry at someone who tries to run him over with a truck, why shouldn't I get angry if a smoker attempts to poison me? The effect is the same, just slower. Of course, all reasonable minds have by now agreed that smoking does, in fact, kill. In early 1979, the Surgeon General, after extensive additional research, revised his earlier finding that "cigarette smoking may be hazardous to your health," to the simple statement that: "There is overwhelming evidence that cigarette smoking causes cancer."

The lungs of an average-size man contain approximately 300 million air sacs, each designed to provide him with life-sustaining oxygen. On behalf of all 300 million of my air sacs, I insist upon—indeed, demand—my right to breathe clean air.

Our intake, compression and exhaust system, which processes up to five or six quarts of air per breath, is a remarkable thing. With all that depends upon it, and with all the work it must do, it needs and deserves all the help we can give it.

Wiring: The Nervous System

Many theorists believe that most human ailments of whatever nature or kind are caused by some disfunction of the nervous system. Our falling out of touch with that system has been hailed as the primary culprit.

Tension, stress, aches, pains, general discomfort and other maladies, both postural and pathological, seem almost always to be either caused or complicated by a nervous system that just doesn't seem to cooperate to the same extent that it once did when we were children.

The realization that the nervous system—which was designed to operate in a drug-free, tension-free, stress-free state—is inexorably related to our general well being, has led to the popularity of holistic approaches to medicine (i.e., approaches that emphasize the total body and its general ability to heal itself naturally). We have been too long in realizing that a system that is sophisticated enough to be both the initiator of the body's muscular activities and the regulator of our mental and physical functions is also sophisticated enough, in most instances, to adjust itself—if only allowed to function as it was intended to function.

"Sensory Man" of millenniums ago has become "Mental Man" of today. Somehow in the process he has divorced his mental and physical existences and fallen out of touch with that portion of him, which is most of him, that thinks and feels without conscious thought.

The brain and spinal cord serve as the system's main base of operations, and from them a prodigious network of nerves spreads to every part of the body. These nerves reach every millimeter of skin surface, every muscle, every blood vessel, every bone, every part of the body from head to toe. They communicate back to the system's base of operations and to each other through billions of electrochemical signals which travel at rates of up to 350 feet per second.

The brain, however, is not to be discounted in its role as initiator and coordinator of this vast system. The brain was definitely not hired for its looks. Soft, gray and furrowed, it looks like an acorn squash and weighs about three pounds. Its outer layer, the cerebral cortex, appears to have been scrunched and unceremoniously stuffed into the 6-by-8 inch vault of the skull. If pulled out and flattened, the cortex would cover more than two square feet in area.

The spinal cord extends downward approximately 18 inches from the brain. Tapered at both ends, it is, at its widest, little more than a half inch across. It is protected by the perforated tunnel of bone formed by the rings of the vertebrae.

Electrochemically, the brain never sleeps. Hence, its need for oxygen is continuous. A disruption in the supply, however subtle, has the effect of destroying brain cells, called neurons. Neurons are irreplaceable. A year-old baby has all the neurons it will ever have. And while the day-to-day loss of some neurons is inevitable, the loss of too many neurons can cause severe and permanent brain injury. Environmental factors such as smoke, alcohol and drugs can, when consumed in excess, reduce the supply of oxygen reaching the brain. Consequently they can destroy neurons, and thus profoundly and permanently affect the brain's ability to function.

But it is "Sensory Man" who deserves most of our attention: the remainder of the nervous system which serves as our complex receptor of the world around us, and which manifests itself in the five physical senses that we rarely develop to the fullest. It is the only system we have—or will ever have—that permits us to fully enjoy physically the world in which we live.

Through our ears we are able to hear sounds when any vibrating object pushes air molecules at a rate of between 15 to 15,000 vibrations per minute. Through our eyes, we are able to perceive light waves which are as feeble as 100-trillionth of a watt. And through our skin we are placed in touch with all that is warm, or soft, or cold or hard around us.

The body's six pounds of skin is thinned out like pie-dough. Its average thickness is only one-twentieth of an inch, yet that skin contains an incredible network of nerve endings. Our hands, for example, contain up to 1,300 nerve endings per square inch of skin.

Although it is perhaps our weakest sense, our ability to smell permits us to distinguish among the four primary smells: fragrant, acid, rancid and burnt. As though to insure that we would not miss too many of the beautiful fragrances this world offers, our sense of smell is fleeting. Sniff a rose and you will smell it for only a short time, even if your nose remains next to it. Soon your body will adjust to that odor and no longer perceive it, thus making room for the nose's ability to perceive others.

Taste is the sense that tells us least. An infant is born with taste buds throughout his mouth, but by adulthood most have disappeared, with mostly only those on the tongue remaining. Yet, despite its frequent need for assistance from the senses of sight and smell, taste permits us to distinguish the four primary tastes of sweet, sour, bitter and salty.

In combination, this system—from the cortex of the brain to the nerve fibers of the spinal cord, to the thin fibers of neurons, to the mechanical marvel of the five physical senses that place us in touch with this universe—provides the marvelously complex system by which we physically relate to ourselves and the world around us.

It is also a system that in the vast majority of instances is best left to its own inherent healing abilities.

Proper Warranty Maintenance

Not surprisingly, there are a few preventive maintenance steps which must be taken by you in order to preserve the life-time warranty on your equipment—nothing fancy, mind you: just the application of basic information to keep your machine properly fueled, polished and cleaned, and fine-tuned for maximum performance.

Recommended Fuel: Diet

When we speak of nutrition, we speak not of food, but of what food contains.

The nutrients upon which the body must rely to exist can be found in the foods that are readily available to most of us. Indeed, part of the nutritional difficulties in America stem from the fact that such foods are *too* available to us. Most of our difficulties stem from not under- but over-eating. Within the United States the trend is clear: we over-consume those types of food commonly regarded as junk foods. In fueling our machine, we would do well to remember a few fundamental principles of good nutrition.

A calorie is a unit of heat. It is the amount of heat needed to raise one gram of water one degree centigrade. A gram of protein, contained in abundance in eggs, milk, meat and fish, is worth four calories. A gram of carbohydrate—starches and sugars—contains four calories; and a gram of fat—butters, vegetable oils, drippings, etc.—contains about nine calories. But our body is not just a stove requiring fuel and stoking. It is more analogous to a computer which must constantly process and apply to various uses the various biologic values of the food it consumes.

All food can be measured in calories. The question then becomes from which type of food should these calories come. Using the basic food categories, we can say, as a rough guide, that first, about 15 percent of our daily calories should come from proteins; second, about 25 percent of our daily calories should come from fats; and third, about 60 percent of our daily calories should come from carbohydrates. Proteins are especially important because they contain many of the essential elements the body must have to rebuild itself.

While fats deservedly enjoy a poor reputation with most of us, we shouldn't forget that their presence is necessary. Fats serve to insulate and lubricate our bodies, and also help our bodies utilize fat-soluble vitamins. Nevertheless, it should be noted that in the United States the rate of fat consumption has increased dramatically. Between 1950 and 1970, it climbed from the recommended minimum of 20 percent to over 40 percent of our diets.

Vegetables, fruits, flours, cereals and sugars are included in the carbohydrate category. Most of us consume far too many carbohydrates. Too many carbohydrates can cause malnutrition and vitamin B deficiencies.

If you really want to get rich quick, and you don't mind killing a few people in the process, I recommend that you invent a new diet and guarantee that it will provide remarkable results. Today such diets are legion. Many people have suffered as a result. Terence's Golden Mean, "Moderation in all things," should apply not only to our consumption of food, but also to our use of new and fancified remedies for excess poundage. At the end of this chapter are tables indicating the amount of fuel your body needs, and the nutritional values that such fuel should contain. In addition are guidelines depicting acceptable weight ranges for varying heights of men and women. Upon examining the tables, you may discover that your weight is entirely normal.

It's just that you're six inches too short.

Care And Cleaning: Rest And Hygiene

It may not increase the longevity of your machine, but keeping it clean, polished, and odor-free will certainly be appreciated by the other machines with which it comes in contact. In modern (but by no means all) societies we have thankfully reached the point where squalor and filth no longer claim lives on a regular basis. Indeed, it seems we've almost reached another extreme: the age of the underarm deodorant. We've crossed the barrier from being just clean to antiseptic; and no doubt the manufacturers of all those things that are somehow supposed to smell better than the human body itself will not stop until we pass from antiseptic to sterile. Personally, I would urge not devices that mask or hide us, but techniques that present us at our cleanest, healthiest best. Old directives come to mind: those we heard as children, which are no less sensible and correct now than they were then. Here are a few of them, well worth repeating. Others you may recall on your own.

1. Use a washcloth and scrub thoroughly.
2. When brushing your teeth, brush all sides
    of your teeth and your tongue.
3. Wash and rinse your hair thoroughly.
    Brush it well and keep it out of your face.
4. Bathe daily.
5. Change your underwear daily.

(If this list sounds embarrassingly basic, take heart. If but one reader chooses to amend his grooming habits as a result of it, the world will be a slightly more pleasant place for us all.)

I suspect that as many Americans suffer from too much sleep as suffer from too little sleep. Depending on our individual metabolisms, our bodies may require from six to eight hours of sleep per 24-hour period. If you sleep more than eight hours per day, you may well be attempting to escape from someone, something, or some situation. Frequently we confuse our need for play with our need for rest. In fact, it's very difficult to broach the subject of rest without also jumping headlong into a dialogue on play. Too often we equate rest with inaction. Yet the process of play is the highest and most beneficial form of rest.

Play is the process by which we, acting as much like children as our adult egos will permit, utilize our bodies in a free and unrestrained fashion toward an inconsequential goal, such as putting a ball through a hoop, or across a goal line. The definition of play varies from person to person. But basically it is what we are individually willing to do for free. It's what we have fun at.

Through fun we rest. Indeed, it is this very phenomenon of re-laxation through use which gives rise to our reverse mileage guarantee.

Reverse Mileage Guarantee:
Longevity Through Use And Exercise

Use it or lose it.

Robert Hutchins, former president of the University of Chicago, was once quoted as saying that whenever he was tempted to in-dulge in a little exercise, he promptly lay down until the inclina-tion passed. Too many of us are similarly inclined. We believe that the only way we can rest, rekindle our energies, or regain our sagging strength, is to sit motionless in front of the Boob Tube, sip cans of carbohydrates, and wait for our youth to return.

Yet, Dr. George Sheehan, who at the age of 59 wrote the remarkable book *Running and Being: The Total Experience*, points out that our youth never really expires. It just gets buried beneath all the unhealthy symptoms of adulthood. But as our bodies age, play inevitably becomes more painful. Our bodies become battle grounds of pulled ligaments, sore joints, stretched tendons and stress fractures. Because of the discomfort associated with such activity, most of us, by the age of 30, abandon any serious effort at fitness.

Yet, the by-product of fitness at any age is health, or as Dr. Sheehan put it, health is what you must pass through on the way to fitness. Our bodies don't deteriorate because of use. They deteriorate because of disuse. They were designed to run, to jump, to play, to feel the world, and not to just think about it.

The relative perfection of the human machine is best demonstrated by this fact: There exists no other machine the con-dition of which actually improves with use.

The human machine demands use. It will deteriorate and die without it. Most Americans exist one short strenuous exertion from death, bordering on a heart attack or stroke, content to avoid any activity which might precipitate the ultimate demise of their machine. The surest form of preventive maintenance is to use that machine.

The jogger is the best example of a person who takes optimum advantage of his reverse mileage guarantee. Using a form of play that is both physically and psychologically right for him, the jogger literally puts miles on his personal odometer by running several miles each week.

Like millions of hack amateur athletes, many of whom are too ill-suited, or too fragile, for other more contact-oriented games, I, too, have become a jogger. I continue to suffer malady upon malady — from stress fractures and lower back pains, to blisters and, of course, stiffness. Yet, as so many other runners, I persist in logging about twenty miles each week, approximately 1,000 miles each year, not because I welcome pain, but because I cherish its by-product: life, and a feeling of freedom, control, and vitality.

The reverse mileage guarantee works not just because it utilizes our muscles and hence improves our physical condition, but also because playing, in any constructive form, permits us to relax and release our emotions. It refreshes and revitalizes our psychological existence as well. Studies have indicated that individuals who perform hard manual labor at work do not enjoy significant advantages over others in avoiding cardiovascular disease. Yet, those same individuals who also participate in forms of play that require strenuous physical exertion do demonstrate markedly better cardiovascular health. The conclusion is inescapable: the more we use, and have fun with, these marvelous machines, the longer they will tend to last, and the better they will operate while we have them.

Abuses Not Covered By Warranty

In this day of increasing product liability suits, even The Manufacturer can't be too careful. What should already be perfectly clear must instead be stated in writing so that there can be no dispute that, should you abuse your machine, you — and not The Manufacturer — are responsible. Here are a few of the many abuses not covered by your warranty.

Overfueling Or Use Of Improper Fuel: Poor Diet

Among the great loves of my life are cheeseburgers, pizza, beer and (occasionally) martinis. In moderation, none are harmful, and, in fact, each possesses certain nutrients which can be beneficial. But in overabundance they can kill. The most common abuse of your machine, not covered by warranty, is overfueling.

No matter what the food, or how good tasting, the consumption of too much of this "fuel" is the surest way known to destroy your machine. Similarly, the over-consumption of junk foods, fast foods, and foods loaded with carbohydrates and fat, are also abuses not covered by your warranty.

The next time you're standing in line at the grocery store, waiting to pay for the food that you will likely consume too much of, examine the magazine rack at the check-out counter. More likely than not, you'll find a small handbook on dieting. Don't purchase those that promise remarkable results in little or no time. Find instead the calorie counters, the nutritional charts — the less spectacular but consistently more effective publications that you can use to establish your own personal dietary guidelines.

Neglect And Overuse:
Poor Hygiene And Rest Habits

Your machine may not break down just because you fail to wash it. However, it may become more susceptible to disease if surrounded by an unclean environment. For that reason, failure to clean and polish your equipment is among the abuses not covered by your warranty. In addition, sleep or inaction alone is not sufficient rest for your machine. It requires recreation on a regular basis — an opportunity to leave behind the stresses and strains of adult living and to engage in action for the sheer joy of action itself. The owner's failure to provide this restful outlet for your machine will void your warranty. Put another way, the type of rest required is affirmative rest: restful action which permits your machine to enjoy itself and the world in which it exists.

Spontaneous Combustion Caused By Disuse:
Stress And Tension

Finally, your warranty does not cover the explosions which can occur if your machine is underused and overstressed. As the owner of your machine, your responsibility is to provide it with outlets by which it may reduce its accumulated stresses and tensions. If you fail to do so, spontaneous combustion, in the form of stroke, heart attack or mental disorder, may occur. Your machine has been designed for many varied purposes, but it was not designed to repress tension and stress. Play is the best method by which to avoid this abuse. The form of play is almost irrelevant as long as it provides a wholesome, active, constructive context in which the machine may find release and entertainment. Through play, the longevity of your machine may be substantially increased, and its operating characteristics and performance substantially improved during your lifetime.

There you have it, folks: the basic information you'll need to get the most out of your machine. Here at Cal's New Body Lot we want your machine to reach its full potential.

Remember to take care of those pumps and hoses. That cardiovascular system needs all the help it can get. The intake, compression, and exhaust systems, while highly durable, will appreciate your help in avoiding impurities and smoke. And the wiring system, although extremely complex, is, more often than not, best left to itself for minor adjustments.

Remember to seek out the proper combination of proteins, fats and carbohydrates in your caloric intake while fueling your machine.

Remember, too, that rest requires not just sleep, but affirmative action and play, and that your machine comes with a reverse mileage guarantee requiring that you put it to use, through play, on a regular basis.

Of course, neither Cal's New Body Lot nor The Manufacturer assumes responsibility for abuses such as overfueling, neglect and overuse, or spontaneous combustion caused by disuse.

Yessiree folks, you've got quite a deal here in this little baby. Go ahead and take her for a spin. If you're not back in an hour, we'll just figure you found the body that was right for you.

Oh, and incidentally, if you need any additional motivation to take extra good care of your machine, you might remember this — it's a detail I forgot to mention before, but it's awfully important.

Once you select your machine, well, you'll never have another chance: because, you see, we're limited to one body per customer.

DESIRABLE WEIGHTS FOR MEN
(Ages 25 and Over)*

HEIGHT (WITH SHOES, 1-INCH HEELS)		WEIGHT IN POUNDS ACCORDING TO FRAME (IN INDOOR CLOTHING)		
		Small Frame	Medium Frame	Large Frame
Feet	Inches			
5	2	112-120	118-129	126-141
5	3	115-123	121-133	129-144
5	4	118-126	124-136	132-148
5	5	121-129	127-139	135-152
5	6	124-133	130-143	138-156
5	7	128-137	134-147	142-161
5	8	132-141	138-152	147-166
5	9	136-145	142-156	151-170
5	10	140-150	146-160	155-174
5	11	144-154	150-165	159-179
6	0	148-158	154-170	164-184
6	1	152-162	158-175	168-189
6	2	156-167	162-180	173-194
6	3	160-171	167-185	178-199
6	4	164-175	172-190	182-204

*Courtesy of the Metropolitan Life Insurance Company, New York, N.Y. Derived from data of the 1969 Build and Blood Pressure Study, Society of Actuaries.

Figure 7-1

DESIRABLE WEIGHTS FOR WOMEN
(Ages 25 and Over)*

HEIGHT (WITH SHOES, 2-INCH HEELS)		WEIGHT IN POUNDS ACCORDING TO FRAME (IN INDOOR CLOTHING)		
		Small Frame	Medium Frame	Large Frame
Feet	Inches			
4	10	92- 98	97-107	104-119
4	11	94-101	98-110	106-122
5	0	96-104	101-113	109-125
5	1	99-107	104-116	112-128
5	2	102-110	107-119	115-131
5	3	105-113	110-122	118-134
5	4	108-116	113-126	121-138
5	5	111-119	116-130	125-142
5	6	114-123	120-135	129-146
5	7	118-127	124-139	133-150
5	8	122-131	128-143	137-154
5	9	126-135	132-147	141-158
5	10	130-140	136-151	145-163
5	11	134-144	140-155	149-168
6	0	138-148	144-159	153-173

*Note: for girls between 18 and 25, subtract 1 pound for each year under 25. Courtesy of the Metropolitan Life Insurance Company, New York, N.Y. Derived from data of the 1959 Build and Blood Pressure Study, Society of Actuaries.

Figure 7-2

FOOD AND NUTRITION BOARD, NATIONAL ACADEMY OF SCIENCES— NATIONAL RESEARCH COUNCIL RECOMMENDED DAILY DIETARY ALLOWANCES,[a] Revised 1974

Designed for the maintenance of good nutrition of practically all healthy people in the U.S.A.

| | Age | Weight | | Height | | Energy | Protein | Fat-Soluble Vitamins | | | |
| | | | | | | | | Vita-min A Activity | | Vita-min D | Vita-min E Activity[e] |
	(years)	(kg)	(lbs)	(cm)	(in)	(kcal)[b]	(g)	(RE)[c]	(IU)	(IU)	(IU)
Infants	0.0-0.5	6	14	60	24	kg × 117	kg × 2.2	420[d]	1,400	400	4
	0.5-1.0	9	20	71	28	kg × 108	kg × 2.0	400	2,000	400	5
Children	1-3	13	28	86	34	1,300	23	400	2,000	400	7
	4-6	20	44	110	44	1,800	30	500	2,500	400	9
	7-10	30	66	135	54	2,400	36	700	3,300	400	10
Males	11-14	44	97	158	63	2,800	44	1,000	5,000	400	12
	15-18	61	134	172	69	3,000	54	1,000	5,000	400	15
	19-22	67	147	172	69	3,000	54	1,000	5,000	400	15
	23-50	70	154	172	69	2,700	56	1,000	5,000		15
	51 +	70	154	172	69	2,400	56	1,000	5,000		15
Females	11-14	44	97	155	62	2,400	44	800	4,000	400	12
	15-18	54	119	162	65	2,100	48	800	4,000	400	12
	19-22	58	128	162	65	2,100	46	800	4,000	400	12
	23-50	58	128	162	65	2,000	46	800	4,000		12
	51 +	58	128	162	65	1,800	46	800	4,000		12
Pregnant						+ 300	+ 30	1,000	5,000	400	15
Lactating						+ 500	+ 20	1,200	6,000	400	15

[a] The allowances are intended to provide for individual variations among most normal persons as they live in the United States under usual environmental stresses. Diets should be based on a variety of common foods in order to provide other nutrients for which human requirements have been less well defined. See text for more detailed discussion of allowances and of nutrients not tabulated.

[b] Kilojoules (kJ) = 4.2 × kcal.

[c] Retinol equivalents.

[d] Assumed to be all as retinol in milk during the first six months of life. All subsequent intakes are assumed to be half as retinol and half as β-carotene when calculated from international units. As retinol equivalents, three fourths are as retinol and one fourth as β-carotene.

From *Recommended Dietary Allowances*, Eighth Revised Edition, 1974, National Academy of Sciences, Washington. D.C., 1974. Reprinted with permission.

Figure 7-3

RECOMMENDED DAILY DIETARY ALLOWANCES,[a] **Revised 1974**

	Water-Soluble Vitamins						Minerals					
Ascorbic Acid (mg)	Folacin[f] (μg)	Niacin[g] (mg)	Riboflavin (mg)	Thiamin (mg)	Vitamin B_6 (mg)	Vitamin B_{12} (μg)	Calcium (mg)	Phosphorus (mg)	Iodine (μg)	Iron (mg)	Magnesium (mg)	Zinc (mg)
35	50	5	0.4	0.3	0.3	0.3	360	240	35	10	60	3
35	50	8	0.6	0.5	0.4	0.3	540	400	45	15	70	5
40	100	9	0.8	0.7	0.6	1.0	800	800	60	15	150	10
40	200	12	1.1	0.9	0.9	1.5	800	800	80	10	200	10
40	300	16	1.2	1.2	1.2	2.0	800	800	110	10	250	10
45	400	18	1.5	1.4	1.6	3.0	1,200	1,200	130	18	350	15
45	400	20	1.8	1.5	2.0	3.0	1,200	1,200	150	18	400	15
45	400	20	1.8	1.5	2.0	3.0	800	800	140	10	350	15
45	400	18	1.6	1.4	2.0	3.0	800	800	130	10	350	15
45	400	16	1.5	1.2	2.0	3.0	800	800	110	10	350	15
45	400	16	1.3	1.2	1.6	3.0	1,200	1,200	115	18	300	15
45	400	14	1.4	1.1	2.0	3.0	1,200	1,200	115	18	300	15
45	400	14	1.4	1.1	2.0	3.0	800	800	100	18	300	15
45	400	13	1.2	1.0	2.0	3.0	800	800	100	18	300	15
45	400	12	1.1	1.0	2.0	3.0	800	800	80	10	300	15
60	800	+2	+0.3	+0.3	2.5	4.0	1,200	1,200	125	18+[h]	450	20
80	600	+4	+0.5	+0.3	2.5	4.0	1,200	1,200	150	18	450	25

[e] Total vitamine E activity, estimated to be 80 percent as α-tocopherol and 20 percent other tocopherols.

[f] The folacin allowances refer to dietary sources as determined by *Lactobacillus casei* assay. Pure forms of folacin may be effective in doses less than one fourth of the recommended dietary allowance.

[g] Although allowances are expressed as niacin, it is recognized that on the average 1 mg of niacin is derived from each 60 mg of dietary tryptophan.

[h] This increased requirement cannot be met by ordinary diets; therefore, the use of supplemental iron is recommended.

Figure 7-3 (Continued)

VIII

Doing It Wrong,
Shattering Myths,
And Doing It Right

> *The pain of the present will never dissolve*
> *entirely. On an occasional day—a good day—it*
> *may slip beneath the surface of our con-*
> *sciousness. On those days, we feel as the wind,*
> *and as close to perfection as possible. But even for*
> *the fittest, it returns.*

If you read just one other book this year, read *Running and Be-ing: The Total Experience*, by Dr. George Sheehan. It is among that small genre of books that causes you to pick up a pencil and underline the important parts until you must restrain yourself after all the pages are thoroughly marked. My copy possesses underlinings, stars, asterisks, exclamation points, notes, and at least one "Amen" per chapter. It is a book like Maltz's *Psycho-Cybernetics* and Frankl's *Man's Search For Meaning*. They don't just interest you, they absorb you. They change you.

Sheehan gives advice on everything from sainthood and asceticism to blisters and shin splints. The book's central premise is simplistically appealing and undeniably accurate: no life can be completely lived without being lived completely on a physical level. Find your sport, he urges. Find your game, your play. Retrace your life to your childhood — to that period when you operated at that level at which the human body was intended to operate. Recall the games that you most enjoyed, and play them again. Pursue your play. Pass through the laziness, the inertia, the inconvenience, the stiffness, and the pain, and emerge as one with the universe, regardless of your age, sex or predisposition toward laughter.

From a sound system of play — a lifestyle that revolves around an intense period of daily relaxation and enjoyment — all other things physical will fall into place. But it must start with play, with exercise, with movement and sweat and flushed faces and callouses and shin splints, and the inexpressible enjoyment that only comes from being physically all you can be. The intellect, writes Sheehan, must surely harden as fast as the arteries. Creativity depends on action. Trust no thought arrived at sitting down.

Meet Mr. Schlock

Meet Mr. Schlock. He's too old to play. Too mature. Too serious-minded and too concerned with work to be worried about his appearance or his diet. No, Mr. Schlock is too important for that. What he does is too important, and besides, he's always late, always busy, always in a hurry.

Another Rotten Morning

Oops, I'm late again. Must have turned off the alarm when it rang. Funny thing. Just can't understand why I never hear it. But no time now to worry about it. Have to hurry to catch my train. No time to shower this morning. Besides, it's cold outside and I don't want to catch pneumonia. I'll work up a sweat ten minutes after walking into the office, anyway.

No time to think about the day or to plan. Just time enough to throw on my clothes and run down to the station.

Well, as always, it looks like I made it with about a minute to spare. The train's not here yet. Time enough to grab a danish and a paper to entertain me on the way into town. Must get some coffee, too. Darn, forgot my DI-GEL™. Hope they have something for this indigestion. No time to worry about it now, though. Here's the train.

Typical morning at work, all right. Gotta get this desk cleaned off one of these days. What I need is more filing space to get all these papers off the floor. Better put my sport coat on. The boss will be around soon. He always is, just to check up on me. Guess he doesn't have anything better to do. Got to remember not to wear this plaid jacket with these striped pants. Oh well, it doesn't matter. I'll just stay seated behind the desk.

Lunch At The Cholesterol Stand

Boy, these tacos are good! I think I'll get an extra one and a soft drink, too. Oops, spilled some sauce on my shirt. It's all right. Matches my tie. Bright red. Better hurry back to the office now. I'm late as usual.

Three o'clock. Is that all it is? Why do these last few hours drag so bad? Seems like there's nothing to do in the afternoons here. Besides, I'm always tired. What I need is a nap, some rest.

Can't believe these guys who go out and play golf or tennis or jog after work. Where do they get all that energy? They must not be putting out a hundred percent at the office, is all I can figure. Like Joe. He's always going someplace after work. Never seems to run out of energy. He must take long naps at his desk.

What's that you say? I don't believe it! Joe got that promotion? Well, I'm not surprised. It should have been mine. But I noticed the boss always spent more time in his office than in mine. Spent more time talking to him than to me. It's politics, I tell you, just politics. It's who you know in this company. It's whose hand you're willing to hold.

Promotions don't have anything to do with how hard you work. Why, look how hard I work! Look how messy this office is! You can tell I'm busy. Why, I was so eager to get to the office I didn't even have time to shower this morning. It's politics, I say. Pure politics.

I Can't Hear The TV Over My Beer

Turn the volume up, will ya'? And bring me a beer. I tell ya' this pace is killing me. Ah, this chair feels nice and soft. Feels good to put my feet up. Where's the paper? Tennis? Not hardly. Why, I've been on my feet all day. I'm just going to sit here till dinner and watch the news and read the paper and drink some beer. And *after dinner—oh look, there's a good show on. We'll just take it easy tonight, and then get some sleep. I need my rest. Yes sir, with as hard as I work, I've got to conserve my energy. Got any pretzels?*

That was a good dinner. I swear these pants are shrinking, or the material's no good. Look at these seams, the way they've stretched. Shine my shoes? Are you kidding? It takes me three days to get the polish off my hands. Besides, that show's about to start, and I'm too busy watching TV.

Well, that's the end of the news. Boy, this world's in sad shape. If I was President I know what I'd do. I'd make everyone slow down. Enough of this running around. They're the trouble makers. Let's see here, there must be something to snack on before bed. Let's heat up that slice of pizza. Yeah, great idea. Got to do something about this heartburn. Keeps me up half the night. I just need more rest, that's all. Got to slow down.

After all, I'm not getting any younger. Yep, that's the secret. Got to take it slow and easy.

Slow and easy.

The Three Great American Myths

They're lies, I tell you, lies!

Three great falsehoods that have led millions to the grave.

Untruths perpetuated upon us, by us. Lies that help soothe, placate, deceive. Lies that we tell ourselves about ourselves. Things that, were we honest, we would know couldn't be true; but things we say nonetheless, in the name of convenience, comfort and our distorted self-image.

Lies, I say. They're lies!

They must be overcome, conquered, eliminated; expunged from the English language, forever banished to the linguistic equivalent of hell—for that is where they deserve to languish for an eternity.

I'm Just Big Boned

You're either twenty pounds overweight or six inches too short. You don't buy trousers that are marked, say, "32 waist, 33 length." No. For you, it's the other way around, and then some.

Perhaps "38 waist, 32 length." From the waist down, there is literally more of you circumferentially than there is vertically. You stand in front of the mirror and you see the bulges. Your spouse puts it as nicely as possible by saying, "You're filling out."

You see the sands shift, the mobility decline, the stamina decrease, and the features fade into a oneness of ever-rounding fat. You are an example of American myth number one: the great lie that has killed so many. You repeat it to all who will listen, regardless of the circumstances or the provocation. At the drop of a hat you'll tell them, because, in addition to being just an excuse, it has also become a source of pride, for somehow bigger is better.

Fact: The overwhelming majority of Americans who are overweight are fat. Plain fat. Their bones have nothing to do with it.

They're on their way to an early grave because they bought lie number one:

"I'm just big boned."

I Can Be Back In Shape In Two Weeks

You lift one heavy box while cleaning out the garage, and you're stiff for days. Your joints seem to ache for no reason at all. The possibility that disuse is the culprit doesn't occur to you.

Your shoulders look smaller and your waist wider than when you were young. The musculature about which you once boasted no longer exists or, if it does, it sags, or is hidden by fat. You can't bend over and touch your toes without bending your knees. You. frequently suffer headaches — mild, but headaches nonetheless. You're often fatigued and winded. When occasionally you must run, which is almost never, you find it awkward. You feel parts of your body bouncing and swaying out of unison and out of touch with what your legs are attempting to do, and with what they used to do so well.

You shoot baskets with your children for ten minutes on a Saturday morning, and the next day your shoulders ache. You attempt calisthenics for two or three minutes once each week — whether you need them or not. You are unable to do more than ten push-ups. You can't conceive of doing twenty legitimate sit-ups. You are unable to sustain any form of constant physical exertion without experiencing some painful malady such as cramps or weak knees or shin splints or blisters or breathlessness.

Yet all the while you harken back to the days when you scored the winning touchdown, made the winning catch, cleared the final hurdle in record time or sank that 30-footer that won the game. You remember those days as yesterday, and hope for those days as tomorrow. And as you continue to deteriorate, you recount to your friends and family, over a beer perhaps, or during lunch, or while you sit and watch the game on TV, how once you did that, too, and were as good, and as lean and as ready to excel.

And as you say these things, you expect that those around you will believe, and so you believe, and in so doing you buy great American myth number two: a myth that will kill you as surely as its predecessor; a myth that may cause you great disillusionment when you test it; a myth that disregards the reality that with increasing age comes increasing discomfort regardless of your level of fitness. A myth that will cause you to abandon efforts at fitness within the first two months, or two years, convinced that something must be congenitally wrong, and that therefore there's no sense trying.

It is the myth to which men in particular are susceptible: once-upon-a-time athletes who knew physical excellence, if only for a year or two, before they discovered cigarettes and booze and staying out late and a dozen other abuses. It is a myth that may kill almost as many Americans each year as do all forms of disease combined.

Yet we say it, we believe it, we live by it, and we die because of it:

"I can be back in shape in two weeks."

I Can Quit Any Time I Want

You watch your life go up in smoke as you light another cigarette. Your fourth of the day, and you haven't even yet finished your first cup of coffee, or finished dressing for work. You suddenly realize you're almost out of cigarettes. Automatically, without thought or resentment, and perhaps intentionally without stopping to consider how insane it is, you rearrange your entire morning's schedule so you'll have time to buy another pack, or carton, or two cartons. But it's all right, you say, because it relaxes you and it's not out of control and it's just a matter of time before you put an end to it.

At night when you return home from work, you automatically reach for a drink. Maybe a beer or wine or a bourbon or a martini. It doesn't matter which. What matters is that you reach for it automatically as a part of your nightly routine. What matters is that whether you're alone or not, you'll drink it. What matters is that you don't consider yourself to be alcohol dependent because you know you're in control. Like the cigarettes, you use the booze of your own free will. You're not like Joe down the street, or that aunt or uncle — the one who lost control and who ruined his life and then tried to end it. You're not like them because you're different. You needn't worry. So you reach for another drink. But it's all right because it's part of your nightly routine. It's something you choose to do and could choose not to do, if you desired.

At bedtime there is, of course, the pill. Not the one you sometimes take in the morning to pick you up, but the one you take now to calm you down. It is a prescription drug, a barbiturate. Your doctor is accustomed to your demands for more. But he maintains a polite suburban practice, and you are one of thousands of patients, and he won't waste too much of his time lecturing you. And besides, he knows that you know you're not dependent upon the drug. So you just keep taking more. And if one pill ceases to have the desired affect, two will do, and the dosage can always be increased still further. And if that doesn't work, it's all right because there is always something stronger on the market. Your doctor will know what to do. And obviously your approach is so reasonable and so logical and so mature that you needn't worry about these drugs ruining your life.

Yes, you are the great American Independent: that rock-hard bastion of self-control. That stalwart example of an individual who can take his conveniences to the limit without going over the line and becoming a slave to them. You are the walking, talking, living, breathing example of the consumer that tobacco companies and distillers and drug manufacturers most want to have. Indeed, you are the image of the consumer that most claim to have: the individual who can take them or leave them, but who freely chooses their use as a matter of personal preference and taste.

And as you light up another cigarette, or pour another drink, or dissolve another pill in your stomach, you mention time and again your independence. You mention it to your spouse, to your children, to your employer, to your employees, to your friends, to all who will listen. And most especially you say it again and again and again to yourself. Because if you say it enough you'll believe it. And if you believe it, that makes it all right. And then your self-image isn't shattered and you can continue relying upon these things without having to worry that they'll kill you; without having to worry that they'll kill those who love you.

And each day, with each additional dosage, with each additional puff, with each additional swallow, you repeat the big lie over and over again; and you believe it and therefore it's true, until it's too late:

"I can quit any time I want."

Doing It Right

Viktor Frankl called it the tragic triad of human existence: guilt for our past, pain in the present and death in the future.

It is at least often, if not universally, true that the older a man gets, the more intensely he regrets his past. Not the affirmative acts taken therein, but what wasn't done: the training that never occurred, the discipline that was never imposed, the constructive habits that were never learned (or that were unlearned). In short, the potential that was never attained. Such guilt exists especially in the ex-athlete: the man or woman who has gradually wasted away his or her physical potential.

Pain increases, too, with longevity. Although unavoidable, it is more often than not misinterpreted by us. We measure our ability to run and jump and play and exert ourselves generally against the way we remember feeling as children, which is to say the way we remember not feeling pain. But that body which was so oblivious to bangs and bumps and bruises has now stiffened, and with that stiffness comes the pain. But with it, too, comes new potentialities: reproduction, strength, stamina.

The pain of the present will never dissolve entirely. On an occasional day — a good day — it may slip beneath the surface of our consciousness. On those days, we feel as the wind, and as close to perfection as possible. But even for the fittest, it returns. The question is never whether, but when and how. And so we must run and play through the pain toward fitness and our full physical potential.

Yet there remains the third tragic specter; death in the future. Unavoidable and undeniable, it waits. But the athlete has already died in dozens of smaller ways, in hundreds of contests against others and himself. And he has risen anew time and again to emerge victorious or to lose with grace. The athlete, and even the non-athletic player — the runner or golfer or Saturday-morning short-stop — has, if his play has been intense enough, acquired his own special sense of mortality, and is undeterred by the impermanence of life. For he seeks perfection in the effort, not the result. And the ultimate effort at our most physical level can best be found in sports.

Initial Evaluation: "Are You Sure Those Aren't Someone Else's Measurements?"

It's the sanest place to start: in the mirror.

To where have the sands shifted? Stare for at least a minute at that image in the glass. Nude and unassuming, let the entire effect sink in. Concentrate most upon those areas over which your eyes have previously slid, not wanting to delay, for fear of what they might discover. The thighs, the buttocks, that roll around the back, that general sag from head to toe.

But don't be content with merely admitting that your dimensions are not what they should be. Find out exactly what they are. Raid the sewing chest and find that tape measure you've been embarrassed to use for the past 15 years. Use it. Don't tuck in that gut too much as you seek to find your distance around.

Obtain as honest an appraisal as possible. Write those measurements down: your chest, your waist, your thighs. Make sure that your scale is accurate, then weigh in. Now determine the measurements you would like to record. Establish specifically your one-year goals for waist measurements, chest measurements and weight. Determine how much you'll have to either gain or lose to reach those goals, and divide the difference by twelve, thus establishing monthly benchmarks to attain along your way to fitness.

Now establish some goals regarding the games you'll play.

Promise yourself at least five hours a week (that's an hour a day, Monday through Friday) of hard play. You pick your sport, your game. Bridge and Canasta should not be on your list. If whatever you do doesn't cause you to work up a sweat within the first 15 minutes, then find another game. It must be strenuous, and it must be fun. The fewer participants required, the better. That way, you'll be less dependent on others in keeping your schedule.

If you have no strong preference, then I recommend jogging. The initial investment is low (you absolutely *must* invest in a high quality pair of running shoes), and there's nothing complicated about the game (just remember the basic rules: left, right, left, right, left, right, as fast as you can for as long as your can). If you haven't run for awhile, and if you're over the age of 25, then invest in Jim Fixx's book, *The Complete Book of Running*, and study carefully what he has to say. Every hour you spend reading it will likely save you ten hours of pain during your running career.

When you start running, don't be discouraged by those who go whizzing by. If it's any consolation, you may take my case as solace. Upon graduating from law school at age 26, I suffered from severe sciatica. In fact, I literally spent my last month of school in traction, and I took my Bar Exams while wearing a heavy metal brace which alone permitted me to remain upright. For a year thereafter I was barely able to walk for more than half an hour without experiencing excruciating pain. Sports and play were out of the question.

Between my 27th and 28th years, I began appreciating how rapidly my body was wasting away due to lack of exercise. The pain remained (as it does to this day), but my fear of an early death occasioned by complete lack of exercise increased. I began walking regularly despite the pain. I moved to Phoenix, where I could exercise outdoors on a regular basis. I began jogging occasionally during my walks, and then began jogging regularly, as far as two or three miles each run, as often as three or four times each week.

But the pain remained. Yet, despite it, I began to feel revitalized, refreshed. At age 29 I began feeling as good as I had when I was 20. Now I run about four times a week. I average five to six miles per run. On off days I lift weights and jump rope. Having quit smoking some time ago, and having held my other vices to moderation, I am as fit now as I have ever been in my life.

Although the pain remains, and likely always will, it is compensated for by an overwhelming feeling of vitality that I would dread living without. I remain a totally ungifted athlete. I am an aggravatingly slow runner. My reflexes are dismal, my timing non-existent. But I am fit, and I have earned every ounce of vitality that I have, and that alone is an enormous accomplishment. And I wish no less for you.

If I can do it, you can do it.

Don't See A Fat Doctor

Dr. Sheehan points out that the jogger has three natural enemies: drivers, dogs and doctors. For that matter, the medical profession is the unintentional natural enemy of all athletic people.

While the athlete, amateur or otherwise, strives for health and fitness, the medical profession strives for the elimination of disease. Yet health is not merely the absence of disease. Health has to do with wholeness, and reaching your level of excellence.

It is because the athlete is healthy that he is medicine's most difficult patient. Medicine in its current form exists to remedy maladies, not to enhance relative perfection. Health is a mysterious balance of all things that are good. So the athlete who presents a stress fracture or a sprain in an otherwise perfectly healthy body presents an irreconcilable dichotomy to the doctor. For all the doctor can do in his wisdom and knowledge, is prescribe the absence of training, so that the aches occasioned by training can heal. Yet it is training that has brought about the fitness of the athlete in the first place. The trouble is that no doctor can specialize in health, since to do so would be to specialize in the universe. It is the healthy athlete, then, who keeps consistently pushing his endurance to the limit that provides the physician with his greatest challenge.

There is no ready solution for this situation. But an awareness of it helps us as we translate our thoughts to action. For example, it is uniformly recommended, if you have not engaged in strenuous physical activity for some time, that you obtain a thorough physical examination before beginning. I would certainly not presume to contradict that advice, but I *would* recommend that you don't see a fat doctor. Don't seek out the advice of any individual, regardless of how well trained, who can't empathize with your desire to be fit.

An out-of-shape doctor is living proof of the fact that what we know logically does not always manifest itself in the way we live. It is not enough that an expert should logically accept the notion that fitness is important. He must live that belief before his advice is worth paying for.

A Sensible Fitness Program

Don't go overboard.

If you haven't been in training for some time, I promise that no matter what you do, or what game you select, if you do it hard for more than 30 minutes the first day, you'll swear the second day you'll never do it again.

Build gradually. Don't use those first few days of training as your personal test to verify your rationalization (and the great American myth) that you, in fact, can be back in shape in two weeks. Don't risk it. The stakes are too high. It's too easy in those first few days or weeks to overdo. An ankle sprain can set you back for months. A pulled ligament can have a similar effect, and a muscle or tendon tear can totally rearrange your physiology.

Take it one step at a time. Find your sport and have fun with it. Measure your progress. Rather than being discouraged at how far you have to go, take pleasure — indeed delight — in how far you've come. Don't ever forget that how fast you run, or how well you shoot, or how squarely you hit the ball, relative to the next guy, is as unimportant as your level of success relative to the next guy. For, as we demonstrated with the Success Environment Formula, the only person against whom you compete is the only person with whom you will succeed. The only enemy that can cause you to quit is the only friend with whom you can share victory. He's the guy whose sweat you'll taste, whose shoes you'll carry, whose heart you'll feel pound, and whose spirit you'll feel soar, as you strive together to be physically all you can be.

As always, you must do it right with the guy in the mirror.

There is a little Mr. Schlock in each of us.

Perhaps it is his tendency to oversleep and to rush in the morning. Perhaps it is his unwillingness to bathe. Maybe it is his diet or his laziness. But wherever he exists in us, he must be exposed and eliminated.

He cannot be permitted to continue to exist in the form of a lie. To say that a lie becomes true if it is told enough times, is itself a lie which has been told too many times. To which of the three big myths are you most susceptible? Which is most likely to kill you? Against which shall you resolve to revolt?

As always, it begins and ends in the mirror as we size up–literally–where we stand, and as we measure our dimensions against what we will become. It begins with seeking the professional advice that is so necessary, but not seeking the opinions of those who do not live what they preach. And it begins with finding a game that is right for us and pursuing it in a gradual, sensible fashion.

These are the things that will cause us to reach the peak of our physical abilities. They are the methods by which we can become all that God intended us to be.

IX

Looking The Part
Of The Successful You:
Grooming, Attire
And Silent Command

*Clothes designers are, God bless them, in the
business of selling clothes . . . . Their ability to
continue to earn an income is based upon their
ability to convince you that what you bought last
year is already obsolete.*

Calvin Cautious was shuckin' and jivin' at the local disco.

At his John Travolta best, Calvin was especially confident
tonight. His disco suit was just back from the cleaner, his hair
greased back in the latest fashion. Calvin had just finished
reading yet another book on body language, his third this week,
and he was sure he could read the signals to select a promising
partner.

Then he spotted her across the dance floor. All the signs said
"yes." Her body spoke a language he clearly understood. Her
elbows said "passion," her ankles said "willingness." That slight
twitch of her shoulder said "promiscuity" and — could it be?
Calvin thought — was that a knowing wink? Calvin crossed the
dance floor toward her.

Suddenly he was there, saying nothing. Within inches of her, he struck his own pose; a gesture of male dominance and preening unsurpassed since Brando wore his T-shirt in *On The Waterfront.* Calvin supplemented his stance with his best Clint Eastwood squint and waited for her to melt into his arms.

To this day Calvin still doesn't understand how any woman could have had such a powerful left hook. He never saw it coming. With half of his Clint Eastwood squint swollen shut, and with his disco suit torn from his tumble over the nearby table, Calvin concludes that he must have missed something in that last book on body language.

Oh well, Calvin. Back to the drawing board.

Don't Go Grubby

That generation of Americans born between 1945 and 1950 — that wave of humanity that fell upon this country as a result of the post-war "baby boom" — has at least two special problems with which to contend.

The first problem is volume. There are too many of them. Having already entered the job market in force, they will be competing with one another for the best career opportunities during their entire productive lifetimes.

The second problem that this generation faces compounds the first: grooming. For them, the Vietnam era changed all the definitions of what was appropriate in grooming. Those who survived the era as teenagers, young adults, protestors, or veterans, found their closets filled with an odd assortment of old suits, blue jeans, flannel shirts and fatigues that are a little too worn and sometimes too symbolic of the '60s to be worn today, even in this the land of Levi Strauss.

Their mirrors are filled, too, with the images of hairy faces: beards left over from long ago, and hair lengths that no one can decide what to do with. The result has been a vast array of grooming and dressing styles that have caused too many members of this particular generation (which incidentally is rapidly becoming the bulk of the work force in America) to assume that any form of attire and grooming is generally appropriate for any type of occasion or career.

Yet the individuals who still exert a profound effect upon the career advancement of the members of the post-war generation are of another era: an era punctuated by crew-cuts, "white walls," discipline, conformity of dressing and grooming habits, and war of another kind that was far more popular.

The members of the post-war generation have learned that in all things we must first please ourselves. Indeed, the Y Factor of the Success Environment Formula is just another way of affirming this basic notion. Yet, the more practical members of that generation realize that the people who hire them, fire them, promote them, or buy from them are often of an earlier generation whose likes and dislikes, and whose grooming and dressing heritage should also be respected.

This section, then, is directed primarily to those products of the post-war baby boom. Its directives on grooming may seem too fundamentally basic to those of earlier (and even to those of later) generations. But this post-war generation should not be blamed for its lack of finesse on the subject. It has been busy enough competing against itself in unprecedented numbers and in dealing with a world that often seemed turned upside down.

Splitting Hairs

John T. Malloy, in his book *Dress for Success* (for men), and his book *The Woman's Dress for Success Book*, reached some startling conclusions about grooming and attire.

Malloy's conclusions are, he insists, based upon research: the kind that determines not what types of clothes or hair styles we like, but what kind cause favorable reactions in others. It is, Malloy says, not a question of right or wrong, good or bad, pretty or ugly, but rather a question of what "tests best."

For example, the type of test Malloy might conduct would be to place two photographs before the senior personnel director of a corporation. The executive would be told that the photographs are of identical twin brothers, and that he should select that brother whom he would be most inclined to hire. Actually, the photos would be of the same individual. However, in one photo he might be wearing, say, a green suit, and be wearing his hair slightly over his ears, and in the other photo he would be wearing a gray pin-striped suit and have his hair more closely cut. Malloy would then record the reactions of such executives to reach his statistical conclusions regarding which types of attire and grooming "tested best."

The results of research by Malloy and others like him have sometimes been surprising. It seems, especially on young men, for example, that even hair which is only moderately long elicits negative reactions from older individuals, even though these older persons might themselves, in their own way, now be emulating such hair styles. Similarly, facial hair tends to test poorly in most corporate environments. As a general rule, the younger a man is, the more likely he is to elicit negative reactions from others for wearing hair that is "too long," or for sporting a mustache, beard, or goatee.

Women are especially vulnerable to encountering prejudice against their hair within the business community. Statistics indicate that within the business community, a woman's hair should be no longer than shoulder length. Hair that is wavy, not curly, is acceptable, and hair that is short but not masculine is acceptable. Hair longer than shoulder length or hair that is too curly (a la *Good Ship Lollipop*) tests poorly within the business community. (Again, it is important to emphasize that here we speak not of aesthetics, but of statistics.)

Some of us resent the suggestion that we adopt a particular hair style in order to effect our ultimate success. It seems almost un-American that such conformity should be pressed upon us. Yet by conforming, we may actually be creating greater freedom for ourselves in achieving our personal goals. For regardless of our own personal preference, it is others who must spend the bulk of the day looking at us and our hair. When we sport styles that cause others to spend their time trying to adjust to our hair, we distract from our business purpose, whatever it may be. Better that we should dress and groom in a manner that makes others feel comfortable, so that they can concentrate on the product, service, or idea that we are presenting to them.

Most men still consider it to be downright unmasculine to have their hair cut by a stylist. They still automatically trudge down to the same local barber, who hasn't taken a refresher course in ten or fifteen years, and whose patrons generally look as though they were either scalped with a dull knife or run over by a lawn mower. Patricia Fripp, in the book *The Joy of Selling*, devotes an entire chapter to the importance of good haircuts for men. One of San Francisco's most successful "lady barbers," she writes:

> *Even in this day and age when hair cuts cost about $17, over an average period of six weeks between cuts, that will work out to be about 40¢ per day for your hair. If the average salesman makes five calls a day, it costs him 8¢ a call to be totally confident in his appearance — at least from the neck up! I wonder how much he paid for parking while he was calling on his prospect.*

Splitting hairs? Possibly. But the advantages of good grooming are undeniable.

Scrubbing Down Daily

There still exists, unfortunately, a small but very noticeable percentage of Americans who have not caught on to the necessity of bathing daily. They seem to believe that accumulated body odors can be covered up with other odors from a can or a roll-on stick, when, in fact, all such additions do is bombard the innocent bystander with additional unwelcome fragrances.

There is also that percentage of Americans who believe that they shouldn't wash their hair daily because it's not good for it. I have no authoritative source on this subject, but I suppose that many years ago shampoos might have been strong enough to have caused some damage if used every day. But I also suspect that today you would have to swim in a vat of your favorite shampoo for hours on end to suffer any damage.

Yet, the real advantage to scrubbing down daily is not hygienic. It is — bluntly — economic. With whom would you rather deal: the sleepy-eyed, semi-shaved, uncombed hack, who, by his lack of grooming and cleanliness, firmly announces to you that he is not even organized enough to set aside 30 minutes in the morning to clean up, or the individual who is scrubbed down, shaved, combed out and well attired, and whose total presence bespeaks a level of organization and professionalism that you can admire, and with which you can freely associate?

Scrubbing down daily. Simple. Fundamental. Embarrassingly basic. Absolutely essential.

The Classic Combination:
Good Health And Good Grooming

I ran in my first 10,000 meter race the other day. Bill Rodgers, the world class runner, was there. He was beaten by Tom Hunt, a fellow I had never heard of until that day, and yet who obviously is an exceptional athlete. They each ran the 6.2-mile distance in slightly less than thirty minutes. As I watched those two young men receive their awards after the race, I was enormously impressed by their vitality. The eyes of each seemed especially clear and alert. Their complexions were excellent. Their muscle-tone, of course, was superb. They were lean, lithe, and relaxed. Their every movement bespoke an athletic elegance that could only come from a superb combination of fitness and health.

I've never seen either of those men in a suit and tie. Their business (to them running is a business) doesn't require that they wear one except on rare occasions. Yet, I could imagine how vital and commanding they would appear in such attire. Rodgers and Hunt were, on that day, excellent examples of the classic combination: good health and good grooming. Just as a vital, athletic, healthy physique will profoundly complement wearing apparel, so,too, will ill health and general lack of fitness be apparent, regardless of the cost or tailoring of clothes designed to hide their presence.

You can't buy vitality. It's not available through Brooks Brothers. It comes only through fitness and health. Grooming serves to frame that fitness. It can be a poorly structured frame, inappropriate for the picture, or it can serve to accent and emphasize the power and purposefulness of the piece of art within. The choice is yours. Let good health and good grooming supplement each other to produce the picture of the successful you.

Threads: Doing It Right

Enough of this disgusting sentimentality!
Enough of this effort to placate the emotions! It's time to get tough! Heartless! It is time to muster our courage, walk into that closet, and begin ruthlessly to eliminate the vast majority of our

wardrobe; to dispose, with cold calculation, of those items that have outlived their usefulness — if, indeed, they ever had usefulness.

Men, it's time that those two-toned shoes you bought in the early '70s were dispatched. Remove them from the premises late at night under cover of darkness, when no one can see that you still actually own some.

Ladies, those mini-skirts will not come back in fashion. Even if they do, they never were appropriate for business wear, and by the time they come back, you'll have six great grandchildren and be playing bingo at the Home.

Yes, men, I promise. That tie of yours that says, "Visit Mammoth Cave!" will never be of use to you again. And ladies, even though you wore that skirt with the poodles on it for your first date, it's time to be cold, cruel, heartless. Put the poodles to sleep permanently.

It's time that we clean out that closet and start doing it right.

E.S.P. —
The Effect You Desire

What you wear on weekends is none of my business. I would not presume to dictate your leisure time life style.

I hope by now we can agree, however, that by carefully selecting our business clothes, we may enhance our pursuit of professional and economic goals. Much has been written on the subject. Many books are available. I urge you to read one or two to confirm your appreciation of the common sense that they contain.

The *E.S.P. of Business Success* summarizes the effect we are attempting to attain with clothes, the reaction we seek from others.

E   represents Enthusiasm. We wish others to know that we are wholeheartedly involved with what we're doing, that we are excited about our work, and that we enjoy helping them. Our clothes must say, "I am enthusiastic."

S   represents Sincerity. It is imperative that others trust us as we trust ourselves. It is important that they understand that we mean what we say, that we'll stand behind our promises, and that they can rely upon us at all times. Our clothes must also say, "I am sincere."

P   represents Professionalism. It is not enough that we are just enthusiastic and sincere. We must also be a pro: well trained, confident, successful at what we do. Subtle and not flamboyant; understated yet elegant; at ease in our environment. Through our clothes we can say these things. We can say, "I am a professional."

The *E.S.P. of Business Success:* enthusiasm, sincerity and professionalism. These are the messages we are attempting to convey with our clothes. With each article we select, we should ask ourselves, "Does this article say those three things?" If not, put it back on the rack and look elsewhere.

What Not To Wear
And When Not To Wear It

Whole books have been devoted to a description of what not to wear. The few paragraphs that we will devote to the subject, therefore, can't possibly be all inclusive.

However, in our Success Environment Seminars around the country, we have found general agreement among our audiences that there are certain dressing transgressions which should simply not be permitted. They are the kinds of things that many of us do unintentionally, but which make others shudder.

For example: men, don't wear short socks. Nothing is tackier than a man who sits down, crosses his legs, and suddenly exposes four to six inches of what is usually a very hairy and very skinny ankle. It not only looks bad, it often looks downright funny. Unless you're a professional clown, I heartily urge you to invest in knee-length socks.

Speaking of socks: ladies, unless you are a nurse and must wear white, don't wear anything other than flesh (or natural) colored hose. John Malloy, in *The Woman's Dress For Success Book,* said that colored hosiery tests so poorly that he wouldn't recommend it as a face mask for a bank robber.

Men, don't attempt to utilize what are essentially sport clothes for business purposes. Shirts should be long sleeved, white or a very soft pastel. Shirt patterns should be extremely subtle. Most patterns should be avoided. Nothing is worse than a man wearing a $200 suit over an $8 shirt.

Accessories are also important. Once, while in the Midwest doing a seminar on dressing, I asked a gentleman if he would lend me his belt. What he offered was a rope, on the end of which was attached a medal he had won in a 1954 bowling tournament.

Belts should be new, should fit the loops on your trousers, and generally should not boast of your success in 1954 bowling tournaments.

Accessories for women are equally important. The over-sized purse, for example, is dangerous. Purses have a nasty reputation. They're known to be filled, in a very disorganized fashion, with a lot of feminine things, none of which can be found when needed. Whether the stigma applies in your case or not, it is worth avoiding.

Carry a leather briefcase instead. You don't have to do without all those accessories in your purse. Just open the briefcase, pour the contents of your purse into it, close the briefcase and throw away the purse. Now you have a funny shaped purse that looks to the rest of the world like a very organized and professional briefcase. Just don't open it in the presence of clients or customers.

The list of little things that should not be done is endless. Women, for example, should in most instances work hard not to display any cleavage. According to the experts, cleavage distracts from your business purpose. Personally, I have nothing against cleavage. In fact, I'm rather fond of it. But, I must admit, as a typical male, that if I were, for example, being given a sales presentation by a woman who wore an outfit that displayed her cleavage, I would more than likely be concentrating less upon the presentation than upon the cleavage. Chauvinistic? No. It would not be my fault if she dressed in a manner which distracted from her business purpose. As a prospect, client, or customer, I have no responsibility to work overtime mentally to overcome her errors. That kind of reaction is not chauvinistic. Just normal.

Women in the business community still have enough obstacles to overcome without deliberately handicapping themselves by dressing inappropriately. European designers, it must be noted, still seem to regard women in business as something of a passing — and bad — American joke. They have, as John T. Malloy points out, never dressed women for the boardroom. They have only dressed women for the bedroom. A designer's label, or the encouragment of a salesclerk, are no guarantee that a particular garment will be appropriate for the business world.

For both men and women, subtlety is the key. While rich, conservative tones are most appropriate for men's suits, the lighter colors are most appropriate for shirts and blouses. We are somewhat prejudiced by our own history. Many years ago, the only dyed colors that less expensive garments could hold were the darker colors. Only the more expensive cloths could accept a lighter dye. Thus poor people, or the "working class," wore darker shirts and trousers, and the more affluent wore lighter garments. This created the distinction between "blue-collar, white-collar" which remains with us even today.

The man who wears a suit with a dark shirt says to us subconsciously, "I'm a blue-collar worker who just happens to have to put on a suit today." We want our apparel to say, at the least, that we are professionals in whom our clients or customers can have confidence. We must thus avoid colors that conjure subconscious lower-middle or working-class prejudices in the minds of others.

What To Wear
And When To Wear It

Clothes designers are, God bless them, in the business of selling clothes. They're not in the business of selling widgets or real estate, or managing a staff or whatever you may do. Their ability to continue to earn an income is based upon their ability to convince you that what you bought last year is already obsolete. As a result, styles often change radically. We are told what is "appropriate," what we should be buying, what we should be storing, and what we should be throwing away by the very people whose incomes depend upon a healthy turnover rate among the clothes in our closet.

Yet it is the very people we listen to most — the designers — who would be least inclined to admit that, *for business purposes,* styles within the United States have changed very little within the last 20 years. For men, the most appropriate form of business attire is now, and will probably continue to be for the indefinite future, the three-piece suit. Usually gray, with perhaps a subtle pin-stripe, sometimes charcoal or blue, this suit is the standard business uniform in most of corporate America. The trousers have flared slightly, the coats have been tucked a little at the waist, but over the years, generally, the style has remained the same; and while the rest of the country was running around buying two-tone shoes, red shirts and white ties, the leaders of corporate America were buying subtle, conservative, elegant suits, white shirts and equally subtle ties.

But what of women? Until recently, there was no standard uniform for women in the business community. Because most women in the business community were, bluntly, secretaries, they wore whatever their company would permit. Yet Malloy now suggests that there is, in fact, a standard business uniform for upwardly mobile female executives. It is the skirted suit, complemented by a man-tailored blouse, a contrasting scarf, an attache case, natural-colored panty hose, and simple pumps no more than two inches high.

Yet, many women, perhaps because they are newer to the executive crunch than are men, seem more resistant to this type of conformity than do men. In discussing Malloy's findings with women around the country, especially with those in real estate, I have found a great resistance because, as they say, such a uniform may not be flexible enough for their particular needs. I have no desire to argue with them or with Mr. Malloy. Rather, I would recommend that you examine carefully what he and experts like him have to say, and then incorporate as many of their recommendations as possible into your personal business wardrobe. Ultimately each individual must be the final arbiter as to what is appropriate for his or her particular business and career.

In sum, there exists a business uniform — one for men and one for women — which is totally appropriate for the vast majority of business situations. It is the uniform we should wear under most circumstances when we want to present our professional best.

Silent Command: Body Language

Not too many years ago, graphoanalysis, or handwriting analysis, was in vogue. You'd go to a party and have your handwriting analyzed by your neighbor. "Oh my God!" she'd say. "You have three weeks to live!"

Of course, you survived the prediction, but the lesson was

clear: a little knowledge can be a dangerous thing. In more recent times, it seems that a good number of people have similarly OD'd on kinesics, or *body language*. Everyone seems to know what one or two gestures "really" mean.

For example, if you fold your arms during a discussion, they'll tell you you're being defensive. If you put your fingers to your mouth while talking, they'll tell you you're lying; and if you stick your thumb in your belt, they'll call that a male "preening gesture." It never occurs to them, of course, that in the first instance you might be cold, in the second your lip might itch, and in the third you may be pulling up your pants.

That's why most experts urge us to consider body language in terms of *gesture clusters*: groups of gestures which provide us with a more accurate picture of what a person is saying on a non-verbal level. For example, we rarely evaluate an oil painting on the basis of just one brush stroke. It is the strokes as seen in conjunction with one another that tells us the total story.

Certain variables also have a profound effect upon gesture clusters: age, fatigue, sex and health are but a few. For example, the young man who places his hands on his hips and stands lightly on the balls of his feet with his chin protruding slightly may most likely be indicating readiness or excitement. An older man, making the same gesture, may very well be indicating hostility. Move the hands which are on the hips of both men back slightly toward the small of the back and you may have a gesture — regardless of age — which indicates, simply, that the subject has a backache.

It is important, therefore, that we do not approach body language piecemeal, but that we attempt to acquire an appreciation for various gesture clusters which may provide us some insight into the thoughts of others. Moreover, we must remember that most of our reactions to gesture clusters are subliminal. We don't consciously evaluate them. Therefore, if we can know generally what certain clusters mean to most people, then we can literally incorporate those movements into our own physical repertoire to help supplement the enthusiasm, sincerity and professionalism we are trying to project.

That First Impression

While you may not make that big sale, or clinch that new client

during the first 30 seconds of meeting him, you can most assured-
ly lose it or him during that period.

Suppose you are meeting two new clients at your office for the
first time. As they walk in the door, you notice that the male
enters first. When he enters the room, he leans forward, hands on
hips, and looks eager to get on with the business for which he
came. Meanwhile, his wife, for whatever reason, is standing
behind him and seems slightly more reluctant to participate.
Under those circumstances you may well wish to greet her first,
acknowledging her presence with a handshake, and only then
turn to the male to help acknowledge his already demonstrated
enthusiasm. Such an approach may help to more readily pull her
into the *selling triangle* you wish to create.

On the other hand, if both partners appear equally enthusiastic
about being in your office, then you might well wish to greet the
member of your own sex first. This establishes instant rapport
with that individual and establishes you as someone who is not a
threat sexually.

The first impression centers around the handshake. A handshake must be firm, warm, dry and sincere. The bubble of privacy
for most Americans is approximately arm's length. Whenever
anyone penetrates that zone around our body without our permission, we feel uncomfortable. The expression "arm's length
business transaction" probably has its origins in this
phenomenon. The result is that while our handshake must be
sincere and warmly felt, it must not be an intrusion into the other
person's bubble of privacy.

In a business context, the handshake is the only acceptable way
we have of touching another person. The handshake was ap-
parently first used on the battlefield. When warriors met each
other to discuss terms, they would hold on to each other's hands
so that neither could reach for a weapon. In later years, the
Romans grabbed each other by the elbow, thus tying up the right
hand of the other. Of course, if the Roman with whom you were
shaking hands was a southpaw, the elbow grabbing experience
might well be your last. From there, the handshake seemed to
evolve into what we customarily regard as the "good old
American handshake": firm, warm, dry and sincere. A sweaty
palm denotes nervousness. Be sure to wipe your hand before placing it in someone else's.

There are two extremes of the "good old American handshake." First is the Fraternity House Crunch. That's the handshake that becomes a wrestling match between two young bucks who want to impress each other with their strength. We see it today especially in young men in the business community who have yet to understand that the purpose of a handshake is to convey warmth, sincerity, and trustworthiness — not pure physical strength. The other extreme of the American handshake is the Wet Fish Touch. It is when two otherwise normal adults offer each other fingers dangling precariously on the end of limp wrists. Neither of these extremes is appropriate in the business world. It is the "good old American handshake" that works.

Women in business should shake hands as freely as men in business. Most of us are admittedly victims of our upbringing, which said you shouldn't shake a woman's hand unless she offers it to you first. Many women don't quite know how to react when a man offers his hand. They frequently look at it as if to say, "I'm not going to touch that hand; I don't know where it's been!" But that's their problem, not yours. Ladies, if a potential male client or customer refuses to shake your hand, I urge you to pawn him off on someone else — preferably another woman in the office you don't like. For if he is unwilling to convey to you a normal form of business greeting, then will he really treat you as an equal in the negotiations which are likely to follow?

For both men and women, that first impression is enormously important. Make it work for you.

What You "Say" To Others

Most of us could learn a great deal by looking at ourselves through our colleagues' eyes.

As a helpful exercise, I recommend that you sit down with several of your colleagues — individuals with whom you are closely associated at work. Ask them to list bluntly and honestly those physical characteristics about you that convey to them a message. Ask them to list on the left-hand side of a page each characteristic, and on the right-hand side of the page to list the message that each characteristic provides. Encourage them to be honest, and not to search for flattering characteristics.

We frequently develop physical traits of which we are often not aware. It is helpful to have those who know us best inform us of their existence. For example, if you are an exceptionally large male, you may find that your posture is considered by some to be domineering. As a woman, you may make a particular gesture with your shoulder, for example, about which you are totally unaware, and which others may interpret as being overly coy.

Ask your colleagues for their input, and share ideas with them about which of your characteristics you should minimize and which you should expand. Many positive gestures (i.e. those gestures that positively influence others) can — and probably should — be manufactured. For example, it is natural, when speaking in earnest to another, to hold one's hands in front of the body, palms upward. This is an automatic gesture of openness and honesty. Similarly, to place one's hands lightly upon one's chest while speaking is an indication of humility and sincerity. Professional speakers frequently use those two gestures consciously, especially at the beginning of their presentations, to establish rapport with their audience and to establish themselves as open, honest, sincere, and reasonably humble individuals. Does the fact that a speaker may consciously use such gestures to establish himself as being open, sincere and honest, make him any the less so? I think not. It only demonstrates that he has acquired skill enough at what he does to know specifically what physical actions are necessary to supplement the message he wishes to present.

Similarly, in sales or management, other gestures may also be appropriate. By obtaining the input of your colleagues, you may determine which of your customary gestures distract from your purpose and which, if further developed, might aid you in the accomplishment of your purpose.

What Others "Say" To You

The mental processes of another may be "read" by examining his gestures. Remembering our admonition above that we must view gestures in terms of clusters, let us examine a few gestures which are customarily inherent to certain types of mental processes.

Decision making is frequently depicted by chin stroking, the absent-minded biting of the tips of glasses, pacing, or pinching the bridge of one's nose with one's eyes closed.

Evaluation is often accompanied by placing a hand to one's cheek, looking down and tilting one's head.

The classic gesture of folded arms frequently denotes *defensiveness*. Women, for obvious biologic reasons, generally cross their arms lower on their torsos than do men. Downcast eyes and a turned-away face also depict defensiveness, as does the placing of a leg over a chair, or the straddling of a chair backwards and using the back of the chair as something of a shield. An individual who crosses his legs away from the person to whom he is listening frequently does so to establish his facing thigh, side, and shoulder as a defensive barrier against the information he is hearing. And, of course, the classic gesture of defensiveness is the small child who, knowing he is guilty, holds his hands behind his back while professing his innocence.

Mental conflict is often accompanied by eyebrows which are turned down, lips which are tense and a head and chin which are bent forward.

Interest is frequently depicted by a critical evaluation gesture cluster much like the statue *The Thinker*. Sometimes doodling denotes interest, and it is interesting to note that an individual's pupils will dilate when he is looking at something at which he is particularly interested. For example, most men's eyes will dilate when looking at pictures of beautiful women.

While talk of such body language may be interesting, it can be hazardous as well. Yet, a basic understanding of the extent to which we can influence others and be influenced by others nonverbally is especially important as we attempt to present our physical selves in as beneficial a light as possible.

The challenge of looking the part of the successful you has been complicated by a number of factors. Since the post-war baby boom of the late '40s, standards of appropriateness for grooming and attire have been turned upside down. Yet through it all, fundamental philosophies have remained. Good grooming is imperative.

Be it right or wrong, conservative hair styles are the most popular within the business community. Scrubbing down daily remains essential, regardless of what the manufacturers of eight-day deodorant pads may say. Good health and good grooming still provide the classic vital combination we all seek. With our attire, we attempt to convey the *E.S.P. of Business Success:* enthusiasm, sincerity and professionalism. We must not wear clothes that distract from our business purpose, or which inflame the subliminal prejudices of others; and in most instances we should utilize to our advantage the standard business uniforms which are appropriate for men and women.

In presenting ourselves non-verbally, and in evaluating the non-verbal language of others, we must not go overboard and presume to know the innermost thoughts of those around us because we are familiar with the "real" meanings of one or two particular gestures. That first impression is especially important. It must say to our new clients, customers, or acquaintances that we are indeed the individual with whom they want to deal; and that handshake should, in a warm, dry, and firm fashion, reinforce that notion.

What you say non-verbally to others can be consciously altered by you. With the help of your colleagues, you can obtain information which will help you adjust certain of your physical characteristics to your greatest advantage; and while evaluating others, you can look for those traits which may provide you with some insight into what they're thinking.

In sum, the task of looking the part of the successful you is both challenging and exciting. It is a never-ending, dynamic process which requires your continuing hard work and research. But the results are worth it. For the world is entitled to know at a glance that you are indeed an exceptional and worthy individual. You deserve nothing less.

There you have it: an overview of the Outside Mini-Environment; that part of our existence which is physical. We have touched upon the proper maintenance and adornment of those "machines" in which we live, and have reviewed their standard performance features. We understand, too, that common sense must be employed in the proper care and cleaning of those machines, and that there are certain abuses simply not covered by The Manufacturer's warranty.

We've met Mr. Schlock, or, as Pogo said, "We have met the enemy and he is us." Hopefully, we have helped to dispel the three great American myths. We've examined the particulars of getting started on a fitness program of our own that will prolong our lives and enhance our enjoyment of each day to come.

Finally, we have explored the methods by which we communicate non-verbally: grooming, attire and silent command. Through all the confusion of the decades, fundamental principles remain. Clothes can be used to convey the message that we are enthusiastic, sincere and professional; and our gestures and demeanor can be consciously altered, so that such gestures supplement that message.

The Outside Mini-Environment is critically important to our total success as human beings. We owe it to ourselves and to the people we love to be all we can be in this enormously important mini-environment. Let's turn our attentions now to what is probably the least understood mini-environment of them all: Home.

X

You, Me And Us

We will never be as close as it is possible to be.
We won't run out of love, just time. We shall
become as us all that we desire only if we become
as individuals all that we should. We shall remain
unable to love each other any more than we love
ourselves.

At current rates, we will run out of families before we run out
of oil.

Thirty-eight percent of all marriages in the United States end in
divorce.

In 1977, 2.2 million adults were divorced in the U.S., and more
than a million children were directly affected by those divorces.

Since 1900 the divorce rate in the U.S. has increased seven-
fold, and it has *doubled* since 1968.

Only 33 percent of Americans believe that most people who
marry expect to stay married. Yet, 80 percent of the American
public claims to value the concept of a life-time marriage.

Our belief in the system is evidenced by the fact that most
people who divorce remarry. In fact, contrary to the male myth,
more men remarry than women. Unfortunately, second marriages
end in divorce at least as often as do first marriages.

Most experts agree that the biggest factor affecting divorce
rates is the newly acquired financial independence of women.
Since 1970, more than half the married women in America have

found work outside the home. The family unit used to be primarily an economic unit. Its members were financially dependent upon the main bread winner—almost always the man—for food, clothing and shelter. With increased opportunities for women to work outside the home, each family member is now less financially dependent upon the others. The sharing of intimacy, love and support have now become the primary functions of the family and the marriage institution. Its purpose is no longer primarily economic.

Make no mistake. Of those women who work outside the home, most do so not because they want to, but because they have to. Yet their very ability to find some form of work has given them a level of economic freedom not heretofore experienced.

But it's no bed of roses. For example, there are six million single-parent families in the United States. That's 18 percent of all the families in the U.S. The mother who takes her children and leaves her spouse, or, conversely, the mother and children who are deserted by their spouse, can expect to maintain a median income of only $7,211 per year. Yet, the freedom that even that relatively small amount of money represents is substantially greater than the freedom enjoyed by most women just a generation ago.

The result is that while the face of marriage has not changed considerably, its substance, in most instances, has been altered dramatically. The word *partnership*, as it applies to marriage, has been reborn. Roles, responsibilities, and duties have been blurred in the process. Yet, one fact clearly emerges: the purpose of marriage in our society today—indeed, the purpose of any intimate man-woman relationship, whether formalized by marriage or not—is *the present enjoyment of love.*

As we explore the Home Mini-Environment, our purpose will be to discuss ideas and methods by which we may maximize our present enjoyment of love. While we pointed out in Chapter II that we all have a Home Mini-Environment, whether we're married or have children or not, our focus will be upon what is still the customary Home Mini-Environment in America—that is, a married man and woman with at least one child. That is not to say that this formula is the preferred lifestyle. If the last 25 years of changing roles, redefined lifestyles and experimentation have taught us anything, it is that there is no one form of Home Mini-Environment that is right for everyone.

It has been generally agreed throughout history that the family, as conventionally defined, is the socio-economic backbone of any society. It is within the family that many of the problems of our society can be solved. Yet, the family seems to have abdicated its responsibility to schools and government bureaucrats.

We live in an age where, as a result of sheer hard work and ingenuity by those who came before us, most of everything we need is supplied by someone else. We no longer bake our own bread, sew our own clothes, kill our own game, tend our own sick. Now it is all computerized, organized, and done by someone else. Of course, because of such specialization, things are done far more effectively and efficiently. But you can't do your family the same way the laundry does your shirts. You can't defrost a frozen relationship with your spouse by pushing the appropriate button on your microwave. There are no gadgets or gizmos that can help us there.

Upon an exchange of vows between a man and a woman, the institution of marriage becomes as compartmentalized and specialized as it will ever be. Only the parties involved can make it work. There are no exterior remedies. Prepackaged happiness is not available at the store. (Children should constitute an extension of, not the destruction of, the original man-woman relationship. We'll treat the subject of children in Chapter XII.)

It all begins with a man and woman: with the "let's get marrieds," and the "I do's," and the high hopes and the promises of "forevers" and "always" and "nevers," and the expectations of a happily-ever-after, which, by the way, is probably the most misleading phrase ever written, since there are no happily-ever-afters that come automatically—just opportunities to work at being happy.

In the context of marriage, love is not a noun. It is a verb. We are not in *love*, we are in *loving*. It doesn't begin with *you* and *me* and end in *us*. It begins with *you* and *me* and becomes *us*, but *you* and *me* remain and grow and flourish. We don't grow so close that we lose our identity and become just one. Instead, we grow together and flourish individually. In the process, we create the bridge that is *us*.

You And Me

So we begin our journey together, aware of what we were, what we are, and what we shall become.

We know without needing to read it in a book that our marriage will be only as good as the relationship we create. Our relationship is the foundation upon which all things will take their value and meaning.

We may buy a home of 100 rooms, but if each is not filled with love by the relationship we create, then the house will have no value to either of us.

We may drive the fanciest car and wear the finest clothes, but if they are not pressed into service for the greater cause of our love, occasioned by the relationship we have built, then they will be of no value and will bring us no happiness.

If we should fill our yard with children, and if their laughs of excitement and joy should fill our ears, they will only echo painfully as a reminder of what might have been, if the rest of our bodies and souls are not filled to overflowing with the loving relationship that we have created.

What We Were

We were alone and lonely and wanting to share our unique version of life with someone else who cared, and who took special pleasure in the things that pleased us most.

We were waiting for that combination of circumstances to present itself in such a manner that we would know the time was right, as well as the person involved, to seek the type of commitment and sharing that we had heard about and hoped for.

We were crammed full of love waiting to get out, and we were looking for someone like each other upon whom that love could flow, hoping—only hoping—that the other person would have the ability and desire to reciprocate.

It was upon our first discovery that each of us had love to share that our relationship took its first tenuous step. For now there was something mutual between us, and our only concern was to discover as many ways as possible by which we could share the love we had to give. So many ways presented themselves that they filled our days and our hearts. The more love we gave, the more we seemed to have to give.

Then it occurred to us that, at least for us, marriage was the ultimate way in which we could share our love. What we didn't know then was that being married was not in itself an act of love, nor was it proof of love, but just a place where we might express our love and keep looking for ways to share it. We were to discover that marriage would be to our future life what the park was when we were courting. A place to go, to be together. A place to say, "I love you."

What We Are

We are individuals.

In the closeness of daily living and in the contest of us against the clock, we know it's too easy to forget that we are each unique, and that if our relationship is sacred, it is only because we, individually, are sacred.

We are busy growing—each in his own way. We each have interests and goals and projects and deadlines which must be met. We are, as Khalil Gibran wrote in *The Prophet*, not one land mass, but instead two islands separate and distinct, washed by the mutual waters of love.

We are aware that growth is inevitable and desirable, but that growth uncommunicated will widen the gap between us, until it is too great to bridge. For us, growth unreported is growth unshared; and each unshared experience pulls us slightly farther apart. Yet words, if soft and unrehearsed, can close the gap: words describing what we feel and to where we traveled in our minds that day.

If we have a tendency to be abrupt with one another during the day, it is because of the intensity with which we pursue the projects so necessary for our growth. We understand that abruptness is, in its own way, a healthy enthusiasm, but we do not let it become an excuse for discourteousness, and we do not let a single evening pass without explaining in as much detail as the other desires the importance to us of our endeavors.

We are good listeners. We know we must be. We listen not just for what is said, but for what is meant. We think hard upon the words we hear from each other, and use them not just as a catalyst to launch into discussions of subjects of interest to us. We listen. We feel what the other person is saying.

We are touchers. We touch our hands, our heads, our lips; and we touch as often as possible, because it's much more fun than not touching, and it gives us each a rush of warmth, however slight, to sustain us until the next encounter.

We are laughers, but mainly at ourselves, not each other. But we are criers, too; most especially when we hurt for each other. We know we must communicate. We know we must share. For we are building a bridge between us which is us, and it is sharing which is the mortar that holds the span together.

What We Shall Become

We shall become even closer and more deeply in love.

Marriage, like success, is a journey, not a destination. We will never be as close as it is possible to be. We won't run out of love, just time. We shall become as us all that we desire only if we become as individuals all that we should. We shall remain unable to love each other any more than we love ourselves.

We shall likely have others to love as well, children and grandchildren and great grandchildren. But our love for them shall not dilute our love for each other. It shall, instead, be merely an extension of it.

We shall become experts at communicating and understanding what the other feels. We shall grow increasingly respectful of the time the other needs to be alone and to be together. We shall each demand from the other that he or she not take the duration of our marriage as proof of its permanence; and we shall continue each day to earn the companionship of the other.

We shall earn the companionship, not the love, of the other, because love is not earned. Love worth having is not granted upon a condition. We shall not say to each other, "I will continue to love you if . . ." or, "I love you because . . ." We shall instead love or *be loving* each other unconditionally and without reservation.

Three Promises To Keep

When I was practicing law, a woman came into my office one day. She wanted a divorce.

I said, "What's the problem?"

She said, "My husband has lost all interest in me. Doesn't listen to what I say."

I said, "Well, what makes you feel that way?"

She said, "Yesterday at breakfast he was reading his morning paper, as usual, and ignoring me, and I was talking to him and I know he wasn't listening to me."

And I said, "How do you know?"

"Because," she replied, "I said, 'Honey, I've decided I want to be cremated.' He didn't even put his paper down. He just said, 'OK, get your hat and we'll go'."

Another wife asked her husband, "Honey, do you still love me?"

He said, "Of course I love you. I'm your husband. It's my job."

These two old jokes point out one of the most common maladies afflicting marriages today: the tendency of one or both partners to assume that the marriage will maintain itself without their active involvement. In other words, frequently, one or both partners believe that their mere presence is proof enough that they love their spouse and are happy with their marriage.

Yet to be successful, any marriage must be based upon at least three promises: promises that require the total involvement and dedication of the parties involved. The goal of marriage, or of the Home Mini-Environment—the present enjoyment of love—cannot be obtained without the making of, and abiding by, these promises. They are inherent to any successful relationship.

Promise Number One: To Make Promises Only Because We Want To, Not Because We Have To

This is a non-promise. It prevents us from entering into indefinite commitments because of our sense of obligation rather than because we genuinely want to.

For example, it would be more truthful to say, "I will work at loving you forever," rather than to say, "I will love you forever." It would be more honest to promise, "I will work at being faithful to you forever," rather than saying, "I will be faithful to you forever."

Once marriage is viewed as a series of obligations rather than as a dynamic growing process, the seeds for its destruction may be planted. The alternate lifestyles of today, where so many men and women live together outside marriage, are, of course, in very large part a reaction to the perception of many that marriage is, in fact, a series of obligations and not the dynamic growing process it should be. But any man-woman relationship, whether formalized by marriage or not, can be viewed in either light. That a man and woman do not engage in marriage vows does not relieve them of obligations if one party chooses to impose obligations upon the other (witness the famous law suit brought against actor Lee Marvin for half the earnings he accumulated while living with his non-wife companion).

The key, then, is that promises, or commitments, must be made, not through a sense of debt or obligation, but freely, flexibly and mutually. It is not the certificate of marriage which makes the relationship sacred. It is not the imposed obligation of one party upon the other that gives it its value. It is, instead, the mutual sharing of promises, dynamic in nature, that are freely given because of what the relationship is, not because that relationship happens to be called a marriage.

Promise Number Two: To Share

It begins after the first few years of marriage: that insidious tendency not to share.

It comes from the knowledge that your spouse knows, generally, what you are doing, where you are doing it, why you are doing it,and even how well you're doing it. It comes from assuming that what went on, for example, at work, is as boring to listen to as you presume it will be to recount.

It's a form of complacency that says, "There's no longer a need to share every minor experience." It is the tacit understanding of the parties that nothing new is happening, that it's been "just another day," that there is "nothing much to discuss." Dinner should be served, TV should be watched, and sleep should be had; and tomorrow shows every indication of being just another routine day.

After awhile, even discussions of the children become routine. News that Tommy broke another basement window gets old after awhile. It's hard to muster as enthusiastic a response the fifth time as you mustered the first. The bills are pretty well paid, and, as usual, there's nothing much to discuss financially. You sit together and watch a show, and you feel there's no real need to discuss it because you both just saw it, and, after all, you know your spouse well enough to know, basically, what he or she thought of it.

The result is that nothing gets shared. The newness is gone. The novelty has escaped, and there simply isn't much to talk about. But whereas discussion begets discussion, so too, silence begets silence. The longer a silence is maintained, the more difficult it is to break. The longer it has been between discussions of consequence, the more awkward the next one will seem. The longer it has been since one spouse felt deeply enough about something to sit the other down and tell him what was really on her mind, the more difficult it will be to do it again.

Promise Number Two is to share, even when sharing doesn't seem necessary. Promise Number Two requires that even if the day seems routine, even if it seems as though nothing new has happened, that each partner accepts as a personal responsibility the task of finding something to discuss with the other. Whether it's a movie, or the weather, or the bills, or the kids, or the house, or work, or play, or your hobby, it must be shared. The tendency to sit and vegetate and to assume that we are quietly in touch with our spouse, even though nothing of consequence is being said, is too devastating, too hazardous, too lethal to marriages to be permitted to continue to exist.

Yet, sharing must not be undertaken on a formalized basis. Discussions between husbands and wives should not be conducted like corporate board meetings. It is during unguarded moments when such discussion should take place, casually, honestly, softly, with the partners sharing, as they really are, the thoughts they really have, without worrying about each word selected, each phrase employed. Such intimacy, such informality, is for most of us an acquired skill. It does not at first come automatically. At first in marriage, we're too frequently caught up in our role as husband or wife to be honest enough to share our doubts and fears, our aggravations, discouragements, hopes, aspirations, dreams. But as we each grow, and as we continue to build that bridge which is us, and as we continue to share, we can lower those barriers and be our true selves with each other.

But it requires that we share.

Promise Number Three: To Work At Being Happy

Happiness is hard work.

It was Lincoln who said that people are about as happy as they make up their minds to be. Nowhere is the importance of attitudes more evident than in marriage. Being happy in marriage requires the same kind of work that being fit requires: a regular and consistently applied program. Much of what we explored in connection with programming our "computer" within the Inside Mini-Environment is especially applicable here.

Too many couples believe that their happiness will be automatic simply by merit of their status as married people. But the fairy-tale ending, the happily-ever-after, never materializes. We become disillusioned upon discovering that married people do not live happily ever after automatically, but instead must work at being happy.

Promise Number Three requires that our expectations regarding marriage be realistic. Marriage is like Weight-Watchers®. You don't get skinny just by joining. You have to use the program and *work at it.*

The best way to be happy is to make someone else happy. Take the case of the smile. It is a devastating weapon. It has won fair maidens, launched careers, won elections, stopped wars, and generally been one of the best things that mankind has ever invented. A smile makes us especially happy when it's on someone else's face, and we know we put it there. Generally, to make ourselves happy, we need simply make our spouse happy in little ways. At least once each day we must find a way to make him or her laugh—not just smile politely, but laugh. We owe ourselves one good laugh a day. It's good for our health, for our sanity, and it's especially good for our marriage.

We must not go to bed angry. Sometimes it's tough. When we're very tired and very angry at each other, it's very tempting to just roll over and go to sleep. But our marriage is too valuable to risk it. Even if it means you'll stay up all night rehashing old grievances that you've been discussing for years, it's better than giving up the ghost, cashing in the chips, and going to bed angry.

Promise Number Three requires that we work at being happy. It acknowledges that the only "happily-ever-after" is the one we make; that to work, a good marriage must contain laughter. And that a spouse who wants his or her marriage to last will not go to bed angry, even if it means they must stay up all night.

Happiness. It's work. Hard work.

But worth it.

Us

Us is what *you* and *me* create. It is that third person that we make even before we make children. *Us* is the way in which we relate to one another. It is the way in which *you* accept the love *me* has to give, and the way in which *me* accepts the love *you* has to give. *Us* is no more important than *you* or *me*. For us to work, *you* and *me* must be whole and complete and happy. Yet it is the success of us that provides *you* and *me* with much of our happiness. It's circular. Interrelated. Complicated. Precariously balanced. Interdependent. Important. Precious.

Sacred.

Is There Sex After Marriage?

Yes, there is sex after marriage. There is even *enjoyable* sex after marriage, if:

First, we recognize that men and women have varying biologic needs at different times of their lives. For example, most men reach the height of their sexual powers at about age 19. By age 29, the sexual potency of men is generally on the decline. Yet it is at age 29 that most women reach the height of their sexual abilities. The result is that as marriages progress into the third decade of the partners' lives, it is frequently the woman who initiates (or who wishes to initiate) intercourse.

Many men are frequently dismayed at their wives' apparent newfound aggressiveness, since they are victims of the notion that, even in marriage, a sexually aggressive woman is a promiscuous woman. Meanwhile, many women are discouraged by what they perceive to be their husband's lack of interest in them. In fact, what they're witnessing is a very normal biologic *changing of the guard*, which happens to all couples at various times and in various degrees.

Second, we relax. During the first few months of our sexual relationship, relaxation doesn't matter much. Both partners are so enthusiastic that sex is frequently intensely enjoyable, even though either or both may have been a bundle of nerves when they began. As the novelty wears down, however, the body will become increasingly less likely to respond to physical stimuli unless it strips away some of the barriers that exist. The most common barrier is tension.

You don't have to be a Ph.D. in physiology to know that, when it comes to sexual responsiveness, men and women are wired differently. Men are aroused relatively quickly, and frequently expend themselves with equal speed. For them, even brief sex can be intensely satisfying. Women, however, build gradually. It is generally not until they are thoroughly relaxed that they can begin to accumulate the passions necesary for their complete enjoyment of sex. Part of relaxation comes from knowing that your partner is not going to rush you simply to appease his own speedier biologic schedule.

But the benefit of relaxation is not limited just to women. Men, too, can find sex infinitely more satisfying if they approach it in a relaxed, well paced fashion. Each partner must do what is necessary to help the other escape the day's tensions. The critical component for relaxation is time. Neither partner must rush. Each must approach the experience as a relaxed and non-competitive interlude. As a general rule, if you spend less than 45 minutes from first touch to completion, you're probably not spending enough time relaxing, and getting to know each other physically, prior to actual intercourse. The result, quite simply, is that you may be diminishing the fun you might otherwise be having with each other. There are, of course, exceptions, but the 45-minute rule of thumb is a helpful, informal, standard.

Third, we use intercourse as a tool for expressing affection, and not just as a method of sexual release. Having a partner with whom to have sex *is* a convenience. Unfortunately, many partners regard it as only that: a method by which they may release themselves sexually without particular concern for the other partner.

More than being a convenience, intercourse is the most biologically natural way we have of expressing intimacy, love and affection. Sexual release is a secondary benefit—a by-product of the physical sharing experience between two people who love each other. Please don't misunderstand. The physical sensations are, of course, enormously rewarding in and of themselves (or as the speaker Zig Ziglar says, he had a lot more fun dating once he realized that when he kissed a girl and she kissed him back, she wasn't doing it for *his* sake).

And *fourth, each partner devotes himself to the satisfaction of the other.* It is a simple fact that does not require substantial elaboration. The Manufacturer, in His wisdom, designed it this way: The harder we work to arouse our partner, the more aroused we become. The better we satisfy our partner, the more satisfied are we.

Sex becomes a whole lot less combative when each partner is devoted to the satisfaction of the other. During intercourse, most of us tend to mentally ask ourselves, "How am I doing?" by which we mean, "How much am I enjoying myself?" In fact, we would be far more satisfied in the long run, both physically and emotionally, if by the question, "How am I doing?" we meant, "How well am I satisfying my partner?"

It's as though our mandate came right out of the language of Positive. Help the other guy get what he wants, and you'll get what you want. The more you give, the more you get. In the movie *Cat On a Hot Tin Roof*, Elizabeth Taylor was having marital problems with her husband, Paul Newman. Her mother pulled her aside, pointed to the bed and said, "That's where you'll solve all your problems. That's where it begins and ends. That's the cornerstone of your marriage."

I'm not sure she was completely right, but I don't think she was too far wrong.

Is there sex after marriage? Thank God, you bet!

How To Say, "I Love You," Without Saying, "I Love You"

Please write down these six words and carry them with you: warmth, respect, encouragement, sex, affection and caring.

These words represent the six qualities or actions we can possess or take in order to say, "I love you," without having to say, "I love you." There's nothing wrong with the words themselves. They're probably the nicest three words there are to listen to. But sometimes we grow immune to just saying them or just listening to them. We require more, a demonstration, if you will, of the feelings the words are intended to express. "Don't tell me," the old maxim goes, "show me."

So how do we show our love without constantly reciting it? How do we display our devotion without acquiring an immunity to the words themselves? The six qualities or actions listed above, it seems to me, provide the answer. Carry your list of these qualities with you. At the end of each day, before you walk in the door at home, read that list aloud to yourself. Then find a method by which you may display each of these six qualities or actions. If each day, in our own way, we can touch upon each of these qualities, however briefly, for the benefit of our spouse, with a word, a touch, a gesture, or some other appropriate action or inaction, we can keep the word *love* alive in our Home Mini-Environment without beating it to death by over-verbalization. Let's briefly explore each quality or action to see how it may apply to our Home Mini-Environment.

Warmth. Warmth is a quality of hospitality. It is a quality that attracts others to us. Just as the family room fireplace, it causes others to relax around us. A pat on the back, the type of laugh that makes others smile, too, or an embrace that says it all are among the many manifestations of the quality of warmth.

Respect. Respect is a frame of reference toward others. It is a quality which permits us to accept the importance of others, their existence, their ideas. It is manifested largely by attentiveness to the ideas and opinions of those around us.

Encouragement. Encouragement is a team quality. It causes us to support others, to cheer them on, to let them know that we not only are aware of what they're doing, but approve of their efforts, wish them well, and genuinely believe in their success. Encouragement is often manifested by such simple statements as, "You can do it," "I have faith in you," or "I know you'll succeed." It is often manifested tacitly by our assumptions regarding others; for example, by our assumption that our son or daughter will graduate with honors. Unspoken, but felt by all, it is a form of encouragement. The assumption that our spouse will, of course, close that big deal is another form of encouragement. But to be encouragement it must, at some level—whether tacitly or verbally —be communicated to our partner.

Sex. Sex is both an action and a quality. As an action it has already been discussed. But as a quality it is perhaps even more important. It is the realization by both partners that, however similar they may become in attitudes, whatever experiences they may share, there will always remain the basic fundamental biologic difference that attracted them to each other in the first place. It is a quality of constructive want, of controlled desire, and it includes the quality of respect for the sexuality of the other partner. The quality of sex manifests itself at home in hundreds of ways: a wink of an eye, a brush of a shoulder, a pat on the rear, a quick kiss that becomes a long kiss, a squeeze, a giggle, a glance.

Affection. Affection is the unrestrained desire to help another. It is a method of displaying concern by converting that concern to action. It, too, manifests itself in many ways, through helping with the dishes, perhaps, through holding a hand, through a hug, or through a laugh or a tear.

Caring. Caring is the quality of continuing concern. It is the process of wanting to know the details of our partner's day, the things that made him or her happy or sad. It, too, is evidenced by listening, but also by seeing, sometimes with our third eye, how we might help, and then in taking such action as is helpful to our partner.

Warmth, respect, encouragement, sex, affection and caring: These are the six qualities we may possess, or actions we may take, to manifest the love we feel at home.

Role Merger And Reconciliation: Men, Women Liberation, Chauvinism And Happiness

There are certain biologic inequalities for which neither men nor women are responsible.

Until the use of cloning or test-tube babies becomes popularized, which I suspect will not occur in our lifetime, women will be left with the task of bearing children. It is no more unjust that this is so than that most women outlive most men.

Yet, I suspect, with the continuing (and inevitable) liberation of women, it is the economic effects of these biologic differences that will be most debated. Should both partners share the financial repsonsibility for maintaining the home? Should both partners accept equal responsibility for child care? Would such a division of responsibility damage the traditional roles upon which the marital relationship has been based? If so, will that effect be positive or negative? Will the blurring of traditional roles impede the abilities of men and women to function normally within the marriage context, or will a new norm emerge, upon which others may model their conduct and relationships?

It certainly appears that within the marriage context, the roles of men and women tend to merge as the years roll by. It has to do, I suspect, with an acceptance of partnership: a realization that the unique worthiness of the other is not a threat to either.

Yet, even in such thoroughly merged relationships as we may find among the elderly, there remains a knowledge of, and appreciation for, the sexual distinctiveness of the partners. It is, after all, that distinctiveness that attracted even the older couple to each other in the first place. It is not chauvinistic (either masculinely or femininely) to take pleasure in that difference.

It *is* chauvinistic to assume that the biologic role to which either partner was born inherently disqualifies him or her from accepting a particular role or responsibility within the marriage relationship. Indeed, *chauvinism* is an unnecessary word. The word *prejudice* was popular long before *chauvinism* fell into vogue. *Prejudice* would suffice nicely to describe our tendency as both men and women to cast each other into thoughtless roles, such as *sex object*, or *insensitive breadwinner*.

While responsibilities and roles must change, and while the entire institution of marriage undergoes continuous upheaval, it will be the very dissimilarity of men and women that will continue to serve in the future—as it has in the past—as the foundation upon which their happiness is based.

I resist the over-simplistic temptation to shout, "Vive la différence!" and to leave it at that. Rather, as we search for new and meaningful methods by which each partner may reach his or her fullest potential, let us never forget that marriage is, always has been, and hopefully always will be, a context in which a man and a woman—as a man and a woman—may love each other as perfectly as their minds and spirits and bodies and souls will permit.

You wouldn't buy a house if you knew it had a 38 percent chance of tumbling down. Yet, every year millions of Americans enter the institution of marriage, even though 38 percent of their marriages will "tumble down."

Of course, we never enter into marriage believing that ours is vulnerable. Love conquers all until the bills arrive, until the children arrive, until we get too tired or too insensitive, or until we stop sharing. Love will suffice until we stop making promises because we want to, and start making promises because we have to, until sex is not fun anymore, until we run out of ways to say, "I love you," or until our image of ourselves gets turned upside down by new demands and new theories and new lifestyles that we don't quite understand, and that we can't quite control.

Yet there is a bright side, too. Sixty-two percent of all marriages succeed; and the partners of each marriage can create their own percentages, depending on how hard they're willing to work.

The institution seems inherent to our status as human beings, and whether the name be changed in years to come, the legal obligations redefined, or the ceremonies for beginning or ending the relationship altered, what will probably always remain the same, and what probably always should, is that most men will continue to possess the capacity to love a woman, and most women will continue to possess the capacity to love a man; and each in his or her own way will find the other.

And together the you's and me's of this world will create the us's that make life so worth living.

XI

Managing Money

*People who claim money is the root of all evil
never had any.*

An old story about the great football coach, Vince Lombardi,
relates that at the beginning of each season he would call his
players together, sit them down in the club house, and stand
before them. Despite the level of expertise represented by the professional players he faced, he would raise a football in the air and
say, "Gentlemen, we're going to start with the fundamentals. This
is a football. The purpose of this game is to move this ball from
your end of the field to the opponent's end of the field."

It is said that on one occasion, one of the rookie linemen in the
front row earnestly raised his hand and pleaded, "Not so fast
coach! Not so fast!"

Like Lombardi's pre-season talk, this chapter is also about the
fundamentals—of managing money. Despite the fundamental
principles contained herein, I suspect there will be more than a
few readers who will, in effect, raise their hands and plead, "Not
so fast, coach. Not so fast."

Next to poor communication, poor money management and immature financial expectations are the primary causes of marital
discord in America. They are a contributing cause to a substantial number of suicides; and are frequently the cause of lifelong
personal bitterness and disappointment.

It is very nearly criminal that our educational system does not provide, as a matter of routine, courses on personal financial management. Every high school should provide a course that covers fundamentals, such as how to balance a check book, what happens when you finance the purchase of an automobile, and how to establish a sound savings program.

Can money buy happiness? Yes. But only to the extent that: first, it buys us the freedom to pursue those projects that we consider most important; second, it provides for the well-being of those we love; and third, it provides security against disaster. It is so easy to say, yet so difficult to practice: money should be a slave to us. We should *not* be a slave to money.

Many of the principles contained in this chapter were first outlined in a brilliant little book entitled *The Richest Man in Babylon*, by George S. Clason. In his book, Clason outlines "seven cures for a lean purse." During this chapter we'll touch, in our own words, upon each of them.

How To Make It

We all know how to get rich fast: invest your money at high risk and be prepared to lose it. But too little has been written on the subject of how to get rich slowly. How do we make our money carefully, steadily, inevitably, without incurring substantial risks to our life savings, our life work, or those we love?

There is nothing inherently evil about financial speculation. There is nothing wrong with taking the "big risk"—if you can afford to. Most individuals who are sucked into get-rich-quick schemes can afford neither the financial nor emotional loss so frequently associated with such deals. High risk, high potential investments have their place within our personal financial plans, but only after we have established a sound foundation of conservative financial management which will provide us with a secure base from which to operate.

First and foremost, we must identify our primary source of income and do everything within our power to increase our skills relative to that primary source of income.

If, for example, you are a salesman, then your primary source of income—the life blood of your personal economic system—is sales. The more you do individually to increase your skill at sales, the more "new money" you will have to work with in building your fortune. Rule Number One, therefore, is: *increase your ability to earn.*

Next, in order to cause our money to work for us, we must press some of it into service. To do so, we must abide by the age-old admonition: *for each ten dollars you receive, spend but nine. Ten percent of all you earn is yours to keep.* It is *that income* which must be pressed into service on your behalf.

How beautifully it can work for you! For example, money invested safely, say, in a savings account at 7 percent annual interest, will, when compounded, nearly double in ten years. Rule Number Two, then, is: *Start now to save at least 10 percent of everything you earn.*

The Purpose Of Money

Freedom is the most valuable commodity that money can buy: the freedom to choose how to spend one's time, the freedom to travel, the freedom that only financial security can bring.

It was the enormously wealthy Andrew Carnegie who once wrote, "The man who dies wealthy is a failure." His philosophy was simple: Make as much money as you can, then press it into the service of others before you die. His attitude depicted another form of the freedom that money buys: the freedom to help others economically.

Money can bring happiness only if it is well earned, honestly received, and carefully spent. Its purpose as a form of monetary exchange is to permit us to buy those things that we personally consider to be of value. Yet, in sum, what money really buys for us is the freedom to choose what we consider to be of value.

Each dollar in your pocket is a slave who should work for you. Your dollars should be your own private army of workers devoted totally to your enrichment. People who claim money is the root of all evil never had any. The Bible, incidentally, does not make that claim. It says the *love* of money is the root of all evil. When we talk enthusiastically about acquiring as much money as we can, we do so not because we love money, but because we love the freedom money buys.

Sharing The Work Load

In today's family, the role of "breadwinner" is often blurred.

As a recent television commercial states, "She brings home the bacon, fries it up in a pan, and never, never, never lets you forget that you're the man."

Most married women work outside the home to supplement the family income. On the whole, wives who work do so not because they want to, but because they feel that financially they have to. Generally speaking, working wives do not earn as much as their husbands.

For example, according to the U.S. Labor Department, in 1977 a family with a single wage earner had a $13,218 average yearly income. In the same year, a family with two wage earners had an average annual income of $20,415.

With most women working outside the home, their independent financial contribution to the family's well-being has become the norm. Obviously, for most families, this is the system that works best. But a word in defense of those wives who do not work outside the home is in order.

The financial value to a family of a well kept home, well prepared meals, and well laundered clothes is not insignificant. In the case of an "average" family, comprised of husband, wife, and two children, it would cost the husband about $6,000 per year, plus the cost of room and board, to replace the in-house domestic services of his wife.

It is, in other words, wrong to assume that a woman who does not work outside the home "doesn't work." Especially among younger families, where both husbands and wives almost always work, there seems to be developing an increasing prejudice against the occasional spouse who does not work outside the home. It is a prejudice that domestic-oriented spouses justifiably resent. It is a clearly established principle, both in law and in common sense, that husbands and wives do not have to bring home identical paychecks to be deemed to have contributed equally and significantly to the economic well being of the family.

There still exist many situations where it just doesn't make sense for both spouses to work outside the home. Frequently, especially in the case of self-employed persons or independent-contractor types, such as commission sales professionals, there is plenty of book work, paper work and scheduling that the "non-working" spouse handles on a part- or nearly full-time basis from the home. But whether the spouse's contribution is directly economically beneficial, or whether that spouse provides the domestic support so necessary for a happy and organized homelife, his or her contribution is entirely significant, and should not be demeaned by those who personally find it more practical or feasible to work outside the home.

The responsibility of providing for the economic well being of the family can be shared many ways. A complete sharing of that responsibility requires only that each spouse work to the best of his or her abilities, in their own way, for the attainment of their mutual financial goals.

How Much Is Enough?

A very wise man once said, "If I get very rich, I'll probably retire and spend my time walking barefooted on the beach. But if I go broke, I'll probably retire and spend my time walking barefooted on the beach."

How much is "enough"? For each of us, it varies. The ultimate question is, "How much will it cost for me to exercise the freedoms I want to exercise, to the extent I want to exercise them?"

It is, for example, one thing to say, "I want enough money to be able to travel," and quite another to say, "I want enough money to be able to travel around the world at will in a jet that I own." The first goal might cost you $12 to get you from Toledo to Youngstown by bus. The second goal may cost millions.

But no amount of money will be "enough" if, at the early stages, you do not acquire the habit of saving at least 10 percent of everything you earn. Contrary to popular myth, it does not become easier to save money the more money you make. If you developed the poor habit of spending more than you took in when your income was at the $20,000 level, then you will more than likely retain that habit when your income is at the $200,000 level. As a result, you do not buy more freedom. You buy more worries. Your troubles are the same. They just have more zeros attached to them.

In deciding how much is "enough," it is essential that we get as specific as possible in establishing our economic goals. When we explore the Work Mini-Environment in the next section, we will discuss the detailed process of effective goal setting. But for now, you may want to list specifically the various material items you wish to acquire. Use the chart entitled "Economic Goals" (figure 11-1) at the end of this chapter to determine how much money you would like to devote to each major personal expenditure category one, five and ten years from now.

For example, you may decide that one year from now you would like to have at least $6,600 per year (that's $550 per month) to invest in housing. Perhaps you would like to spend no less than $300 monthly (that's $3,600 annually) on your automobile, or $100 a month ($1,200 per year) on travel. Decide how much money you'd like to spend annually on all the things there are to spend money on, one year, five years and ten years from now. Then at the bottom of each column add up your totals to determine how much disposable income you'll need (*after taxes*) each year to sustain that life-style. Remember: your savings should equal at least 10 percent of all the other categories combined. You may wish to conduct this exercise with your spouse. Hopefully, it will provoke some discussion and thought.

How much money is "enough"? Only you can decide.

How To Spend It

The third fundamental principle of personal financial management is this: *You must budget your expenses so that you have enough money to pay all your bills without spending more than nine-tenths of your income.*

If, after adding up all of your current bills, you discover that you cannot afford to live on just nine-tenths of your income, then you are living beyond your means. Period. Merely increasing your income won't help you if you do not immediately break the pattern of spending everything as it comes in. If you spend too much, there will never be enough money, regardless of your income level. It never becomes easier to budget your money. Indeed, as your income increases, it gets harder to budget, because you find more and more terrific things upon which to spend it. Regardless of your income level, *now* is the time to budget.

Fourth: *You must invest your money only where it may be reclaimed, if desired, and where it will collect a fair return. Consult only with those who are experienced in the profitable handling of money.*

Don't buy into the hairbrained schemes of distant relatives or neighbors, no matter how good they may sound. *Money pushed too far, too fast, in pursuit of large short-term gain tends to evaporate.* Put your money only where it can be reclaimed.

Seek professional advice, and pay for it. Free advice from well-intentioned friends and self-appointed experts is worth exactly what you pay for it: nothing.

Fifth: *Own your own home.* Nobody likes inflation, but owning your own home is the best hedge you may ever have against it. Will Rogers said of land, "They ain't making any more of it." The demand for homes, especially in the Southwest and West, is absolutely incredible.

In 1978, in Phoenix, Arizona, for example, the average home increased in value more than 15 percent (that's more than 1 percent per month). Therefore, if you owned a $100,000 home, its value would have increased at a rate of more than $1,000 every 30 days! New homes in the Phoenix area increased in value at an even faster rate—closer to 20 percent annually!

Of course, diminishing the effects of inflation is not the only benefit of home ownership. By owning a home, the interest and tax portions of your payment will be deductible from your federal income taxes. If, for example, you make a total mortgage payment of, $500 per month, over a 30-year term, it is likely (especially in the early going) that as much as $450 of that amount will represent your payments toward interest and taxes. That would constitute total interest and tax payments, over a 12 month period, of $5,400. If you are in the 30 percent federal income tax bracket, by deducting that $5,400 from your income, you will literally save 30 percent of that amount, or $1,620 in taxes! Meanwhile, of course, while enjoying these tax savings you are accumulating the equity (increased value) we discussed above.

In sum, a home bought at a fair price, in a good neighborhood, that you personally work hard to maintain, is one of the safest and most profitable investments money can buy.

Paying Cash Is NOT Un-American

Calvin and his wife, Cathy, walked into the local appliance store and began looking at a new home video recording system.

The salesman walked up to them, smiled, and said, "It's a pretty little model, ain't it? You pay $5 down, take it home today, and pay nothing for six months."

Calvin's wife looked at him and said, "Who told you about us?"

A lot of thinking Americans these days believe that in the face of ever-increasing inflation it is wisest to finance their purchases whenever possible, rather than save to pay cash with money that a few months or a few years down the road will have greatly depreciated in value. There is much to commend that approach — within limits. Most of us, for example, leverage our money in similar fashion when we put a minimum number of dollars down on our house and finance the rest. We finance our cars the same way as well. Or perhaps we may finance the remodeling of our family room, or the installation of that backyard swimming pool.

The use of financing for the purchase of such major capital items seems eminently sensible. But that is not where most of us cut our own throats. Where we commit financial suicide is when we finance the purchase of the smaller items like TV sets, appliances, home video systems, stereo equipment, and a host of other consumer items that can be bought on time with plastic money. Then, of course, there is the ultimate insanity: borrowing money that it will take two or three years to repay to finance a vacation that will last two weeks.

If there is one sales closing technique that should be outlawed, it is the close which declares, "You'd better buy it today. The price is going up tomorrow." It is a variation of the "impending disaster" close, but now, because of the frequency with which it is used, it deserves its own name: the inflation close. How many millions of people have been induced by that closing technique to finance the purchase of billions of dollars worth of goods can't be accurately ascertained. But we all possess some property which we purchased, whether financed or not, under the threat of "higher prices tomorrow." Whether prices increase tomorrow or not (I am convinced that the use of that closing technique serves as self-fulfilling prophecy which, in fact, increases prices) it is *not* foolish, or un-American, or uneconomical, or old fashioned, to wait until you can pay cash for an item before buying it.

Financial maturity is the ability to distinguish between one's ability to finance something and one's ability to afford something.

Within our Home Mini-Environment we attempt to create a setting in which we can love and be loved, and in which we may encounter a minimum of barriers distracting from the love we wish to express or receive. By exerting a modicum of patience, we can prevent our purchase of that new TV, or that new refrigerator, or that new washing machine, or that new jacket, from interfering with the love we intend to express or receive at home.

The temptation to over finance can be overwhelming. It can best be resisted, however, if we simply remind ourselves of those things which are in fact of most value to us in our marriage. For most of us, the newest electronic gadget, or fancy coat, or overly-expensive car does not even appear on the same list as does the love and affection and security of our spouse and family.

When it comes to money, patience and maturity are not just virtues. They are qualities of hardheaded discipline that save marriages.

When It's Wise To Finance

Many of us should undergo major plastic surgery to have our credit cards removed.

As a general rule, most of the consumer items that we purchase on revolving credit terms should not be purchased on such terms, but rather should be purchased only on a cash basis. Revolving credit through a store or through one of the major credit card companies should be used only sparingly for consumer items, and only in the case of an emergency. Major purchases such as homes, automobiles, remodeling and other capital improvements can reasonably be financed as long as we can afford the payments. The financing of these major items is generally enough to keep us pretty well strapped.

Most Americans are, without question, over financed. It has been estimated that the average American family would stay afloat for approximately 60 days if its primary breadwinner lost his job, and did not receive any other form of compensation. After about 60 days, the creditors would begin closing in. Most families do attempt to be cautious in the amount of financing they do, but wind up over financing anyway. The problem is they do not accurately anticipate their monthly cash needs for miscellaneous items when trying to determine how much room is left in the family budget for another monthly payment. The result is that there is no money left for contingencies such as emergency repairs, new shoes, hair cuts, or dinner out.

Although experts disagree as to the exact percentage, as a general rule, no more than 50 percent of our monthly income should be earmarked for payments on credit (such payments would include house payments, car payments, revolving charge payments, non-current credit card payments, etc.). The remaining 50 percent of the family income should be devoted to current payments for items such as savings, food, clothing, entertainment, recreation, and miscellaneous repairs.

Priority Planning: Avoiding Frustration

We seem to be particularly susceptible to the hazards of over financing, because we allow our desires to well up inside us and then explode without our prior planning.

Over a span of several weeks or months, we may accumulate the desire for a number of consumer items. We may not clearly make up our mind which of those items we would like to purchase first. Instead, we wander down to the shopping center with no clear intention of what it is we wish to buy, and even perhaps with the avowed intention not to buy anything. We begin to window shop and are exposed to some of the very items we have been thinking about. The result, of course, is that by the time we leave the shopping center, we are the proud owners of any number of things which, had we planned ahead, might have been relatively low on our list of priorities. And all of them may be financed.

It is very educational, although sometimes a little frustrating, to sit down with your spouse, pen in hand, and mutually list all the items you wish to purchase. Next to each item, list its cost; then determine how much money you will have available each month to set aside for these items. Most of us find we have more items than money available. We must then priorize our items and determine which we shall purchase first. This process helps keep our financial expectations for the coming year realistic, and prevents us from purchasing expensive impulse items which might not otherwise have been at the top of our list.

How To Save It

The sixth rule of money management, from Clason's *The Richest Man in Babylon,* provides: *You must put what you save to work for you so that it will create a steady stream of new revenue.*

Your savings must be placed into service on your behalf. The temptation to push your money too far, too fast, in pursuit of large short-term gain must be resisted. Instead, the money that you save and invest to work for you must be regarded as the strongest viable hope you possess for future wealth. It must be guarded zealously and invested conservatively.

The seventh principle of financial management provides: *You must plan in advance for the needs of your old age and for the protection of your family.*

This, in modern times, requires that we be adequately insured, so that our families will be adequately protected in case of our death. All men and women above the age of 30 should have affirmative, active programs by which they are saving money for their retirement. The vast majority of elderly persons in America today find themselves — regrettably — to be financial burdens upon either the government or loved ones. Those who find themselves in that humiliating and dependent position did not plan it that way. They just did not begin early enough to set aside the money needed for their retirement.

Yours To Keep

That 10 percent of your income which must be set aside must remain inviolate, protected against all intrusions and all pressures. It is, in fact, your most viable hope for future wealth. Betray the integrity of that 10 percent and you betray yourself, your future, your wealth, your security, and your freedom.

Ten percent of everything you earn is yours to keep. Period. It is not to spend on a TV, or a car, or a dishwasher, but to save, to invest conservatively and to put to work on your behalf.

The individual who overspends, regardless of his income level, and who fails to contribute at least 10 percent of his annual income to form a permanent savings, is a wage slave, and will die dependent upon his ability to report to work on time and earn his weekly paycheck. Only the individual with enough discipline to set aside at least 10 percent of his income has any hope of creating a source of income for himself that is not directly dependent upon his labor.

Ten percent of everything you earn. Yours to keep. The pressures are, from time to time, enormous. But your resolve must be complete. I urge you to resolve today, with your spouse, that, effective immediately, 10 percent of all you earn will be placed into service to work for you, to create a steady flow of new revenue which will provide you with prosperity and security in the years to come.

If It Sounds Too Good To Be True . . .

Lawyers are, of course, paid cynics.

By training, they have come to suspect everyone and everything. It is not surprising, then, that I first heard the following piece of advice from a lawyer who was, at the time, my professor of taxation in law school.

He said: "If it sounds too good to be true, it probably is."

Many fortunes could have been saved by that advice. Many sums have been lost without it. The tendency to squander our money on get-rich quick schemes that have no realistic possibility of success is not limited to those among us who are particularly idiotic.

During my tenure as a practicing attorney, I encountered many sad cases that were brought to me by clients who had bought into what they were at first convinced were sure things.

A 65-year-old former school teacher lost $33,000 on a real estate syndication plan that "couldn't fail."

A 45-year-old man, with an advanced degree and a good position with a major corporation, lost $18,000 on a new "miracle" cleaning compound.

An intelligent, conservative family man in his early 30's lost $9,000 on a computer soft-wear "break through."

When investing that 10 percent that you've worked so hard to accumulate, be critical. Be cynical. Do not trust every seemingly legitimate promoter who offers a "special opportunity."

Remember, if it sounds too good to be true . . .

Classic Investments:
Advantages And Disadvantages

When making investments, seek the advice of paid professionals, and be willing to pay what they charge. Seek independent counsel from someone who will be paid for his advice whether or not you buy whatever is being offered.

Do not feel compelled to remove your money from the bank and invest it immediately. While its rate of return may not be the best, a certificate of deposit, even short term, provides a reasonable return and complete safety. Treasury notes are similarly safe.

Major corporate stocks represent fine long term investments. But market fluctuations make the short-term profitability of such investment questionable — even if you bring with you to the market a very high level of expertise.

The recent glut of "reproductions of art" makes investment in that field hazardous. Investing in art can be very lucrative. But because most of us (myself included) know so little about it, our ignorance tends to compound the risk. As a family undertaking, you may choose to educate yourselves by taking courses in art, and then beginning a conservative, cautious, program of investing in pieces that hold a realistic promise of reasonable appreciation in years to come.

Real estate probably remains the finest investment opportunity available today. Inflation alone makes it attractive. But before jumping into investment real estate (commercial properties), take the time to educate yourself thoroughly in this complex field. A course or two now, at the local university or night school, can save you tens of thousands of dollars a year or two down the road. Speculation in real estate is exciting and usually profitable, if combined with good sense, caution and energy.

Most successful real estate investors do not make their fortunes through rents; they make their fortunes through the accumulated equity which is caused by inflation and increased market demand. Successful investors frequently take properties of depressed value, fix them up or otherwise make them more attractive for other investors, and then sell them. This type of approach requires skill, hard work, and a reasonably good understanding of current market conditions.

Do not be overly swayed by the professed tax advantages of each real estate transaction. Indeed, there are many tax advantages to be had, including accelerated depreciation, which enable you to show a paper loss for tax purposes, although, in fact, the property upon which the depreciation is taken generates a positive cash flow. But be especially careful not to get caught in the "negative cash flow" trap: when that property that was designed to show a loss on paper shows a loss in fact, and you find yourself pumping money into the project that you didn't plan to spend.

Skill, education and hard work are the keys. You can acquire all of them on your own, or you can seek the help of an expert. Many real estate sales professionals are simply not equipped to handle complex commercial real estate transactions. Many others are. Be sure you find an agent who knows what he or she is talking about, who can provide you with all the information you'll need, and who can help you interpret the data.

Real estate is *the* classic investment. But, as always, be cautious. And be sure you fully understand the consequences of each step you take.

Vince Lombardi had a good idea: The basics. The fundamentals.

We would all do well to remember the fundamentals of personal financial management.

Remember the seven fundamental principles first outlined by George Clason: *First,* for every $10 you receive, save one; *Second,* budget your expenses so that you can actually live on that nine-tenths of your income; *Third,* put what you save to work for you, so that it will create a steady stream of new revenue; *Fourth,* invest what you have only where it may be reclaimed if desired, and where it will collect a fair return, and consult only with those experienced in the profitable handling of money; *Fifth,* own your own home; *Sixth,* provide in advance for the needs of old age and for the protection of your family; and *Seventh,* cultivate your own powers to become wiser and more skillful at what you do, since it is your primary source of income.

We enjoy genuine financial wealth when our money works for us, generating new sources of income. Learning to pace our demands, to pay cash, and not to over finance, are among the critical ingredients to our financial success, independence, and security.

Priority planning — the listing and priorizing of those items we wish to purchase — can help us avoid frustration.

Remember, that 10 percent of everything you earn is yours to keep. Invest it only in the cause of generating additional income for you. If an idea sounds too good to be true, then it probably is. Don't feel compelled to pull your money from the safety of a savings certificate, treasury note, or the like, and to place it into another form of investment until such time as you are completely satisfied that the investment will be both safe and profitable. Utilize the classic investments that are available to you, with the help of qualified professionals. But always remember that there are advantages and disadvantages to every investment, and that each one must be thoroughly examined and evaluated on its own merits.

Money. The root of all evil? Hardly! Just the potential source of complications and heartaches if it is not handled properly.

Money. It must work for you, for your family. You've earned it. You're worth it.

You deserve it.

ECONOMIC GOALS

Annual Disposable Income: Allocation	1 Yr. Monthly	5 Yr. Monthly	10 Yr. Monthly
Housing & Utilities......	_____	_____	_____
Auto..................	_____	_____	_____
Food.................	_____	_____	_____
Clothes..............	_____	_____	_____
Insurance............	_____	_____	_____
Entertainment.........	_____	_____	_____
Travel...............	_____	_____	_____
Other...............	_____	_____	_____
_____.....	_____	_____	_____
_____.....	_____	_____	_____
Savings..............	_____	_____	_____
Monthly Total......	_____	_____	_____
	× 12	× 12	× 12
ANNUAL TOTAL	_____	_____	_____

Figure 11-1

XII

Family: Making It Work

Too many adults play "parent" 24 hours a day.
They bury that part of them that is also a husband
or a wife, and most especially they bury that part
that is a child—the part that wants to play games,
not roles.

Family:

A. The most instinctive, fundamental social or reproductive group in man and animal.

B. A group of individuals with enough of a past to expect a future.

C. A bunch of people who have the right to inconvenience each other.

D. A group committed irrationally to each others' well being.

E. None of the above.

F. All of the above.

Select the definition of your choice. They're all correct. Or, if you selected line E, "None of the above," you may write your own definition. The ability of *family* to meet many definitions and to adapt to changing times has contributed significantly to its survival over the years.

A family needn't be composed of mothers and fathers and children. People who have simply grown to love each other, whether they live together or not, and who, at some levels, rely upon each other for love and companionship can constitute *family.* But the family to which most of us most closely relate is the one that involves mothers and fathers and children.

About two children per couple is the average just now, although that figure fluctuates a few percent from year to year. We may be witnessing a resurgence of our emphasis upon this type of family in America. In 1978 there was, for the first time in years, an increase in the rate of childbirth, which had for quite some time bottomed at a level below the zero population growth rate. Is this the beginning of a trend? Perhaps. The pendulum is bound to swing from one extreme to the other. Perhaps it will swing a little less far each time as we grow increasingly mature as a civilization.

Yet the family remains, because it remains flexible. Years ago, the primary purposes of the husband-wife-children type family were economic and educational. The children would be fed and clothed and housed and trained at farming or trading or whatever the family did, and in exchange they were expected to contribute in whatever way possible to the family's economic well being—by working on the farm perhaps, or by helping in the store. The mother, of course, was responsible for childbearing and rearing, and for housekeeping, while the male assumed the role of bread-winner, and was responsible for putting new currency into the family's income.

But most of these functions have now been stripped away. The family no longer relies upon itself for sustenance, except in very rare circumstances. There is no real threat of starvation in America today. Every American family knows that should it be faced with such a threat, someone, some institution, or some government agency would help them. Electric appliances have, of course, freed women from the drudgery of never-ending domestic tasks, thus giving them more time to pursue other goals; and giving them, for the first time in recorded history, enough time to consider what else they might like to do. As educator, too, the family has been replaced by schools and teachers and buses and aptitude tests and entrance exams and a vast multi-billion dollar education industry.

Yet, despite the stripping away of these traditional responsibilities, the need of every individual for intimacy, love and support remains. In fact, with the family having to spend less time as a unit upon economic and educational functions, it can now devote itself more fully to providing its members with the intimacy, love and support that they desire. The result is that the goal of the American family has become, more now then ever before: *the present enjoyment of love.*

The Rights Of Children

Calvin's wife, Cathy, was having problems with their two strapping teenage boys. They were good kids, and generally well behaved, but they had one shortcoming: they swore too much around the house.

Cathy went to the child psychologist at the school to ask her advice. "You must lower the boom," the psychologist said. "Let those two boys know, in no uncertain terms, that you simply will not permit their use of profanity around the house!"

"Right on," Cathy thought. "From now on I'm going to take control of the situation!"

The next morning, the two boys stampeded downstairs to breakfast. First the big, strapping, 16-year-old sat himself down at the breakfast table. "Ma," he said, "give me some of them damn cornflakes."

Cathy was just a little thing, but without getting angry, she walked up to the 16-year-old, wound up, and belted him. The boy flew off the chair, hit his head against the wall, and fell to the floor. His eyes were as big as saucers. He didn't know what hit him.

Then, remaining poised, Cathy turned to her almost-as-large 15-year-old son,who was seating himself at the breakfast table. "And what would *you* like for breakfast?" she asked.

He leaned forward across the table, looked at his older brother down on the floor, looked at his mother and said, "I don't know, but I sure as hell don't want *any* of them damn cornflakes!"

Children have rights, too. Not the least important among them is the right to know specifically why they're being disciplined. Sometimes we assume our children understand our every move and motive, when, of course, they don't. They have enough difficulty just understanding themselves. Self discovery is a full time job for them. As a result, the parent who simply assumes that his children will "figure out for themselves" the reasons or motives behind any particular act is likely to be disappointed.

For some reason, teenage boys seem particularly dense. Conversations with them tend to begin and end with words and phrases such as: "Huh," "I don't know," "Ya know," and other nondescript grunts and groans. They lie around a lot, and take up space. They spend countless hours staring at the ceiling. Everything they eat turns to hair. Yet, they have a right to be as they are, just as children of all ages have a right to be as they are.

Children of any age, in fact, possess at least three inherent rights: the right to grow as children, the right to learn, and the right to love and be loved.

The Right To Grow As Children

Children are not always pleasant to have around. In fact, sometimes they're downright inconvenient. They have a tendency to demand attention when attention is least convenient to give.

Yet, their demands are part of a growing process that is as inevitable and natural as the growth of a flower or tree. One of the saddest phenomena imaginable—and one that we've all witnessed from time to time—is the sight of a parent who expects too much from his child, too soon. Children *don't* necessarily understand things the first time they are explained to them. Their lack of understanding is not a function of any lack of intelligence; it is simply a reflection of their lack of experience. The child who must be shown two, three, or four times how to cut his meat properly is not necessarily inconsiderate, uncaring, or dull. He's just a child who didn't catch on the first few times. Children have a right to grow as children, individually, at their own speed. They have a right to expect that adults understand how hard it is to learn things for the first time.

Children, otherwise known as *rug runners, curtain climbers, cookie crumblers,* or *screen scratchers,* admittedly can be relied upon to provide certain physical phenomena around any home. From time to time they will provide sticky globules of unidentified substances on floors and countertops. They will leave dirt marks on walls, usually in the general vicinity of (but by no means immediately next to) light switches. They will leave crumbs in the milk after drinking directly from the container. They will wear a trail on any carpet, regardless of how expensive or of what quality, which will coincide logistically with the shortest possible route between their bedroom and the refrigerator.

While children, of course, do not have the right to deliberately or maliciously disrupt a home, they do have the right to live with parents who understand that a certain amount of unintended disruption is inevitable. The right to grow as children includes the right to make mistakes: the right to be a *typical* 4-year-old, or a *typical* 8-year-old, or a *typical* 12-year-old, or a *typical* (God forbid) 16-year-old. Children are not miniature adults. They have the right to be what they are, to learn at their own rate, and to enjoy the world as only children can.

The Right To Learn

Inherent to the right to learn is the right to be disciplined. Knowledge without discipline is very nearly worthless. Discipline is required to sort out, to evaluate, and to logically and responsibly apply what is learned. Children have the right to have parents who care enough about them to provide the discipline necessary for constructive and meaningful learning. It is the responsibility of parents to absolutely insist that their children work hard on their lessons at school, and on their assignments at home. This requires that parents remain involved, and that they be aware of what their children are studying, and what their classroom and homework requirements are.

Yet, as important as formal education is, what a child learns informally will most profoundly affect his life. A child has a right to learn that his parents love him. He has a right to learn that his future is bright, and that his potential is virtually unlimited. He has the right to learn how little things are done, and the right to have parents who will explain those little things to him. He has the right to explore, to ask questions—some of which may be inconvenient or embarrassing—and to receive honest answers to those questions.

The right to learn extends beyond the initial curiosities of a child. For curiosity is a quality that can be encouraged and expanded. A child's right to learn, therefore, includes the right to be encouraged by his parents, the right to be rewarded for working hard at learning, and the right to be told time and again how proud his parents are of his willingness to learn. If childhood has one overriding purpose, it is to learn. Thus, learning is inherent to the status of—and unquestionably a right belonging to—children.

The Right To Love And Be Loved

Children have a right to show adults how much they need them, and how much they love them. By the same token, they have the right to be shown how much they mean to adults.

The suppression of emotions has no place in the raising of children. The father who won't hug his son for fear of "sissifying" him should be shot. Such a father, the experts say, probably does more to contribute to any "sissification" process than does a father who openly and honestly expresses his affection. Children have a right to be told they are special. They have the right to be kissed and hugged and loved and made to feel, through touches and caresses, that the adult members of their family are glad they're there. They have a right to live with adults who work at openly and honestly expressing their love, so that they can emulate those techniques and better express the love they feel for those around them.

Children have a right not to have to assume that they are loved. They have the right to be told, and to be with parents who in many little ways tell them many times each day that they are part of a unit in which love flourishes, in which they are loved, and in which they may freely love others.

The Rights Of Parents

Primarily, parents have the right to be something other than parents.

Parents do not lose their identity as human beings simply because they have children to look after. They retain their likes and dislikes, their individual characteristics, their hopes, dreams, and personal aspirations. Too many adults play "parent" 24 hours a day. They bury that part of them that is also a husband or a wife, and most especially they bury that part that is a child—the part that wants to play games, not roles.

Too frequently, parents don't act as themselves. They act instead as they think a "parent" should. They present that role to their children. Unfortunately, the role itself acts as a barrier between the parent and child. Parents, of course, retain the responsibility for providing discipline and control to the lives of their children. But their even greater responsibility is to view the world through their children's eyes and to enjoy it with them, explaining —each step of the way—the significance of what the child sees.

The Right To Grow As Adults

Whereas children are not just miniature adults, adults are, to the extent that they are still growing, just big children.

The need to explore and to learn and to grow does not stop with an individual upon his becoming a parent. Indeed, parenthood can, and often does, serve as a catalyst for growth. Parents retain the right to continue to grow as adults. Since growth involves change, parents, by implication, retain the right to change. Yet, radical change is not necessarily involved.

Because parents feel an almost instinctive obligation to present a consistent image to their children, they often fear change and, therefore, fear growth. Yet, the most worthwhile *consistent* image that we parents can present to our children is the image of consistent adult growth. Many children perceive adulthood as something static. They conceive it as a non-dynamic process, as though once you become an "adult," that's it. To many, adulthood is where hardening of the attitudes sets in. Since children instinctively imitate adults, they may view adulthood as a period in which they will "get mature," settle down, and cease to grow. They then proceed to do just that. They become very dull, non-growth-oriented adults who beget other children, who emulate *their* parents and become dull adults, etc.

The solution to this depressing cycle is for this generation of parents to break out of the static mold, and to geniunely pursue the process of dynamic growth. Consider the effect upon children of such a change. Rather than entering adulthood convinced that their life as parents should be static, they will instead enter adulthood desiring, at least subconsciously, to emulate the dynamic, growth-oriented adult life process to which they were exposed as children. To leave our children with that heritage is far more valuable than all the static, "consistent" parent role-playing we have mustered to date.

The Right To Enjoy Each Other

Do you remember how much fun the two of you had together before the kids arrived? How ironic it is that so often the very products of a loving relationship are the cause of its disintegration.

Suddenly the children arrive, and we are steeped in our self-imposed role as parent. We feel some level of guilt when we attempt to enjoy, at an adult level, the companionship of our spouse to the exclusion of our children. So we confine our husband-wife relationship to those few precious minutes between the time our children go to bed and the time we retire as well. Yet, parents have the right to enjoy each other more often than that. The trick is to do so in such a way that the children do not feel excluded, and the adults do not feel guilty for spending adult time together.

The best solution is to urge upon our children from the very outset the notion that they are not the products of their mother and father, but rather of a relationship that their mother and father created. That relationship will continue to exist long after they are grown and gone, and have developed a relationship of their own with someone else. Children can—and should—be taught that the relationship deserves to be preserved, and requires considerable work and effort. After all, almost any child can understand that a relationship good enough to have produced *him* must be pretty darned important, and worth preserving.

Parents, for example, generally have the right to talk together alone for a few minutes, as one or both arrive home from work, before being deluged with children and childlike things. Parents have the right to incorporate a consideration of their adult needs when planning their days, secure in the knowledge that their children will prosper and thrive if they live under the umbrella of a genuinely loving adult relationship. Parents have the right to go out from time to time, to have fun, and to enjoy each other as they did before they began assuming the role of parent.

Parents, then, retain the right to enjoy each other. Indeed, their ultimate ability to function well as parents—their ability to provide a loving adult relationship within which a child may flourish—depends upon their doing just that.

The Right To Pursue Their Own Interests

Our tendency as parents to believe that the world revolves around our children is, at times, overwhelming. Yet realistically we know that in a certain number of years the children will be gone and on their own. If, by that time, we, as individuals, have not pursued and developed interests of our own, we will be about as exciting to live with as a loaf of bread.

Parents as individuals—and not necessarily as couples—must pursue their own interests. The independent growth discussed in Chapter X, which is so essential for a meaningful and long-lasting relationship, does not become any the less essential simply because a relationship is complicated by the presence of children. More than being merely a right, the independent pursuit of interests is a responsibility that each individual owes to himself. A family must strive to provide its members, including the parents, with the time and space necessary for each member to pursue what interests him most.

Quality Time

It is not enough that, as a family, we merely be together. It is not enough that we be in the same room at the same time. We must share, and grow, and learn from each other.

It is much more easily said than done. The distractions are many. The competition is great. There are dozens of things happening at school that occupy the thoughts of our children. Both spouses have a host of distractions from work which continue to occupy their thoughts, even after they get home. The TV set blares. The radio plays. We bury ourselves in separate sections of the newspaper, and we call that "being together."

More than anything else, the American family needs *quality* time: the kind of time that families used to spend together before radio and TV were invented. We are told that back then, with nothing much else to do, families *had* to enjoy each other—and they did. They worked at their relationships and at their family games and projects, and they sang together and talked together and told stories and listened to what each other had to say. It will never be quite the same, now that TV and radio and automobiles, and a host of other distractions, are with us. But we still need something that we can fairly call *quality time:* time together, with each other, that we spend together on purpose, not because we have to, but because we want to; time that involves family discussions and games and projects that are at least as entertaining as prime-time TV, and more rewarding to boot. Quality time. Time together. Time to grow. Time to love. Time to share. Time to be a family.

What "Being Together" Means

Togetherness seems to be more of a mental process than a physical one.

We've all seen large families crammed into small cars with each person inside looking either out the window or away from those next to him, indicating that their thoughts are somewhere other than in the confines of their automobile. Yet we've also known people who seem very "together," although separated by hundreds—perhaps thousands—of miles. The closeness is mental, not physical.

Less extreme, but no less real, is the family that sits together all evening in front of the Boob Tube not uttering a word to one another. Physically they are "together," but they might just as well be oceans apart. They are not thinking of, or talking to, each other. They are just sharing space, electricity, and a TV set. Being a family must mean something more than that. Being together must be far more worthwhile than being merely physically near one another.

Being together—really being together—may well be a lost art. It needs to be re-discovered, revitalized, and re-used. For, being together, in a meaningful sense, means that the parties want to be with one another, that they enjoy one another, and that they are relaxed and spontaneous and comfortable and eager to enjoy what each other has to say.

Being together, like success and marriage and life, is a dynamic process. It is the process of ideas being bantered back and forth, conversation floating about the room, laughter echoing in everyone's ears, all amidst a pervasive feeling of warmth and affection. That is not to say that "being together" requires noise. It can be very quiet. But the quietude must grow from an appreciation of the presence, both mental and physical, of other family members. There is a genuine "being together" aspect to Mom in the kitchen, preparing dinner, Dad in the living room, finishing his paper, Sister upstairs completing her homework, and Brother in the garage, finishing his chores, if all members of that family are experiencing that sense of community which causes each to look forward to seeing, and sharing with, and touching, the others.

"Being together" is what every family requires. Indeed, there can be no "family" without it.

Family Projects

The bicentennial era inspired many helpful works in the area of family life, not the least of which was the very pleasant little booklet entitled *Family Time*. It was prepared and published by the Family Communication Committee of the Million Dollar Round Table, and written by Grady Nutt. In it are listed a number of family type projects and experiences that can be shared by all family members. Among the suggestions included in that booklet are these:

Sponsor a family "how to" night. Depending upon the ages of the children, some of the subjects which might be covered can include: how to use a telephone; how to dial an emergency number; how to use the nearby pen and pad to take phone messages; how to write a check; what the family budget is and how it works; what manners are and how they should apply at, say, the dinner table; and how to operate various tools and appliances around the house (for example, how to load the dishwasher, how to run the vacuum cleaner and change the vacuum bag, how certain tools work, how to change a car tire, how to utilize the bathroom plunger, or how to change a fuse).

Sponsor a family discussion night. Use cartoon characters, or characters from TV, and have every family member select that character with which he or she most closely relates. Then have that member explain why he or she relates to that character. Or play spin the bottle with your family. The person to whom the bottle points must explain what he or she most particularly loves about another family member. A particularly thought provoking movie or television show might also serve as the foundation for a family discussion on crucial issues. In such discussions avoid the tendency to moralize or to preach. Instead, just share ideas and approach the discussion with the notion that "everyone is entitled to his or her opinion."

Sponsor a family awards night. Using miscellaneous pieces of paper, cardboard, cloth and old cups, have each family member fashion an award for every other family member, to congratulate him or her on some special accomplishment, or some special quality that is particularly appreciated.

Enjoy a musical night together. Explore the many ways in which music may be enjoyed. Experiment with records, tapes and radio. Sing together in unison and in harmony. Fashion homemade instruments, such as combs, spoons, and pans, and do your own "arranging." Discuss each others' theories on how music might first have developed, and what kind of musical instruments people 100 years from now might enjoy. Record each others' voices on the tape recorder and discuss the miracle of sound.

Sponsor a family game night, complete with puzzles, riddles, board and card games. Select games that all family members will enjoy, making sure that no one member will have to sit out too long if he loses a game or round.

Of course, not all family projects need to be undertaken within the home. Outings, picnics, camping trips, sporting events, visits to state and national parks, and trips to the zoo, to concerts, or to plays, are, of course, always appropriate, and often provide quality family time. We are limited only by our imagination. Indeed, a helpful family project would be to have all family members sit down together and list those projects that they would like to see the family undertake. Some planning is required. Some effort is needed. But the results are well worth the time and energy involved.

For What They Are

Love is, as we mentioned earlier, noncompetitive and unconditional. But the parent must often correct his child. As a result, it is easy for the child to believe, even though told the contrary, that it is only because he acts in such a fashion, or refrains from misbehaving, that he is loved.

First and foremost on our list of priorities for establishing quality family time together must be our promise to each other that we will love each other for what we are. Each individual within a family, be he an adult or child, has the right to grow at his own rate. Each will make mistakes and learn from them, and continue to grow. But in the meantime, through it all, each family member must enjoy the others for what they are.

Children will eventually stop being children. It's ironic that parents who very frequently wish to accelerate the rate at which their children mature suddenly regret the arrival of young adulthood in them and wish they had taken more time to enjoy them as they were. For it is the total acceptance of another, with all his or her imperfections, that love is all about. And it is this acceptance that is the foundation upon which relationships are built, and upon which families flourish.

The family, as conventionally defined, still remains the very foundation upon which our civilization exists. But it doesn't occupy its important status because it has remained static over the years, but because it has adapted itself to ever-changing demands.

Now, more than ever before, the family has become the focal point of our never-ending quest for the *present enjoyment of love*.

Into this environment come our children with the right to grow as children, the right to learn, and the right to love and be loved. The parents, as creators of the environment, do not lose their rights as individuals upon its creation. They, too, retain the right to grow—but as adults; and they must enjoy the right to enjoy each other and to pursue their own interests.

Happiness as a family requires more than that mere space and time be shared. It requires involvement with each family member, the fashioning of family projects of mutual interest to all, and the acceptance of each family member for what he or she is.

The Home Mini-Environment, that part of our existence where we go to love and to be loved, is that one aspect of our lives that gives the rest of our lives meaning. For without home base—that sanctum to where we can retreat and grow and think and share—the rest of our existence would not mean much, if it meant anything at all.

It begins with you and me—what we were, what we are, what we shall become—and ends with us. It is perpetuated by promises—the kind of promises that help, not hinder, our relationship; and it is nurtured by our constant effort to find ways to say, "I love you," without having actually to say the words.

Its success depends upon our maturity, especially upon our financial maturity. We must distinguish between our ability to afford something and our ability to finance something, and we must maintain a conservative and realistic approach toward all things financial.

Finally, "Home" is an environment involving the rights of both children and parents. Its success requires that all parties work together at building quality time to share.

Home: that beautifully complex and confusing environment. Yours deserves to be nothing less than a treasure of shared warmth, respect and love.

W

XIII

Getting On Target
And Staying On Target

*The establishment of unrealistic goals can be
profoundly demoralizing. It is an agony to which
we need not subject ourselves. We need only approach the business of success realistically—one
step at a time.*

Calvin Cautious had just returned from his annual deer hunting
trip.

"Calvin, next year I'd like to go deer hunting with you," his
wife, Cathy, said.

"That's great!" Calvin said. "I'd love to have you come! We'll
spend the whole year preparing. I'll teach you everything I know
about deer hunting. I'll take you out and buy you a new deer hunting rifle, and teach you how to shoot it. I'll get you a new deer
hunting outfit. I'll buy you a pup tent and teach you how to put it
up. It'll be great!"

They spent the entire year preparing. The big day finally arrived,
and they made their way up into the mountains. They were about
half way up the first mountain when they came to a salt lick.

"Now this is where I want you to set up camp," Calvin told
Cathy. "When the deer come by here to the salt lick, you can take
your game. But remember," he warned, "there are a lot of trophy
hunters in these hills, so don't you let anyone talk you out of your

227

game. If you bag something, it's yours. Don't you let anyone talk you out of it.''

Calvin walked a few steps further and turned. "Now, I'm going up to the top of the next hill to hunt elk," he said. "But don't worry. If I hear any shots or confusion, I'll be right back down to help you out.''

No sooner had Calvin made it to the top of the next hill than a shot rang out from down below, and a tremendous argument filled the valley.

Calvin ran down to the salt lick. What he found when he got there was his wife, rifle poised, holding a man at bay.

The man had his arms in the air, and he was saying, "OK, lady! It's your deer! It's your deer! It's your deer!" Then he looked down at the dead animal beside him. "Just let me have my saddle!''

We've got to know what we're shooting for—especially at work!

In this chapter and the next, we will explore the specific techniques we can use to get on target—and stay on target—in our Work Mini-Environment. You will find many of the principles discussed here applicable to the three other mini-environments as well. But, as a practical matter, they will have their greatest application in our pursuit of professional and economic goals.

Please take the time to conduct the few exercises contained in these chapters. The exercises are based upon fundamental goal-setting and time management principles. They are simple and extremely helpful—but only if used. Without them, we, like Cathy, may appear to be prepared, but may, in fact, lack the one or two critical pieces of information so necessary for our success.

Yes, we've got to know where we're going to get there.

Our self-adjusting success mechanism (Chapter V) can't get us from where we are to where we're going until it has a target or a goal at which to shoot. Run a steam-roller across an asphalt parking lot on a warm summer day, and it may do no damage at all. Send a 112-pound woman in a pair of high-heeled shoes across that same parking lot, and she will likely poke holes all the way across it.

The difference in effect, of course, is caused by the fact that, whereas the weight, or energy, of the steam-roller is dispersed, the weight, or energy, of the woman is refined and funneled to that small point that touches the pavement—her heel. The results are a classic example of the effect of channeling energy through a fine point.

Similarly, a shotgun blast at one hundred yards, while uncomfortable, is rarely fatal, since its energy is dispersed by the tiny pellets that move gradually away from each other. A single round from a conventional rifle, however, might well be deadly at many times that distance. The difference, again, is accounted for by the channeling of energy.

Talent is a form of energy. We each possess a different combination of the stuff, and some possess more than others. Yet the *quantity* of talent that we possess is as irrelevant in determining our success as was the weight of the steam-roller in making an impression on an asphalt parking lot. It is how we *channel* the talent that we do possess that makes all the difference. What other phenomenon could possibly account for the divergent results obtained by so many people with so many different combinations of talents?

We've all met those people who, on a talent scale of one to ten, rank minus four, but who, nevertheless, have acquired great wealth and otherwise achieved enormous success. It's disheartening to discover that Joe Flabeets, the guy who was voted "least likely to succeed" by your high school graduating class, now owns the local taco stand down at the corner. That's not the discouraging part. He also owns the shopping center in which it is located, a chain of laundromats, and the local bank.

On the other hand, we've all known individuals who were loaded with talent. On a talent scale of one to ten, they might rank plus fourteen. Almost everyone who meets them assumes that they are on their way to great accomplishment and great fortune. Yet, during their lives they never quite assemble all the abilities they have and channel them in a specific direction. They never use the potential they possess. They are much like the steam-roller in our example. Although they have enormous amounts of energy available, it is unusable because it is unrefined. But the Joe Flabeets of the world are like the woman's high-heeled shoe. They channel and refine whatever talents they have, and take their best shot. As a result, they succeed.

This chapter is devoted to channeling your energy—especially at work. Its purpose is to help funnel your talents through as small a space as possible, so that their intensity—and effectiveness—might be increased 100 fold. It all begins with deciding specifically—exactly—on the direction in which you wish to channel the talents you possess. You can always change your mind at a later date, but the process of getting on target and staying on target must, by definition, begin with selecting a target. That target must not be vague, as in the case of the individual who says, "One of these days, maybe I'll make a lot of money." It must be specific, exact, refined. With this in mind, let us begin to explore the *actual mechanics* of effective goal setting.

The Characteristics Of Goals

It's what goals are NOT that is especially important.

They're not promises, hopes, wishes, dreams or whims. A goal is a specific destination. It is an affirmative, realistic and specific target. It is something that we must so clearly visualize that at times it seems to be already within our possession.

A goal effectively set becomes very nearly an obsession. Not that we must lose all perspective in our pursuit of the desired end result, but an effectively established goal becomes so intense, so real, so compelling, that it will, if strong enough, and vivid enough, and believed enough, begin quite automatically to generate the qualities within us necessary for its accomplishment.

To be effective, goals must be constructed in such a way that they will withstand our tendency to stray off course, to forget our initial intention, and to seek the line of least resistance when we begin encountering obstacles. Goals must have an independent existence of their own, so that they can exist for as long as needed as guide posts to which we can return time and again, as we seek to continually refine our direction.

To meet these requirements, a goal, when established, should have at least three characteristics: it should be written, it should be realistic, and it should be affirmatively specific.

Written

When our goals aren't written down, where we can look at them and they can look at us, it's too easy for us to—perish the thought—rationalize. It's just too easy to forget the commitment we intended to make.

Many of us hesitate to write down our goals because the process seems so permanent. Yet, I am only recommending that your goals be written on paper, not chiseled in stone. As we grow, we may want to change our initial goals, and that's fine; but the decision to change should be a rational, conscious decision, weighed against standards previously etched with commitment and preserved with desire. The process begins with a piece of paper, a pencil and you. When a goal is not written, it becomes something less than a goal: a resolution, perhaps (as with those eminently forgettable New Year's resolutions), a hope, a dream, a desire, a wish.

In addition to viewing a goal as a destination, it is also helpful to view it as a tool. Its purpose is to help us chisel away at our tendency to either procrastinate or stray off target. We have all, during do-it-yourself projects, suffered the frustration of not being able to find the necessary tools. When we fail to write our goals down, the result is much the same. That "tool" is just not there when we need it, and we wind up devoting our energies to "finding it" again, rather than using those same energies to pick up that tool and use it to help us build the future upon which we have decided.

Realistic

Not long ago, I was conducting a seminar for insurance salesmen on the west coast. During one of the breaks, an especially young member of the audience came up to me, pumped my hand, and said, "Thanks to you, I've established my financial goals for the coming year!"

"Great!" I said. "What are they?"

"During the next 12 months I'm going to make a million dollars!" he said.

For all I knew, he was fully capable of doing what he intended. Yet, I had the feeling that he really hadn't stopped to analyze just how productive he would have to be in order to earn one million dollars in commissions. I was confounded by his statement. On the one hand, I didn't want to say or do anything that might serve to discourage his pursuit of such a lofty goal. I did not want to play the role of *Wishy-Washy Positive* to this young man. Yet he seemed so green that it might not have been fair to turn him loose with that attitude, without at least breaking that goal down for him into manageable units.

"Terrific!" I said. "Now, the next step is to break that goal down into smaller units so that you can stay on target each step along the way."

"Great idea," he said.

"Let's see," I continued. "You will earn one million dollars during the next 12 months." I whipped out my pocket calculator. 'That's an average income of $83,333.33 per month. Now, there are an average of 4.3 weeks per month. That means you want to earn, on the average, $19,379.84 per week. This, of course, presumes that you will not take a vacation any time during the next 52 weeks. Do you intend to work on Sundays?" I asked.

"Well, no," he said. "I'll probably take Sundays off."

"How about Saturdays?"

"Yes, I'll work Saturdays," he said. "It looks like I'm going to have to."

"O.K.," I continued. "That's $19,379.84 per week, divided by six days per week, which equals $3,229.97 per day that you must earn. You must earn that amount 6 days per week, 4.3 weeks per month, 12 months per year, without fail, in order to reach your goal of one million dollars this year. Tell me," I asked, "how long have you been selling insurance?"

"Three weeks," he said.

"And what's the most money you've ever earned in a single day, so far, selling insurance?"

"I earned $147 yesterday!" he said.

"That's great!" I said (and I meant it). "All you have to do now is continue to earn that $147, plus an additional $3,082.97 per day."

I put away my pocket calculator and watched him as the information sank in.

"You know," he said, "that goal might be a little high this year."

"You may be right," I agreed.

"Yep," he said as he walked away. "I think I'll only make $800,000."

God bless him. I hope he does exactly what he says, but the point the young man *may* have missed was that our goals must be realistic.

By establishing realistic goals, we are not condemning ourselves to a life-time of less than extraordinary results. We are simply approaching the process of success in an incremental and realistic fashion. Our goals can—and should—have goals of their own. In other words, as we reach a milestone that we have established for ourselves, we can always expand our horizons. But better that we should have to constantly expand our goals, than to have to accept defeat as we constantly fall short of the less realistic goals that we have established.

A man's reach, it is written, should exceed his grasp. But growth does not require that we at all times strive for things which are probably unattainable. Instead, it requires only that we establish, and then reach, our goals one step at a time. As we find ourselves reaching the goals that we've established, we may impose even higher (yet still realistic) standards for the future. The establishment of unrealistic goals can be profoundly demoralizing. It is an agony to which we need not subject ourselves. We need only approach the business of success realistically—one step at a time.

Affirmatively Specific

It is not enough to say, for example, "I hope to lose 20 pounds during the next six months." Even if that statement is written down, it won't do us much good, say, three months from now.

In the first place, it's not affirmative. It does not reflect the intensity with which you have decided to achieve your goal. Instead, the word "hope" implies that the statement is nothing more than a wish. Moreover, this statement is inherently negative. It implies the *loss* of something. Why not emphasize what will be *gained* by the accomplishment of the goal?

Therefore, rather than saying, "I hope to lose 20 pounds . . .," we should say, "I will weigh 160 pounds . . ." The difference is subtle, but critically important. First, at all times our goals should begin with the words "I will." Next, they should reflect, affirmatively, the nature of the accomplishment we are pursuing. Finally, they must be very specific. For example, the statement, "I will weigh 160 pounds *in six months*," is inadequate because it is not specific enough. As written, the statement provides us with the convenient cop-out of being able to say, four months from now, that our goal will be reached six months from *then.*

Instead, a goal must specifically state the date upon which it will be accomplished. Therefore, the statement which originally read: "I hope to lose 20 pounds during the next six months," should more properly read: "I will weigh 160 pounds on or before January 1, 19__." This statement is affirmative because it uses the phrase "I will," and because it does not emphasize the loss of something, but rather the attainment of a specific goal (i.e., the weight of 160 pounds); and it is specific because it states the date on or before which the goal will be attained.

The importance of a goal being both affirmative and specific cannot be overemphasized. When a goal fails to possess these qualities, it affords us with numerous opportunities to "escape," to rationalize away our initial intention. Moreover, by being affirmatively specific, the statement of the goal itself serves as an affirmation contributing to its accomplishment. When we repeat our goals each day, as we should do, once each morning, once each afternoon, and again just before going to sleep, we create a personal positive affirmation. We thus positively program our computer (see Chapter VI) for the accomplishment of the goal that we have written.

What Do You Really Want?
"The End Is Near" Test

In his book, *How to Get Control of Your Time and Your Life,* Allen Lakein proposes that we should consider what we would really want to do with our remaining time if we knew we would be struck by lightning six months from today. His emphasis upon obtaining a clear picture of our true desires is consistent with our earlier observation that the extent to which we are able to clearly establish our own priorities is inversely proportional to the time we have previously spent trying to please others.

In establishing our personal goals, it is imperative that we strip away what we perceive to be the expectations of others. Our inquiry must focus upon these issues: What do *I* want to accomplish? Where do *I* want to spend my time? What do *I* want to be doing for the rest of my life?

By considering what we might want to do if we *knew* we had only a limited amount of time to live, and by comparing those projections with the goals we might otherwise set, we can measure the *Goal Gap* that we have created. Our *Goal Gap* is, namely, the difference between the goals we would pursue if we knew our time was very limited, and the goals we would otherwise pursue while expecting a life of normal duration.

What If You Had Exactly One Year To Live?

You've just seen your doctor, and he has given you *The Word.* There is no doubt about it. There is no cause for false hope. You'll feel okay until then, but exactly one year from today you'll be cashing in your chips, canceling your subscription, checking out, kicking the bucket, buying *The Big One.*

You have 12 months to live. How will you spend them? Assume your death arrangements are already made. What will you do during this last year of your life?

On the top half of the *Goal Gap Exercise* (Figure 13-1) at the end of this chapter, list all the things you would like to do. Using the mechanics discussed above, list at least one goal for each mini-environment of your life. Be sure they are written, realistic, and affirmatively specific.

Exactly what goals will you want to accomplish before your year is up? Are there old friendships to rekindle? Extra money to be made? A special trip to be taken? Decide now how you would spend that time.

"One Year From Today I Will . . ."

But you probably have many years in which to live, to pursue your full potential, to utilize the gifts that God gave you.

Given the fact that you expect to live a reasonably long life, what do you intend to accomplish during the next 12 months? Using the bottom half of the *Goal Gap Exercise,* list the one major goal you intend to accomplish during the next 12 months in each of your four mini-environments. Remember: you are now anticipating a longer life. Your goals may not seem as desperate, your deadlines may not be as rigid.

Reconciling The Difference

Now compare the two lists contained on the *Goal Gap Exercise*. In the first, you determined what you would do if you had only 12 months to live. In the second, you established goals based upon a normal life expectancy.

How different are the goals that you set in each? Compare the goals of each mini-environment carefully. If there is a substantial difference between the two in any mini-environment, then the following important question must be asked: if the goals you listed in *The End Is Near Test* portion of the *Goal Gap Exercise* tend to reflect the things you would most like to do with your life, then why aren't you doing them anyway—even if you may have substantially longer to live?

Of course, the answer to that question is often obvious. For example, work-related goals may become virtually irrelevant to an individual who knows he has only 12 months to live. A person expecting a longer life, however, will probably continue to focus his attention upon his work, so that he may acquire the wealth he desires.

On the other hand, a substantial difference between the two sets of goals may be cause for alarm. It may indicate that (since we rarely anticipate our early demise) we are pursuing goals which don't really bring us much happiness. We pursue these latter goals in the name of what is expected, or what will help us reach some very distant destination. I do not recommend that you retire to Tahiti just because doing so was one of the goals you listed on *The End Is Near Test*. However, I do recommend that you seriously evaluate the goals you set on the *One Year From Today I Will* segment, to determine whether they genuinely reflect your innermost desires.

The purpose of this exercise is to help us clearly distinguish between those goals that we might establish simply because we assume they are expected of us, and those goals we really would establish if we were genuinely trying to please ourselves. If the difference between your two sets of goals is too great, then I suggest you seriously re-evaluate the directions in which you are heading, and attempt to articulate goals that genuinely satisfy the real you.

Goals Statements

So what do you *really* want to accomplish in each of the four mini-environments of your life?

We may now construct a specific *Goals Statement* for each mini-environment.

Please examine the form entitled *Goals Exercise* (Figure 13-2) at the end of this chapter. Note that in the upper left-hand corner a space is provided to list one of the four mini-environments. Make four copies of this form and list a different mini-environment in the upper left-hand corner of each.

The purpose of the exercise we are about to conduct is to force us to consider, in a limited amount of time, the goals we would like to have accomplished at certain intervals of our life. The exercise does not cause us to priorize the goals. We'll do that later. Rather, it will simply help us get our mental wheels turning. On the form, there is room to list lifetime goals, one-year goals and 30-day goals. It is best that you limit yourself to three minutes for each durational category while listing your goals. In other words, take three minutes to list your lifetime goals, three minutes to list your one-year goals, and three minutes to list your 30-day goals for each mini-environment.

We impose a time limit because of the familiar phenomenon known as Parkinson's Law. Parkinson's Law provides that work will expand to fill the time allotted for it. In making the difficult and often life-changing decisions involved with goal setting, we frequently procrastinate as long as possible. But since this is merely an exercise which can be redone at will, and since it is, after all, written on paper, not chiseled in stone, it is best that we impose a severe time limit on ourselves, so that we do not labor indefinitely over each decision.

Take three minutes for each durational category on each of the four separate *Goals Exercise* sheets that you have duplicated from this book. List all the goals you can think of for each mini-environment. Repeat the exercise for each mini-environment until you have four separate *Goals Exercises* completed.

Now examine what you have accomplished on each sheet. Do the 30-day goals logically lead to the attainment of the one-year goals? Will the one-year goals logically lead to the attainment of the lifetime goals? Hopefully, yes. If not, I suggest you re-evaluate your intermediate and short-term goals. They should be closely related to the accomplishment of your lifetime goals.

Now please review each of your *Goals Exercises* a final time. It is necessary that you priorize your goals in each durational category, for each mini-environment. You must select from among all the goals you have listed the one goal in each durational category that is most important to you at this time. Remember, this exercise can, and should, be conducted on a regular basis—monthly, quarterly, or annually. Your decision now, that a particular goal is currently more important than another, will not prevent you from changing your mind the next time you conduct your exercise. But for now, select the one goal in each durational category (lifetime, one-year or 30-day), for each mini-environment that is the most important goal to you.

If you have priorized your goals by placing an asterisk or other symbol next to that most important goal in each category, then we are ready to prepare *Goals Statements* to reflect the direction you wish to take in each of your four mini-environments.

Lifetime

The purpose of a *Goals Statement* is to provide a check-at-a-glance of the goals you have deemed to be most important in each of your four mini-environments. They also give us an opportunity to write out, in our own words, the goals we intend to reach.

Please examine the form entitled *Goals Statements* (Figure 13-3) at the end of the chapter. Note that it is divided into thirds, depicting the durational categories of *Lifetime, One-Year* and *30-Day* goals. First, in the *Lifetime* category, list, where indicated, the most important goal that you have established for each mini-environment.

For example, your entry for the Inside Mini-Environment might read, "I will have mastered the principles in the great book *Think and Grow Rich* by Napoleon Hill." Your entry for the Outside Mini-Environment might read, "I will have maintained an exceptional level of fitness." The entry for the Home Mini-Environment might read, "I will have had a very warm and happy family life"; and your entry for the Work Mini-Environment might read, "I will have a net worth of one million dollars."

Below those entries are the words, "During my lifetime I will":
After these words, using language of your own, insert in full
sentence form what it is you intend to accomplish in all four mini-
environments during your lifetime. For example, your statement
may read, "During my lifetime I will: *Have mastered great principles of independent thought and success, have taken great care
of my body, have maintained a warm and caring and loving relationship with my spouse and children, and have accumulated a
substantial amount of property and wealth from which they will
benefit after my passing.*"

You have now clearly established the direction that you genuinely wish your life to take. You have, perhaps for the first time,
on a single sheet of paper, listed the very guts of the things you
wish to accomplish during your lifetime. You have, by utilizing
goals that were realistic, written, and affirmatively specific, implied that you are fully capable of reaching these goals; and thus
you have defined the outer limits of your potential. It is an important step—critically important to the full utilization of your talent
during your lifetime.

One Year

Our use of one-year and 30-day durational categories is arbitrary. We could just as easily have resorted to three-year and
six-month categories. But the shorter the time frame with which
we deal, the more easily we may be specific about the goals that
we establish.

Using the *One-Year* section of your *Goals Statement* form,
please list the most important one-year goal you have in each of
your four mini-environments. For example, your one-year Inside
goal might state, "I will master and clearly apply Napoleon Hill's
first principle." Your one-year Outside goal might say, "I will
weigh 160 pounds." Your Home one-year goal might state, "I will
have established the habit of spending at least one hour of quality
time with my family each day." And your Work one-year goal
might declare, "I will have the Bagley commercial transaction
completed and closed."

Therefore, your *One-Year Goals Statement* might read: "No
later than one year from today I will: *Have mastered and applied
the first principle of Napoleon Hill's book, have attained a fit*

weight of 160 pounds, have devoted myself one hour per day to the love of my family, and have substantially enhanced my career by successfully completing the Bagley transaction."

Now compare your one-year goals to your lifetime goals. Are they consistent? Will the one-year goals logically lead to the completion of the lifetime goals you have established? If not, you should rework your one-year goals. If so, you are right on target in accomplishing your top-priority lifetime goals.

Thirty-Day

Play it again, Sam. This time with soul.

We may now complete the exercise by listing the most important 30-day goals we have in each of our four mini-environments.

Your 30-day goals might read as follows: "I will re-read Napoleon Hill's book and carefully outline the first three chapters" (Inside). "I will weigh 178 pounds" (Outside). "We will have a family discussion on potential family projects and will have undertaken at least two of those projects" (Home). "I will submit to Jones a preliminary plan for the Bagley transaction" (Work).

Your *30-Day Goals Statement*, then, might read, "No later than 30 days from today I will: *Have re-read and carefully outlined the first three chapters of Napoleon Hill's book, have reached the weight of 178 pounds, have clearly established a project game plan for my family, and have begun the process of refining our approach toward the Bagley transaction.*

Now for the big question: Will your 30-day goals directly help you accomplish your one-year goals? If so, you are right on target. If not, your 30-day goals should be re-evaluated. The goals within each of our durational categories should supplement the others. Our 30-day goals should logically lead to the accomplishment of our one-year goals, and our one-year goals should logically lead to the accomplishment of our lifetime goals as well.

Obviously, this type of goal setting is particularly beneficial as it applies to the Work Mini-Environment. Income, production, and quotas, are things easily quantifiable. By conducting exercises such as these on a regular basis, we can specifically identify our targets for many years ahead. Of course, we'll always retain the right to change our minds and refine our directions. Indeed, these exercises are not intended to tie us down, but rather to free us up. They are designed to give us a meaningful and knowledgeable basis upon which we can measure known alternatives.

It is, after all, how we refine our energy, not the energy itself, that will determine the extent to which we reach our full potential as human beings. We may take a shotgun approach to life, heading in many directions at once, knowing that our energies will consequently be dispersed; or we may proceed as might a bullet—steadfastly and directly toward a predetermined target. But to do this we must have goals. Our goals must be written, realistic, and affirmatively specific.

We must ask ourselves, openly and honestly, "What is it that I really want? If I had just one year to live, how would I spend those 12 months? How might I compare the way I would otherwise spend my life, if I knew my time was limited, with the way I choose to spend my life now? How may I reconcile that difference?" These are tough questions, but they must be asked—and answered. For ultimately it is that guy in the mirror we must please. The goals that we establish must genuinely reflect the life he wishes to live.

Our goals must be especially precise. To obtain that precision, we must re-do our *Goals Exercise* and our *Goals Statements* on a periodic basis. Monthly is best, but at the least we should sit down for an hour or two once each quarter to reassess our direction, to reaffirm our life's purpose.

Congratulations! If you have conducted these exercises, you are well on your way toward getting on target and staying on target. But how do we translate these goals into the affirmative conduct that will lead to their accomplishment?

I'm glad you asked. It's as simple as A-B-C.

Goal Gap Exercise

"The End Is Near" Test

What if you had exactly one year to live? Within the next 12 months (list one major goal for each mini-environment):

I will _____

I will _____

I will _____

I will _____

"One Year From Today I Will . . ."

Assume you have many years to live. *Now* what goals will you accomplish within the next 12 months (list one major goal for each mini-environment)?

I will _____

I will _____

I will _____

I will _____

Compare and reconcile the goals you have listed in each category.

Figure 13-1

Goals Exercise

MINI-ENVIRONMENT: _____ DATE: _____

Lifetime Goals List

1. _____   6. _____
2. _____   7. _____
3. _____   8. _____
4. _____   9. _____
5. _____   10. _____

One-Year Goals List

1. _____   6. _____
2. _____   7. _____
3. _____   8. _____
4. _____   9. _____
5. _____   10. _____

30-Day Goals List

1. _____   6. _____
2. _____   7. _____
3. _____   8. _____
4. _____   9. _____
5. _____   10. _____

Figure 13-2

Goals Statements

DATE: _____

Lifetime Goals Statement

INSIDE: _____   HOME: _____

OUTSIDE: _____   WORK: _____

DURING MY LIFETIME I WILL: _____

_____

_____

_____

One-Year Goals Statement

INSIDE: _____   HOME: _____

OUTSIDE: _____   WORK: _____

NO LATER THAN ONE YEAR FROM TODAY I WILL: _____

_____

_____

_____

30-Day Goals Statement

INSIDE: _____   HOME: _____

OUTSIDE: _____   WORK: _____

NO LATER THAN 30 DAYS FROM TODAY I WILL: _____

_____

_____

_____

Figure 13-3

XIV

The A-B-C's
Of Managing Your Time

*While it is hard to predict exactly, for each
minute we spend planning in advance, we will
probably save at least ten minutes of confusion,
distraction and anxiety during the coming week.*

It's easy to get disorganized.

Take the case of Cassius Cautious, ancestor of Calvin. Back in
the days of yore, there existed a system of justice known as trial
by ordeal, wherein the accused would have to pass certain tests
to prove his innocence. If he could pass the tests, he would be considered innocent, but if he couldn't . . . it usually didn't matter,
because he died trying.

On one occasion, Cassius Cautious was arrested and charged
with a serious offense. The judges handed down the edict that he
would have to pass three tests in order to prove his innocence.
First, he'd be thrown into a room containing four vats of wine, and
he'd have to consume them all within four minutes. Next, he'd be
thrown into a room containing a 565-pound Bengal Tiger with an
impacted wisdom tooth. He'd have to extract that tooth from the
mouth of the tiger—again within four minutes. Finally, he'd be
thrown into a room containing a 97-year-old woman, whom he'd
have to meet and seduce—again within four minutes.

Cassius, like Calvin, was an eager fellow. He said, "Okay, let's get the show on the road!"

The guards threw him into the first room containing the wine, and slammed the door behind him. Three minutes and 55 seconds later, Cassius stumbled out, having successfully consumed all four vats of wine.

Next, the guards threw him into the room containing the 565-pound Bengal Tiger. Again they slammed the door behind him, and from within the room they could hear terrible, horrifying cries and screams of anguish. Nevertheless, three minutes and 57 seconds later, Cassius staggered out, completely disheveled, his clothes torn from him, scratches all over his body, and he said:

"Okay, where's the old lady with the bad tooth?!"

Yes, it's easy to get disorganized.

That's why we need a plan. Goals alone are not enough. We've all known people who had no shortage of goals, but who never bothered to translate their desires into practical, affirmative conduct. Instead, they stopped on a dream and forever failed to take the affirmative steps necessary to accomplish the goals they had set.

The process of planning involves managing our time. The application of fundamental time management principles is especially important, not because it will tie us down to a certain method of doing things, but because it will free us to spend our energies on the more creative pursuits required for the accomplishment of our goals.

In approaching the concept of time management, it is important to disclaim any notion that we wish to become "efficiency experts."

Instead, our goal is *effectiveness*. How long it takes you to perform a particular task is not nearly as important as that you are spending your time upon those tasks that are most important to you. Time management helps us work smarter, not harder. Yet, there is nothing particularly complicated about the process. In fact, building upon the exercises we conducted in the previous chapter, we may now effectively manage our time through the use of a simple three-step process.

Always Make A List Of Activities For Accomplishing Your Goals

Each morning, five days a week, for 20 years, Emanuel would appear at the border station in the small town of Nogales on his way from Mexico to the United States. Each day he would arrive with a wheelbarrow filled with sand. Each day the border guard, who knew that Emanuel had never done an honest day's work in his life, would insist upon sifting through the sand to determine what it was that Emanuel was smuggling into the States.

"You think one day I'll grow lax," he would say. "You think I'll stop examining the sand. But you're wrong. For as long as it takes, I'll continue to sift through it until I discover what it is you're smuggling across the border."

The process went on for 20 years. During that time, Emanuel became a very wealthy man, with elaborate homes on either side of the border. The border guard never found a thing in the sand.

Finally, one day, well after the border guard had retired, he saw Emanuel on the street and stopped him.

"Please," he said. "It keeps me awake nights not knowing what you were bringing across the border. I know that it must have been something illegal. I know that you were smuggling something across. Please tell me, Emanuel, and give me peace."

Emanuel smiled and asked, "Do you promise not to tell anyone else?"

"I promise," the guard said. "I'm retired now, and I won't get you into any trouble."

"In that case, if I have your word," said Emanuel, "I will tell you what you want to hear. During the past 20 years, I have smuggled 5,200 wheelbarrows across the border."

Sometimes we get so caught up sifting through the sand that we fail to recognize the obvious realities before our very eyes. Much has been written on the subject of planning and time management. Frequently, like a search through sand, it has grown over-complicated and has strayed from the central issues at hand. In fact, there is nothing complicated about it. It begins, quite simply, with us making sure that we *always maintain a list of activities that will help us accomplish our goals*. With such a list, we can begin the process of priorizing our activities and scheduling them into our weeks and our days.

Activities Defined

It is especially important to distinguish between activities and goals. An activity is a specific, affirmative act. It is something we do. On the other hand, we don't *do* a goal. It is, instead, something we attain. An activity, then, is a form of conduct.

In order to manage our time effectively, we must constantly search for those activities that will lead us directly to the accomplishment of our goals. Once we list as many activities as we can imagine, we may then priorize those activities, schedule them into our weeks and our days, and begin the process of constantly evaluating which among them will be most effective in helping us reach our goals.

Possibility Lists

It was, I believe, the Reverend Robert Schuller who coined the phrase *Possibility Lists* in conjunction with his positive theology of *Possibility Thinking.*

The Reverend tells the story of how, when he first moved to southern California, he was very young and very broke. He knew only that he wanted to begin his own ministry. His financial situation was so desperate that on one occasion he collected all the unused postage stamps in the house and took them to the Post Office in an attempt to redeem them for grocery money. It was then that he made the startling discovery that the Post Office does not redeem postage stamps.

Nevertheless, his goal was clearly established: his own ministry. He sat down, and on a single sheet of paper listed all the things he could do to find a place to preach on Sunday mornings. Of course, he needed a hall for free. So he listed such activities as "Call on the VFW, see if the town hall is available, contact other churches, contact synagogues,"etc. As an afterthought, and without much hope that it would be a particularly good idea, he wrote, "Contact drive-in theater."

The Reverend followed up on his Possibility List and called upon all those places listed. They all turned him down. As a last resort, he called upon the owner of the drive-in theater. The owner regarded the request as a rather unique use of the premises, and gave his consent.

Today, the Reverend Robert Schuller is pastor of the spectacularly beautiful Garden Grove Community Church. The sun literally never sets on his ministry. It serves millions of people around the globe. And it all began with a kid who was so poor he tried to redeem his postage stamps—and a Possibility List.

Please examine the Possibility List (Figure 14-1) at the end of this chapter. Note that there is ample room to list up to ten possible activities for each mini-environment. At the top of each mini-environment list is room for you to insert the top-priority 30-day goal you have already established for that mini-environment in the last chapter. Please insert the goals you established on the appropriate lines of the Possibility List. (I urge you to make duplicate copies of your forms throughout, and to use the copies so that you may repeat the exercise as often as you desire).

Now take two minutes for each mini-environment, and list all the activities you can think of that might help you accomplish the goal you have established for that mini-environment. Now is *not* the time to evaluate the activities you will list. That will come next. Instead, this is your opportunity to brainstorm, to list as many activities as you can possibly think of in the two minutes allowed (feel free to list more than ten in each category), that will help you accomplish your goals. We impose a brief time limit here for the same reason we imposed a time limit in the preceding chapter: it helps prevent procrastination. Start now, and spend two minutes per category listing all the activities you can think of that will help you accomplish your goals.

Finished? Great! You've just taken an extremely important step for the accomplishment of your goals.

The Priority System

At this stage, the planning process can appear especially frustrating. Suddenly we have at least one clearly established goal for each of our four mini-enviornments, and we may have more than 40 activities listed that will help us accomplish those goals—all of which we want to start on simultaneously.

"Great," you think. "I already had too many things to do before I began the exercise. Now I've got 40 new activities to start on, to boot!"

It is because we obviously can't begin so many tasks at once that we must impose a priority system to determine which activities are most important to us now. Many such systems have been proposed. Allen Lakein, in his *How To Get Control of Your Time and Your Life*, proposes the A-B-C system. In it, he assigns an A value to high-priority activities, a B value to moderately important activities, and a C value to unimportant activities. Other authors recommend numerical systems that may extend from one to three, from one to five, or from one to ten, depending upon how complex the system.

Personally, I like stars. I always enjoyed drawing them as a little kid, and getting them if I did well in school. For our purposes then, let's use the three-star system. It is just that arbitrary. In priorizing our activities, we could use A-B-C, 1-2-3, asterisks, exclamation points, or just about any other design that happens to appeal to us. But we'll use the three-star system. We'll assign a value of three stars to any activity that will lead directly to the accomplishment of our 30-day goal, and which can be meaningfully started sometime within the next seven days. We'll assign a value of two stars to any activity that is of only moderate relative importance in helping us accomplish our goal; and we will assign a value of one star to any activity that is not directly related to the accomplishment of our goal.

The decision is up to you. Only you can decide which of the activities you have listed should be classified as three-star, two-star, or lone star activities.

It is important to note that the status, or rating, of an activity may change from week to week, or month to month. The ultimate question for today, however, is, "Which of the activities I have listed will directly lead me to the accomplishment of my 30-day goal, and which can be meaningfully started upon sometime within the next seven days?"

Return now to your possibility list, and assign a value of three, two or one star to each of the activities you have listed for each mini-environment. There is no firm time limit for this exercise, but it shouldn't take you more than a couple of minutes.

Have you assigned a priority to each of your activities? Great! Now for the ultimate question: of the three-star activities you have listed, which one activity in each mini-environment is the most important activity to you right now? Return to your possibility list and select one three-star activity for each mini-environment. Circle it to set it apart from the others.

Congratulations! You have now not only clearly established a top-priority 30-day goal in each mini-environment, you have (through a simple yet effective process of elimination) logically selected the one activity which is most likely to lead you to the accomplishment of your goal in each mini-environment. Our next step is to be sure we set aside the time necessary for the undertaking of the activities we have listed.

Be Sure To Schedule Your Activities Into Your Weeks And Your Days

Three boys went to the doctor's office for their annual shots. As they sat in the waiting room, each boy picked up a different magazine and started thumbing through it. The doctor came out to the waiting room and saw the boys sitting there.

He walked up to the first little boy and said, "Bobby, what would you like to be when you grow up?"

Bobby was reading *Field and Stream*. He said, "I'd like to be a guide and take people to the wilderness where the big game is, and where the fish bite."

The doctor said, "That's very nice." He turned to the second little boy and said, "Tommy, what would you like to be when you grow up?"

Tommy was reading *Popular Mechanics*. He said, "Oh, I'd like to be an engineer and build great bridges and make airplanes fly."

The doctor said, "That's very nice, Tommy." He turned tó the third little boy and said, "Calvin, what would you like to be when you grow up?"

Calvin was reading *Playboy*. He didn't look up. He just thought a minute, and said, "I don't know what they call it, but I can't wait to get started!"

Having clearly established our goals, and having priorized the activities that will lead us to the accomplishment of those goals, it is time that we, like Calvin, get started on their accomplishment. We do so by taking a few minutes daily to plan. We must be sure *to schedule our activities into our weeks and our days.* But beware: The scheduling that we do will only be of value to us if we use it. Our world is filled with dozens of often well-intentioned distractors who wish to bleed away our time on projects and activities that we would never have listed on our personal priority list of things to do. We must therefore regard our scheduling as the process by which we set aside time that we will treat as sacred, inviolate, for the accomplishment of our goals.

Horizontal Planning

Regardless of what you do for a living, I urge you to invest in a Week-At-A-Glance Professional Appointments Book. It is a type of calendar where, by flipping any page, you can see an entire week at a glance. The days are represented by long, vertical columns. Each column is divided into 15-minute segments. It is a wonderfully inexpensive planning tool, and is especially useful for the scheduling technique known as horizontal planning.

As the name implies, horizontal planning is simply the process by which we block into our weekly calendar the various high-priority activities that we have listed on our possibility lists. For example, suppose you are a sales professional, and that your most important three-star activity for the coming week is to practice your sales presentation. You might therefore block out an hour each day on, say, Monday, Wednesday and Friday, from, say, 8:00 a.m. until 9:00 a.m. The effect of such planning, predictably, will be a series of horizontal blocks across the vertical columns in your calendar. Similarly, we schedule our other top-priority three-star activities into our calendar in the same fashion.

This form of weekly horizontal planning is best accomplished on Sunday afternoon or evening. Many individuals will do their planning Friday evening before leaving the office. Others will wait until they are fresh Monday morning, before leaving for work. Regardless of the exact time you choose, the process is relatively simple and straightforward. Adequate horizontal planning requires that we spend just a few minutes reviewing our possiblity lists, that we select the highest priority activities from that list upon which we wish to spend time during the coming week, and that we block out the time we will spend upon them in advance.

Although it is simple, the importance of this process cannot be overemphasized. By planning in advance, we are suddenly in control of our coming week. We are acting upon, rather than reacting to, the world around us. We have established our priorities and blocked out the time that we will spend pursuing those activities during the next seven days. While it is hard to predict exactly, for each minute we spend planning in advance, we will probably save at least ten minutes of confusion, distraction and anxiety during the coming week.

But we shouldn't go overboard with our horizontal planning. Remember such things as calendars and Possibility Lists are tools designed for our use. They are not prisons from which there is no escape. When doing your weekly planning, don't block in activities too tightly. There will, of course, be some distractions and unexpected events. Leave yourself enough time to react. Call a family meeting and eliminate antagonisms before they begin, by explaining to all present that there will be certain hours of each day that you will be working on projects that are especially important to you, and that other contingencies should be postponed until after those projects are completed.

Furthermore, we all, according to Lakein, possess an internal biologic clock which causes us to concentrate best on certain kinds of activities at certain times of the day. For example, in the morning hours, we may be best equipped for handling paperwork and performing tasks that require heavy concentration. In the afternoon, we may be best suited for dealing with people, answering phone calls, and the like. Whatever your biologic timetable, by planning in advance, you can make it work for you. Schedule appropriate activities into those times of day when you will be most mentally equipped to handle them. Give yourself time to breathe. If you know that as a matter of routine you require 30 minutes of quiet time in the afternoon, be sure to schedule that in. If that mid-morning break is a must, allow time for it.

If used regularly, horizontal planning can unlock more time than we ever suspected we had.

Daily Planning

Most of us make *to-do* lists, but only occasionally: when we're especially busy perhaps, or when we are planning a particularly complex project. But to-do lists are most valuable when we use them every day. Indeed, there is probably no other time-management tool available to us, at any cost, that is as valuable on a day-to-day basis as the to-do list.

The beauty of a to-do list is that it allows us to concentrate on getting things done, rather than upon trying to remember what needs to be done in the first place. The amount of time required to write a good, daily, to-do list is ridiculously small—10 to 15 minutes perhaps, at most. Measure those few minutes against the hours that can be saved each day by advanced planning, and it suddenly becomes apparent why to-do lists enjoy such popularity among successful individuals.

Many successful executives will not leave their offices at the end of the day until after their to-do lists for the coming day are completed. Others will complete their to-do lists just prior to going to bed, so that during the night their subconscious minds will have an opportunity to build enthusiasm for the coming day's activities. Others of us enjoy making our lists over that first cup of coffee in the morning. There is no hard and fast rule as to the "best" time of day in which a to-do list should be completed. It is, however, important that it be completely done before we arrive at work. If our list is not done by then, if we do not at least have the opportunity to think about the activities we have listed as we drive to work, the chances are good that within 30 seconds after we enter the office door, our day will be out of control.

Indeed, many of us have an aversion to to-do lists, because their use is inconsistent with the "reaction mentality" that we have developed at work over the years. Our reaction mentality causes us to believe that because we stay busy reacting to the events of the day, we are therefore constructively contributing to the success of our company and ourselves. We view our job as an opportunity to "put out fires" on a continuing basis, to react to one crisis after another. With such a mentality, we honestly don't know what we're going to do as we go to work. Once at work, we spend our entire day reacting at a gut, knee-jerk level to one situation after another. When we get home, we find it very difficult to recount exactly what we've done, because there was no consistency of purpose to it.

A simple to-do list can help us avoid all this. We need simply sit down with the horizontal weekly plan that we have already made, extract from it the top-priority three-star activities that we have already listed, enter those activities on our daily to-do list, and plan the rest of our day around them. Thus, we will have completed the planning process from (1) the establishment of goals, to (2) the listing of activities, to (3) the selection of high priority activities, to (4) the scheduling of those activities on a weekly basis, to (5) their final insertion into our daily schedule. By working around our three-star activities, and by entering them on our to-do list first, we insure that we will provide our high-priority activities with the time necessary for their accomplishment. We may then plan the rest of the day around them.

Characteristics Of An Effective "To-Do" List

Most of us make our to-do lists on scraps of paper. That habit can be more disorganizing than not having a to-do list at all. It is far better to utilize a standard form. Such forms make our task of organizing the day much simpler.

Please examine the Daily Work Plan, To-Do List (Figure 14-2) at the end of this chapter. I recommend it to you. I suggest you make 30 copies of the form, use it for a month, and then adapt a form of your own that more particularly fits your life-style and business. There is no right or wrong format for a to-do list. However, a particularly useful list will have at least these characteristics:

First, it should provide a section where you can write out or symbolize your goals. This helps remind us, at a glance, what it is we're trying to accomplish. Notice that our to-do list devotes three lines to the listing of goals. Also, you will note a blank line in the upper left-hand corner. On it you may wish to place a symbol for the one overriding goal you are attempting to accomplish that week, month, or year. I urge your use of a symbol because, after all, to-do lists are intended to be used. They should be laying about in clear view of yourself and those who work with you. It is entirely possible that you do not want the entire world prying into your personal ambitions. If so, just resort to a mark that is meaningful to you, and that will serve as a reminder of the things you are attempting to accomplish. Notice, too, that on our form we have left space for brainstorming and the making of a mini-possibility list, so that as we get new ideas we'll have a place to write them down.

Second, it should provide space for daily scheduling. Notice that the left-hand column of our form does just that. Of course, the left-hand column should be pretty well filled out before we get to work. We should enter the three-star activities that we have listed on our horizontal plan first, and then insert other activities as well. Notice that on this form our *Appointments and Project Time* extends from 8:00 a.m. until 8:30 p.m. That these hours extend beyond normal working hours is not to imply that you should remain at work 12½ hours a day. It is to imply that, as a practical matter, the activities we perform which relate to three of our four mini-environments must generally be confined to the early morning and evening hours, and to weekends. Our Work Mini-Environment consumes the majority of our day. Unfortunately, most of us use to-do lists only for work-related activities. Yet the very fact that we must squeeze so many non-work-related activities into such a relatively brief period of time speaks loudly in favor of listing those activities relating to our Inside, Outside, and Home mini-environments as well. Indeed, the importance we should attach to leisure-time and family activities compels us to use to-do lists on weekends as well. When, by mid-week, an entire family can sit down for a few minutes and plan out the weekend, all members have the convenience of knowing in advance what time must be set aside for joint family projects, for chores, and what time will be available for individual activities. Animosities and arguments are averted, and the family's attention can be devoted toward creating quality time together, rather than toward haggling over the quantity of the time to be employed.

Third, it should provide space for the listing of miscellaneous ideas and priorities. The upper right-hand vertical column entitled "Priorities and Deadlines" is an opportunity for us to list important items that might not otherwise appear on our list:"back burner" items that we know we will eventually have to devote ourselves to, but which do not appear on today's list. It is an area in which we can make notes to ourselves, perhaps in preparation for the next day's to-do list. As our day progresses, we can, of course, cross off those items on our to-do list that we have completed. The simple act of crossing off such items is positively reinforcing. It helps encourage us to use and reuse the list.

Finally, our list should provide space for the listing of messages and notes. The lower right-hand corner of our list is devoted to phone calls and notes. The average three-piece suit has 11 pockets into which a man might slip phone messages and notes. If the wearer of the three-piece suit received just five phone calls per day, he could, theoretically, have to search through 55 pockets to find his messages. Although women have fewer pockets, it doesn't matter. They need merely drop their messages and notes into the dark abyss of their purses, and they are gone forever. By placing all our messages in the lower right-hand corner of our Daily Work Plan, we will lessen the risk of such messages becoming lost, and we will have a convenient method by which we can relate our phone calls and notes to our activities of the day.

But regardless of the precise format that you choose for your to-do list, its value will be small if you don't use it. To-do lists are made to be used. They are made to be kept out in clear view, where we can constantly refer to them, and where we can constantly cross things off them and add things to them. We may never complete all the activities on our to-do list. But we shouldn't try to cross off every single item on it. Rather, we should concentrate on crossing off the important items. Be sure to accomplish your three-star tasks first. Then and only then devote your time to two-star activities. Only when your two-star activities are complete, should you concern yourself with the unimportant lone star projects.

Constantly Evaluate The Most Effective Use Of Your Time Right Now

After concluding that they could make a fortune at it, my two friends, Null and Void, decided to go into the hay moving business.

They invested in a small pick-up truck. Then, each day they drove to the country and bought 50 bales of hay, which is all the truck could hold, at a dollar a bale. They then drove the truck to the city, where they sold the hay for 75 cents a bale. This went on for several weeks. Gradually Null and Void began to recognize that they were losing money.

"What do you suppose we're doing wrong?" Null asked Void.

Void pensively stroked his chin. Suddenly he snapped his fingers, and his eyes lit up. "Aha! I've got it!" he said. "We need a bigger truck!"

So they went out and bought a semi. But because they kept losing money, they got out of the hay moving business. Then, one day, they saw a truck break down in the middle of town.

"What can we do to help you?" they asked the driver.

"Well," he said, "I've got a trailer full of penguins here that I'm taking down to the zoo. If you want, I'll give you $100 to take these penguins to the zoo."

"You've got a deal!" Null and Void said in unison.

They pulled their truck up alongside the broken-down rig and opened the doors to both. The penguins waddled off of the first truck and waddled on to the other. Null and Void collected their $100 and headed toward the zoo.

A couple of hours later, the first driver had his truck repaired and was driving through the city near the zoo. He saw Null and Void walking down the sidewalk on the main street of town. All the penguins were waddling along behind them.

The driver stopped his truck, jumped out, and ran up to Null and Void. "What's the story here?" he asked. "I thought I gave you $100 to take these penguins to the zoo!"

"We did," Null said, "but we still have $47.53 left, so we're taking them to the movies!"

Null and Void finally got out of the trucking business. They had to. They had difficulty reading the highway signs. Like the day they saw a sign that read, "Clean Rest Rooms Ahead." They cleaned 147 rest rooms. But that wasn't as bad as the day they saw the sign that said, "Wet pavement."

Let's face it. Some folks you just can't help. They're just too dumb to evaluate the most effective use of their time right now. Nevertheless, for those of us who are not quite so dense, here are some ideas that will help us *constantly evaluate the most effective use of our time right now:*

The 80-20 Rule

The concept has been with us for many years. Its origin is lost in obscurity. But its premise has been proved repeatedly ever since man first realized that some activities are simply more productive than others.

While we may quibble over the exact percentages involved, and while we may believe it is true to a greater or lesser extent, it is undeniably a fact of life, and something about which we should be painfully aware. The 80-20 Rule provides, simply, that *80 percent of our accomplishments are the result of 20 percent of our activity, while we attain the remaining 20 percent of our accomplishments*

with *80 percent of our activity*. Another way of saying it is that 80
percent of your income is generated by 20 percent of the things
that you do, and only 20 percent of your income is generated by 80
percent of the things that you do. Put even more bluntly, the 80-20
Rule tells us this: *when it comes to money, most of us waste about
four-fifths of our time*.

What is the 20 percent of what you do that generates the 80
percent of what you earn? If, for example, you are a real estate
sales professional, then your income is generated when you're out
in the neighborhood getting bloody knuckles, knocking on doors,
and "pressing the flesh," as Lyndon Johnson used to say. Your
income is generally not earned when you are sitting back at the
office flipping through Multiple Lists, reading the real estate
section of your paper, shooting the breeze with your fellow
associates, or generally performing other activities that
are designed to make you feel busy without actually being productive. It is often said that good salespeople are notoriously "poor
with details." It's not that such people would be unable to
handle details if they wanted to. It's just that they know what
generates their income, and—nine times out of ten—it's not
details.

The 80-20 Rule applies even to individuals in more predictable
occupations. While the percentages may not be exactly the same,
an attorney, for example, must put in many hours in order to accumulate four to five hours of legitimate billable time each day.
Miscellaneous distractions, telephone messages, and even the
time it takes to walk to the coffee-pot or to the drinking fountain,
are all factors that reduce our productivity.

After carefully analyzing that 20 percent of what we do that
creates the 80 percent of our income, we can move to expand the
percentage. Make a list today of those activities that generate for
you the greatest amount of income. Make another list of those activities that are generally time-wasters, and that do not directly
affect your income. Post both lists conspicuously, side by side,
where you can see them frequently. Check them from time to time,
and measure your conduct against them. Remember: the most effective use of your time at work will be the undertaking of those
activities which produce the vast majority of your income.

The Pal-Enemy Syndrome

So far, you've done everything just right.

Your to-do list is made for today. You're showered, shaved, well dressed, and at the office on time. You sit down at your desk and begin to pull out the papers relating to that first three-star activity of the day.

Then Jones walks in the door. Jones, your buddy, your pal, your chum. He sits down by your desk, puts his feet up, sips his coffee and commences to share with you a stroke by stroke description of his golf game last weekend. Then he describes, in minute detail, the bladder operation he had three years ago, and ends, 65 minutes later, with a particularly fascinating account of his upcoming family vacation.

But it's okay, because Jones is your pal, your buddy, your chum. You go back a long way. He knows that when he feels like talking, he can come share his time with you, and that when you feel like talking, you can do the same. But here's the rub: that pal, that buddy, that chum who burns up your time at the office, is, in fact, among your worst enemies. He limits the income you earn. He limits the food you put on your table, the clothes you wear, the vacations that you take, and the education that you buy for your children. All this he does while sipping his coffee and discussing his golf game.

How ironic it is that so many of us, after taking such great pains to get to work in the first place, will permit someone else to burn up our day with trivia that is totally unrelated to the accomplishment of the goals that we have set. Indeed, it is important to work well with those around us. There's no doubt about it. It is important to maintain friendships. But such friendships needn't be maintained at the expense of your potential as a human being. We must each, in our own way, identify and isolate that pal, that buddy, that chum, and tell him or her in no uncertain terms that we came to work to work, and that until we are through, they should, quite simply butt out.

Avoiding Procrastination

We had originally intended to treat this subject earlier in this chapter, but we put it off.

There are at least three fundamental techniques that we can all use to help avoid procrastination.

First, be honest. We must be mature enough and disciplined enough to confront directly our tendency to procrastinate. From time to time we all find excuses for not doing things. That's fine. Our mental health may require such diversions. But at the least we should be honest enough to admit it. If we suddenly switch from a high priority task to a low priority task, we should take the time to stop and admit openly to ourselves that we are spending our time on a less productive undertaking. Take time, in other words, to feel a bit guilty. A little constructive guilt can go a long way. Take time to consider how many things will not be done because of the time we are currently wasting. First and foremost, then, *we must be honest and confront directly our tendency to procrastinate.*

Second, we must chip away at those major undertakings that we tend to put off. Allen Lakien calls this the *Swiss Cheese Method.* He suggests we poke holes in that major project. Whatever the terminology we employ, the desired end result is that we whittle away one piece at a time at that major high priority task that we might otherwise put off. High priority tasks are almost always going to be more complicated to do than low priority tasks. If they were easy, they would probably have been done, perhaps by someone else, a long time ago. Instead, we must chip away at our tendency to procrastinate. If you have that major report to write, for example, don't write it, but at least pick up a pencil and a pad of paper. Since you have the pencil in hand and the paper in front of you, why not go ahead and make a few notes? Since you are making a few notes, you might as well reduce them to outline form. Since the outline is very nearly complete, you might as well translate it into paragraph form and . . . suddenly, your report is done. One step at a time, *we must chip away at our tendency to procrastinate.*

Finally, if all else fails, we can choose to do nothing for five or ten minutes. Absolutely nothing. Just sit in a chair. Don't eat. Don't drink. Don't smoke. Don't look out the window. Don't listen to TV or radio. Just sit and do nothing. Sometimes we forget how lucky we are to be busy, how lucky we are to have dozens of projects upon which we can freely choose to work. From time to time it helps to sit for a few minutes, do absolutely nothing, and reflect upon this opportunity. It gives our mental batteries an opportunity to recharge; and, surprisingly, after even just a few minutes, we are often refreshed and ready to take on new challenges with renewed vitality and effort. So, if all else fails, *do nothing for a few minutes.*

The process of effectively managing our time is not particularly complicated. It requires just a few minutes a day. But, as we remember the ordeal of Cassius Cautious, we are reminded of the confusion that can be avoided through proper planning. It is literally as simple as A-B-C.

A. *Always make a list of activities for accomplishing your goals.* Remember that activities are fundamentally different from goals, in that they are affirmative, accomplishable *acts.* Make your Possibility Lists for each mini-environment of your life. Use those lists as an opportunity to brainstorm all conceivable activities that might help you toward the accomplishment of your goals. Finally, priorize those activities lists by utilizing a system of your choice, such as the three-star method that we employ.

B. *Be sure to schedule your activities into your weeks and your days.* Don't stop on a dream, as so many do. Instead, invest in a Week-At-A-Glance Professional Appointments Book. Horizontally plan your week in advance so that you act upon—rather than react to—the world around you. Create the habit now of daily planning. The few minutes each day required for effective daily planning will save you hours of your precious time during the week. Utilize a formal to-do list. Use the form in the back of this chapter for now. But after awhile adopt one of your own that more particularly suits your needs. Stop at your local printer and have several hundred copies run off, then use them—and use them up. Get into the habit of utilizing, each day, every day, what is no doubt the most important weapon you possess in your time management arsenal—the simple to-do-list.

C. *Constantly evaluate the most effective use of your time right now.* Don't be like Null and Void. Recognize and utilize the 80-20 rule. Remember, 80 percent of your income comes from 20 percent of what you do. Find that 20 percent, build on it, and watch your income increase dramatically. Beware of the Pal-Enemy Syndrome. Socialize with that good friend on weekends or in the evenings, but at work let him know, in no uncertain terms, that you both have responsibilities to meet and goals to attain, and that the socializing will have to wait. Finally, employ the three fundamental techniques for avoiding procrastination. Be honest with yourself. Do absolutely nothing for a few minutes. And chip away at those major projects that look so ominous from the undone side.

It's as simple as A-B-C.

Possibility Lists
30-Day Goals

DATE:_____

Inside: My 30-day goal in my Inside Mini-Environment is:

_____

Possible Activities: Inside

1. _____   6. _____
2. _____   7. _____
3. _____   8. _____
4. _____   9. _____
5. _____   10. _____

Outside: My 30-day goal in my Outside Mini-Environment is:

_____

Possible Activities: Outside

1. _____   6. _____
2. _____   7. _____
3. _____   8. _____
4. _____   9. _____
5. _____   10. _____

Home: My 30-day goal in my Home Mini-Environment is:

_____

Possible Activities: Home

1. _____   6. _____
2. _____   7. _____
3. _____   8. _____
4. _____   9. _____
5. _____   10. _____

Work: My 30-day goal in my Work Mini-Environment is:

_____

Possible Activities: Work

1. _____   6. _____
2. _____   7. _____
3. _____   8. _____
4. _____   9. _____
5. _____   10. _____

Figure 14-1

Daily Work Plan 80-20
To-Do List

DAY: _____ DATE: _____

MONTHLY GOALS: _____

WEEKLY GOALS: _____

TODAY'S GOALS: _____

POSSIBLE GOAL-RELATED ACTIVITIES: _____

APPOINTMENTS AND PROJECT TIME	PRIORITIES AND DEADLINES
8:00	
8:30	
9:00	
9:30	
10:00	
10:30	
11:00	
11:30	
12:00	
12:30	
1:00	
1:30	
2:00	PHONE CALLS AND NOTES
2:30	
3:00	
3:30	
4:00	
4:30	
5:00	
5:30	
6:00	
6:30	
7:00	
7:30	
8:00	
8:30	

Figure 14-2

XV

Your Work Environment: Overcoming Obstacles

A go-getter might view a prospect and ask, "How may I profit from him?" A go-giver will view the same prospect and ask, "How might I help him — profitably?" The prospect will sense the difference.

It was Friday, and, as usual, Calvin stopped by the pay window to collect his envelope.

He reached inside for his check, and was surprised when he found attached to it a small notice which read, "You are about to receive a raise!" Calvin was delighted. He ran home and told his wife, Cathy.

"Look," he said, "I'm going to get a raise! We can make those car repairs now, and remodel the basement! You can buy that new outfit, and we can take a vacation! It's about time this company started paying me what I'm worth!"

Calvin went to his easy chair and sat down. He pulled out the pay envelope and reached inside again to re-read the notice. But this time he pulled out a second notice that he hadn't seen the first time.

It read simply, "Your raise becomes effective when you do."

Work. It's where we spend at least 2,000 hours each year. It's where we produce the income that puts the bread on our table. It is where we relate to others in pursuit of professional and monetary goals. It's that part of us that puts aside the child and competes as an adult. It is called work, but it shouldn't be. For it is where we utilize our talents in a mature, competitive, commercial context.

While every job has certain things about it that we dislike, by and large our work should be as great a source of pleasure to us as is our existence in any other mini-environment. But, as always, it is not so much the challenges we face at work that will determine the extent to which we enjoy ourselves there, as it is the manner in which we choose to meet those challenges, that will be the controlling factor. The difference, after all, between a job and a career is largely attitudinal. A job is something we work at. A career is a job with a future. A career is something we live.

The employee who says, "I'd be a whole lot more enthusiastic if I just got a raise," misses the whole point. You don't get your raise first and build your enthusiasm second. As Calvin learned through the notice in his pay envelope: your raise will become effective when you do.

At work, three factors profoundly affect the extent to which we reach our full potential. They are: our ability to deal with others, the manner in which we manage and organize our immediate work area, and the extent to which we *self-actualize* on the job.

Dealing With Others:
A Corny Concept That Works

Cavett Robert brings this message to more than 200 audiences per year: "Above all else," he says simply, "we are in the *people* business."

"Only 15 percent of our success at work," he says, "is attributable to our product or technical knowledge, while 85 percent of our success at work is attributable to our people knowledge. The company that believes it is in the transportation business, or the widget business, or the insurance business, or the calculator business, or the real estate business, is doomed to failure, for we are all in the same business: the business of solving people's problems."

It is a corny concept that works. Indeed, it works incredibly well. For the vast majority of successful people, the Work Mini-Environment is not the cut-throat, win-at-all costs arena that it is so frequently characterized as being. Instead, it is nothing more than a series of opportunities to help other people and to make a profit in the process.

Solving other people's problems has always been, and will probably always continue to be, the one approach that consistently works above all others. "Help the other guy get what he wants, and you'll get what you want," says the language of Positive authors — the Dudley-Do-Rights. It is not necessary that we be naive or gullible, or that we serve as the softest touch on the block for every client or customer who doesn't wish to pay his bills. There is no requirement that we operate at a loss. Indeed, very few clients or customers will ever resent our profits, as long as those profits are derived in the process of solving *their* problems.

That Type Of Person

It boils down to this: we must be the type of person with whom others wish to deal.

Too many of us labor under the misconception that we are paid for what we *know*, when, in fact, we are paid for what we *do*. People don't care how much we know until they know how much we care.

Lawyers, generally, are classic examples of a misplaced emphasis upon "expertise." In a recent survey, lawyers were asked to identify what they thought clients considered to be the most important factors in the setting of fees. The majority of lawyers said that the results they obtained for their clients were most relevant in setting fees. Yet, when a cross-section of clients were asked to list what they felt were the most relevant factors in fee-setting, only 6 percent of them listed results! On the other hand, 47 percent of clients listed the attorneys' *efforts* as being the most important factors in the setting of fees.

Further studies have indicated that lawyers who tend to be rehired by their clients are friendly, prompt and business-like, courteous, are not condescending, and keep the client informed. Those attorneys who were not rehired are impersonal, bored or indifferent, rude or brusque, maintain a superior attitude toward their clients, and fail to inform them of progress on their case. While results obtained by a lawyer are not totally irrelevant in building client confidence, according to the clients themselves, results were a relatively small factor when compared to the more important elements of friendliness, courteousness and caring.

While lawyers may offer the most extreme example, they are by no means alone in their overemphasis upon expertise and results. Every successful business professional knows the importance of listening, of expressing a sincere interest in what the client, customer, or prospect has to say. What a potential client searches for is not someone to *sell* him something, but someone to *help* him with something. Whether or not a particular individual possesses slightly more or less technical knowledge than another becomes almost irrelevant in the face of a warm, caring and courteous attitude toward others. Once a client or prospect knows that we care about him, he will also, by implication, know that, should he ask us a technical question we can't answer, we will *care* enough to find out the answer.

In the last analysis, being the type of person with whom others wish to deal is many times more important than being a veritable warehouse of stored technical information.

Incorporating The Other Mini-Environments

There was a time when the prevailing theory of personnel management was that each employee was capable of checking his personal problems at the door before he came to work. We know better today.

We know that our performance at work will be profoundly affected by our dealings in the other mini-environments of our lives. Yet, while we recognize that the other mini-environments may frequently *negatively* affect our performance at work, we very rarely take affirmative action to see to it that, when possible, they *positively* affect our work performance.

Some of us, for example, consider it unfashionable, or unprofessional, to partake in recreation during our lunch hour. Rather than racing down to the club and squeezing in a quick game of handball and a shower, we find it more appropriate to sit almost motionless, eating a heavy lunch in a dimly lit restaurant. Similarly, perhaps because we feel their presence might be unprofessional, many of us blush at the idea of involving our families more thoroughly at work. Indeed, there may already be enough confusion in your office without toddlers underfoot. But programs at work that involve the families of employees are enormously important. The opportunity for spouses to meet each other, for children to make friends, and for fellow workers to visit on an informal basis at company social events, or at company-supported civic projects, cannot be underestimated in their importance to the total well-being of the organization.

Most of us enjoy dealing with a well-rounded individual. By permitting the more positive aspects of our other three mini-environments to shine through into our Work Mini-Environment, we can demonstrate that we are, in fact, the type of complete person with whom others most like to deal.

Your Level Of Enthusiasm

We are faced with the constant challenge of pulling the rest of the world up to our level of enthusiasm, rather than permitting it to pull us down to its level of complacency.

Generally, we do not sell our products, services or ideas. We sell our depth of commitment to those products, services or ideas. If others can perceive that we are genuinely enthusiastic about what we do, they will trust us as being deeply and legitimately committed to our cause, whatever it may be. Long after the world forgets the strength of our logic, it will remember the depth of our commitment to that logic.

Our level of enthusiasm is probably the most fundamentally important element we bring with us each day to work. Nothing shows more quickly than a deflated level of enthusiasm. What those around us need to see, in order to be lifted to our level of excitement, is pretty much what an audience needs to see in a speaker before he ever utters a word. There should be an aura of commitment to what is about to be said or done — an honest display of sincere enthusiasm regarding what is to come. Others can perceive quickly whether we're bogged down mentally, or whether we're on top of things and thoroughly committed to the task at hand.

In our dealings with others, that special level of enthusiasm must show through. It must manifest itself in our every thought and deed.

Managing Your Work Area

The second factor affecting our success at work is the extent to which we retain control over our work area. Many of us labor under the misconception that the messier a desk is, the more important its occupant must be. It's the old "I must be important; look how busy I am" syndrome.

Yet, studies have indicated that just the opposite is generally true. The more cluttered an individual's desk, the less income is he likely to earn. Most major executives, for example, maintain a clutter-free desk, not because they have nothing to do, but because they know they can concentrate on only one thing at a time, anyway. By keeping extraneous papers outside the periphery of their vision, they are better able to concentrate on the task at hand.

Your work area is the point at which you generate your income. Its every detail should serve to support your efforts.

The Clutter Catastrophe

We've all walked into offices that have been literally overrun by manila folders. Somewhere behind and amongst them all sits a harried executive, usually middle or lower-middle level. He invites you to sit down. You must remove a stack of folders from a chair in order to do so.

"Where should I put these?" you ask.

"Oh, anywhere," he says.

Then you begin to wonder. "Here I am," you think, "to seek this individual's advice or help. As soon as I leave this office, I'm going to become one of these manila folders. He's not going to be able to find me or my problem — much less a solution to it."

We've all fallen victim to the clutter catastrophe from time to time. It is something we must constantly guard against. Paper tends to flow at us in bunches, and it tends to accumulate in bunches on our desk.

As a general rule, it is imperative that we keep all unnecessary paper out of our line of vision while we work. A small shelf or desk behind us is very helpful in keeping unfinished projects out of view. It is not that we want to forget the projects represented by the papers that we place behind us. It is simply that we want to concentrate upon one project at a time, so that we can effectively accomplish each.

Similarly, desk drawers frequently become depositories for unused, or unusable items. In my own desk drawer, for example, I have just this moment discovered, among other things, the following items: an unused calendar from two years ago, keys from an apartment that I used to live in a year and a half ago, business cards from when I used to practice law in a prior life, three dried-out magic markers, the keys to a 1973 Comet that I sold years ago, the operating instructions to my camera, a canceled bank book, a plastic coaster with a picture of a man holding a martini and pinching a woman, one unused tube of grape-flavored lip balm, an empty plastic aspirin bottle, and a half unwrapped throat lozenge.

And that's just the first drawer. It is not surprising, then, that we find so many objects within our immediate work area that distract us.

Another malady closely related to the clutter catastrophe is that we tend to place our office utensils in the wrong spots. If you are right-handed, for example, your phone should sit on your left side so that you can answer with your left hand and take notes with your right. Many of us nearly hang ourselves every time we answer the phone, simply because it is on the wrong side of our bodies. Also, if we are right-handed, our calculator and dictating equipment (if we use them) should likely be on our right-hand side.

Family portraits are always appropriate (I knew a young, single, divorce-lawyer who borrowed someone else's portrait of wife and child, just to keep out of trouble with his clients). But one or two pictures are generally plenty to let the rest of the world know where we're coming from with respect to our Home Mini-Environment. There is no need to turn our desks into family archives, as so many of us tend to do. The overly photo-laden desk is especially common among older women who have gone back into business to ward off retirement. Their desk tops often support the photos of eight to twelve darling grandchildren, as well as a number of sons and daughters. Whenever I see such a desk, I'm afraid to go near it, or near the owner, for fear that they'll have a cute little story to tell me about each of the photos displayed.

A final note: people who steal tape, paper clips, and staplers from other desks should be summarily executed. If your company is so cheap that you must constantly borrow one another's desk equipment, then either (A) find another company, or (B) invest in a few of the items yourself, mark your name on them, and cut off the hands (at the elbows) of anyone who touches them.

Handling Paper Once

The rule is simple to state, but difficult to apply: the best way to avoid the clutter catastrophe is to handle each piece of paper only once. This requires, however, that you be prepared to work upon the project that the paper represents as it crosses your desk.

Many of us plan our whole morning around the arrival of the mail. We just can't wait to see what has arrived. We tear everything open, give it a glance, and then throw it into a pile for future action. The result is that we wind up handling each piece of paper — and frequently the envelopes they came in, too — at least twice. If you are in a position to do so, have your mail screened before it reaches your desk. Have your secretary discard all junk mail and have her place items of intermediate importance in a separate file for your perusal at a later time. Then have her deliver to you the top-priority items already opened with whatever papers, forms, or files that might be involved in your reaction to them already attached. Whenever possible, reach for each piece of paper only once. React appropriately to whatever project the paper represents. Then remove it (or have it removed) from your work area.

Frequently a piece of paper represents a project that cannot be completed in one handling. A separate file, or bin, for incomplete projects is appropriate, so long as each time you pick the paper up, you take as much action as you can on it at the time.

Unfortunately, our tendency to handle paper more than once is often supported by an inadequate filing system. Most healthy, growing businesses are plagued by inadequate filing systems, simply because their systems cannot keep up with their growth. As we expand in many different directions and begin accumulating correspondence and notes on new ideas and projects, we frequently find ourselves with no file in which to put them. But our entire filing system does not have to be reorganized every time our business takes a slightly different direction. We need only have a *new projects* cabinet, wherein we can place some of the more recently established files. Then, once each half year or so, we can re-work the filing system and incorporate the new files into it. In the meantime, we will have a specific and organized location for all the new material we accumulate.

File 22

We've all heard of File 13. It is the wastepaper basket, the circular file. It is where the junk mail winds up, as well as every other disposable, used up item in the office.

I propose that you also begin a *File 22*. Use one of your desk drawers, preferably the least convenient to get to. By checking some of your lower desk drawers, you will probably find, as I have, that they contain next to nothing of immediate importance to the business. Clean one out and use it as the place where you will put all papers representing low priority projects.

In his book, *How to Get Control of Your Time and Your Life,* Allen Lakein calls this the *C Drawer*. His recommendation is that you place all *C* (as opposed to *A* and *B*) activities in the *C Drawer*. Using our terminology, it is where we should place all papers relating to our lone star activities. Throw them in the drawer and let them sit. A low priority activity will very rarely become a high priority activity without some advance warning. In the meantime, you have it placed out of the way where it can't distract you. Periodically, perhaps once a month, review the papers in your *File 22*. You'll be amazed to discover that the vast majority of them have solved themselves. They may then be thrown away and forgotten. By placing papers in *File 22*, you are assuming that you will take care of them *by not taking care of them*. It's a file with a Catch-22 philosophy.

Most of us like to work on lone star activities because they are nice time-fillers. Having just spent an entire section emphasizing the importance of a clean work area, let me retreat slightly by stating that our need for order should not serve as an excuse to keep us from working on more substantive projects. Many is the time, for example, that we have all cleaned our desks with the reasoning that, "Once I get this area squared away, I can really concentrate on that big project." Of course, it never seems to quite work that way. There is always an abundance of lone star activities to be done.

Rather than freeing us to concentrate on our more important activities, our emphasis upon such low grade activities tends to tie us down. It creates the sensation of progress without the reality. Better that we should simply file those lone star projects away. Then, from time to time when we need a mental break, when we need to work upon something that is not too demanding, we can pull a project out of our *File 22*. In this respect, lone star activities can be slightly therapeutic. Such activities tend to have clearly identifiable beginnings, middles, and ends. They are simple to perform. Consequently, when we find ourselves knee deep in the details of that overwhelming three-star activity, and we need a break from it, we can rely upon our *File 22* to provide us with a suitable, temporary diversion.

Self-Actualization On The Job

By far the most challenging obstacles we face at work are the limitations we place upon ourselves.

Throughout this book we have emphasized the cause of these limitations: at some level we abdicate responsibility and permit others to determine the extent to which we will utilize our full potential. Too often, rather than being self-actualizing, we are, in fact, self-destructive. We *assume* that there is a pecking order in the company, and therefore we can't get promoted ahead of the next guy. We *assume* that a limitation in our education will automatically prevent our receiving a higher salary. We *assume* that our lack of experience will prevent us from closing a particular sale. We *assume* that despite the theories and the books and the protestations of so many to the contrary, there is a certain level of success at work beyond which we cannot climb.

Perhaps it is the economy we blame, or the boss, or our fellow workers, or the drive back and forth to work each day, or the weather, or Lord knows how many other dozens of things. Regardless, we always seem to find a method, sure enough, to rationalize away our lack of success at work. But in the last analysis, we know that we must be self-starting. It has been said, with much truth, that if you really want to succeed, you should look around, find out what everyone else is doing — and do precisely the opposite. Yet, ironically, we continue to look to others for a lead, a hint, a clue, as to what initiatives and directions we should be taking. But it is, as always, that guy in the mirror to whom we must look.

We can enhance our ability to self-start by recognizing three things: first, that our *competition* is an unmixed blessing; second, that *go-givers* generally succeed; and third, that it is our right—and responsibility—to choose extraordinary productivity and success at work.

Special Obstacles: Competition

In the long run, the only person against whom we really compete is the guy in the mirror.

Externally, there are two species of "competitors" around us. First, there is the competition from across the street, or across town — that other company that seems to keep constantly cutting into our business. Many of us waste a lot of energy over-worrying about what that competition is going to do next. Rather than positively and constructively concentrating upon how we will improve our own product, service or idea, how we will better meet the needs of our clients or customers, or how we will better help solve their problems, we worry instead about how we will react to the competition's next move. Our attitude becomes defensive, reactionary. We begin competing, not against our own abilities, but against what we *think* the competition *might* do next.

The second species of external "competition" is that fellow down the hall — the co-worker who is vying for that special promotion, or that additional income that you also seek. We frequently perceive that person as a threat to our success, rather than as a natural catalyst who will help propel us toward the realization of our fullest potential. We worry about what *he's* going to do, or say, next. We weigh our decisions at work against how they will enhance our perceived competitive position relative to that person.

But we don't really compete against either the person down the hall or the company across town. There is no denying that they may help to set some of the social parameters in which we operate. They might be players upon our stage, as Shakespeare might have said. But in this play, *we* write our own lines, and in the last analysis it will not matter much how well we did relative to others. All that will matter is the extent to which we utilized our own potential.

By concentrating solely upon doing just that, our efforts will likely become apparent to those with whom we work. We will be the type of person with whom others wish to deal, intent upon self-growth and oblivious to the petty banalities of inter- and intra-office politics; and, as a result, we will likely—quite auto-matically—obtain the status, prestige and income to which we aspire.

Go-Getters, Go-Givers, And Already-Gotters

We won't be able to sustain a self-actualizing approach if we enter each day as a *go-getter*. The trouble with being a go-getter, as the name implies, is that he is constantly trying *to get* — to take — something from another.

The bright, ambitious young man who is described by others as "a real go-getter" may at first regard that term as a compliment. But later he may discover that those who use it most frequently to describe him seem least inclined to deal with him. The problem is that others may see him as an individual who has earnestly turned his talents into getting what he wants (which in and of itself is not evil), without a corresponding emphasis upon giving others what *they* want.

Being just a go-getter can be frustrating. The people with whom you wish to do business may know you are loaded with talent, but they may refuse to deal with you on a regular basis because they sense, perhaps without knowing consciously, that you are not gen-uinely channeling your efforts to their benefit.

The kind of person with whom others most wish to deal is, of course, a *go-giver*. He is the individual who, rather than turning his talent and enthusiasm toward getting for himself, turns toward giving to others. A go-getter might view a prospect and ask, "How may I profit from him?" A go-giver will view the same prospect and ask, "How might I help him — profitably?" The pro-spect will sense the difference. People literally stand in line to do business with a go-giver. They do so not because they believe they may take advantage of him, but simply because they know that his emphasis will be, first and foremost, upon serving them.

It is much easier to sustain our self-actualizing behavior as a go-giver than as any other classification of business professional. For the go-giver is constantly reinforced by the positive and encouraging expectations of others.

Yet a word of warning is in order to those go-givers who presume that they can rest on their laurels — those individuals who have achieved some measure of success and status within their industry, but who now believe that they can sit back and cease to give because they have accumulated what they perceive to be enough *position power* to protect their status indefinitely. These are the *already-gotters*. These are the individuals who at one time performed well on the firing line, but who, having accumulated a few past victories, now content themselves with being uninvolved with those around them. They are a sad breed, the already-gotters, because they tend, at a most critical period of their lives, to sit upon potential which, if properly used, could be all the more valuable since it is tempered by wisdom and experience.

Self-actualization requires that we become a go-giver and stay a go-giver until the day they re-crate us and ship us back to The Manufacturer.

The Right To Choose

Finally, self-actualization requires that we always remember that we each clearly possess the most important right — the ultimate freedom: the right to choose.

It is totally within our domain and power to choose either success or failure. We may choose mediocrity or excellence. We may choose to adopt a reaction mentality and be over-concerned with external "competitors", or we may devote ourselves fully to reaching our own potential — and let the positive results take care of themselves.

We can choose to be a taker — a getter — and not a giver. In the short run, that approach might be profitable. But in the long run it is self-defeating, for we will be quickly recognized as being that type of person with whom others do not wish to deal.

Our right to choose stems from the fundamental responsibility that we have to accept responsibility for — and exert control over — our existence in all of our mini-environments. Nowhere is that responsibility more clearly established than in our Work Mini-Environment.

By applying a few fundamental principles, we can overcome the three major obstacles we face each day at work.

Our success in dealing with others can be greatly enhanced by the corny notion that is so undeniably true: above all else, we are in the *people* business. We must be the type of person with whom others wish to deal — enthusiastic, sincere, and professional. People will not pay us for what we know. They will pay us for what we do.

We must permit the positive aspects of our existence in our other mini-environments to show themselves in our Work Mini-Environment, so that we can present ourselves as positive, well rounded individuals with whom others most like to deal. Our enthusiasm must remain inviolate, protected against the rest of the world's efforts to diminish it.

In managing our work area, we must make a common sense effort to avoid the clutter catastrophe. Find and use a filing system that works. Clean out those desk drawers once a decade, and handle those pieces of paper just once, if possible. Establish your own *File 22* for the collection of non-priority projects, and watch as many of them solve themselves.

Finally, our self-actualization on the job requires that we recognize that guy in the mirror as being the only significant competition we face. It demands that we be a go-giver, constantly seeking ways to help the other fellow get what he wants. In return, as the Dudley-Do-Rights have insisted all along, we will get what we want as well. And we must remember that we have clearly within our power the ability to choose success or failure. The results that we obtain, and the extent to which we overcome the obstacles that we face, are totally up to us.

We must get on target and stay on target by clearly establishing our goals and by insuring that they are written, realistic and affirmatively specific. We must constantly ask ourselves, "What is it that I really want with my life? How can I best reconcile what

I am doing now with what I would otherwise do, if I knew my time on this planet was severely limited? What are my goals — for this month, for this year, for this life?"

We must translate our goals into specific and affirmative conduct. We must not permit ourselves to stop on a dream. Instead, we must utilize basic notions of time management to get the job done. It is, indeed, as simple as A-B-C. A, always make a list of activities for accomplishing your goals. Complete possibility lists on a regular basis and priorize the activities you've listed. B, be sure to schedule your activities into your weeks and your days. Utilize the technique known as horizontal or weekly planning. Use a to-do list on a daily basis — not just to keep track of work-related activities, but also to keep track of all activities relating to the other mini-environments as well. And C, constantly evaluate the most effective use of your time right now. Remember the 80-20 Rule: 80 percent of what we earn is earned by 20 percent of what we do. Beware of the Pal-Enemy Syndrome. Be on guard against those individuals who would burn up your time and your future. And take what simple actions are necessary to help avoid procrastination.

Finally, in overcoming obstacles at work, remember to be the type of person with whom others wish to deal. Remember to keep your work area orderly and well organized, and always remember that you are in charge. *You're* in control. By choosing now to apply these fundamental principles at work, you can — and will — accomplish all that you've ever dreamed of — and more.

Y

XVI

"Y" Me, Lord?

To the extent that money is a measure of the ser-
vices we perform for others, its accumulation is
noble. To the extent that we press our money into
the service of those we love . . . its disbursement
is inspired and divine.

When Calvin awoke, he was, pardon the expression, scared to death.

"This must be it," he thought. "I must have died and gone to heaven."

He looked around. Everything was so vast and white and hazy that it was hard to tell for sure. But it looked like, well, it looked like a big garage.

"Calvin Cautious?" a voice asked from behind him.

Calvin was startled. He spun around. Behind him stood a large, bearded man, wearing white overalls. He was carrying a clipboard.

"Where did you come from?" Calvin asked.

"I work here," the man said.

"But a moment ago you weren't here."

"We travel differently up here," the man said.

"Up here?" Calvin asked. "Where is this place? Where am I? Am I dead? Is this heaven?"

"No, no," said the man. "You're not dead, and this isn't heaven. This is simply a way-station, a check point. You're here for warranty service and to answer some questions on a new survey we're conducting."

"A survey?" Calvin asked.

285

"Yes. It's a new policy. Ever since we sent the Ralph Nader model down, we have to keep closer track of consumer satisfaction. The Manufacturer says we better clean up our act before we get sued."

"Are you . . . are you . . .?" Calvin asked.

"No, I'm not Him. I'm just one of the Engineers. My job is to ask you some tough questions, Calvin."

Calvin kept looking around. "When can I go back?" he asked.

"When you answer the questions."

"Just any answer?" Calvin asked.

"No. You must provide me with the correct answers, Calvin." Suddenly The Engineer had Calvin's full attention. "You see, it's a new policy. We see no sense wasting space down there on equipment that won't be used properly."

"Do . . . do you mean," Calvin stuttered, "that if I can't answer the questions the way you want me to, I'll be dea . . . I'll be dea . . .?" Calvin couldn't quite bring himself to say the word.

"That is correct," The Engineer said. "Your warranty will be revoked, and you will be permanently recalled. Are you ready for your questions, Calvin?"

"'I guess so," Calvin nervously answered.

"Very well, sit down, and we'll begin."

Do You Really Believe You Were Put Here To Fail?

The Engineer examined his clipboard. "Tell me, Calvin, what is your purpose down there?"

"Well, I . . . um . . . you know," Calvin mumbled, "I want to work hard and not hurt anyone, and I want to get along with folks and stay out of trouble."

"But what about your talents, Calvin, your talents?"

"Well, what talents I have—and they're not much—I take good care of. I kind of pace myself, you know."

"No! No! No!" The Engineer shouted. "Your answer is all wrong. Don't you remember the story of the talents?"

"Yes, I think so," said Calvin. "The Manufacturer gave each of three men a different set of talents. To one man He gave five talents. To another man He gave two talents. And to the third He *gave but one talent."*

"That's right," The Engineer said. *"And some years later The Manufacturer checked up on each of those three men. He checked with the man who had five talents, and was pleased to find that he had multiplied his five talents many times by working hard, and by applying each one. He checked with the man to whom He had given two talents, and was equally pleased to see that he had labored hard, used his talents, and multiplied them. But when He checked with the man to whom He had only given one talent, He became very angry. For that man had buried his talent in the name of protecting it. And it was then that The Manufacturer uttered some of the harshest words He was ever to utter. 'Thou wicked and slothfull servant!' He shouted. 'How dare you not use the gifts that I gave you!' Do you get the point of the story, Calvin?"*

"I think so," Calvin said. *"I think so."*

"I don't know what we're going to do with you, Calvin. I just don't know."

Is It Wrong To Be Rich?

The notion has been with us for thousands of years: poverty either produces or proves purity. The notion may be correct, but there is nothing inherent in it that implies that poverty is the only road to salvation, however we personally define the term.

I suspect that the belief that wealth is wrong is more social than scriptural. It is a rationalization imposed upon us by many of those who choose not to earn much wealth. It is a philosophy with which we have all had to live at some level during our lifetimes. Is it inherently wrong to be rich? Of course not. It is no more inherently wrong to acquire material wealth than it is wrong not to acquire wealth if we truly don't desire it. It's what we do with money that matters. It's how we get it that counts.

To the extent that money is a measure of the services we perform for others, its accumulation is noble. To the extent that we press our money into the service of those we love, to provide them with as warm and as comfortable and as secure an existence as possible, its disbursement is inspired and divine.

Do You Have To Go Through Hell
To Get To Heaven?

Each Sunday he sits on a red velvet throne, on a gold stage, in an ornate old theatre in the heart of Harlem.

As he expounds his message to the faithful, the hearts of his listeners are filled with hope, while their wallets are simultaneously emptied. He is "the Reverend Ike." By and large, the members of his congregation consider the personal expense a fair exchange for the hope that he provides.

He is immensely popular with his followers because he hits, time and again, upon a theme with which they all agree. Those who are genuinely poor know, much better than the rest of us ever will, the truth of the statement which, through repetition, the Reverend Ike has made famous: *You don't have to go through hell to get to heaven.*

Incredibly, large portions of the human race still believe that for an individual to experience an eternity of happiness, he must first experience a lifetime of unhappiness. We must suffer, they say, to earn our reward. Yet, how tremendously inconsistent it would be to accept such a philosophy. On the one hand, we find ourselves placed upon this planet, fully equipped to contribute significantly to our own individual success. Yet the psychology of suffering would require us not to use the very tools and talents we were given.

If our being here proves anything, it is that we must accept the challenge of using the tools and talents that we possess. Our purpose is to make our lives as successful and as happy as we possibly can. Rather than being a mantle of suffering, we should view our existence here as a dress rehearsal for the eternity of happiness we deserve.

Isn't Being Here All The Permission You Need?

An old Jesuit saying provides, "It is better to ask forgiveness than permission."

Mediocrity, you will recall, is at all times expected without someone else's permission. But excellence, it frequently seems, requires another's expressed approval. This phenomenon seems to spring from our belief that somehow we are not individually worthy of success, without someone else's expressed permission.

The belief may stem from the conformity which is thrust upon us from childhood. Educators call it the "socialization" process. It is the time it takes for a child to learn to stand quietly in line, to answer his name when it is called alphabetically, to speak only when called upon, and to otherwise conform to the codes and expectations imposed upon him.

But to succeed requires that we step out of line, away from the pack, and march to the sound of our personal distant drummer. So we wait for the voice of some subconscious teacher to excuse us from the room before we begin. Yet that voice will never come — unless it comes from us.

Although being here is all the permission we need to succeed, we still feel unworthy because we see others who seem inherently more deserving of success. Yet no one is *inherently* more deserving of success than another. Others may do more to earn it. They may work harder at it. But no one begins more entitled to it than another. Being here is all the permission we need.

We find ourselves in a world filled with challenges just waiting to be taken on. We find ourselves equipped with the talents necessary to meet those challenges. Does not that combination of challenges, and the abilities to meet them, tell us something about why we're here? Doesn't it confirm, finally, once and for all, that no other voice will be forthcoming, and that our existence alone is all the permission we will ever need to succeed?

Who Will Control Your Life?

The Engineer jotted a few notes on his clipboard. Then he looked at Calvin.

"Calvin," he asked, "who is in charge of your life?"

Calvin knew he had the right answer to this question. "I am!" he said. "I'm in charge of my life."

The Chief Engineer remained expressionless. He made another note on his clipboard. There was a long pause. Calvin grew nervous.

"With, of course, a few exceptions," he finally said. "I mean, it's not my fault the way my parents treated me when I was a kid. You know, one time I came home and I wanted to tell them I had made the football team and gotten an A on a test, and I couldn't get

either of them to listen to me. And I'm not responsible for the fact that my boss is a real bear. He won't allow me to accept much responsibility. Once I proposed a new sales plan, and he assigned a younger man to administer it. Yeah, I'm responsible for my life—but with a few exceptions. I mean, sometimes you just don't get the breaks, you know? Sometimes things just don't come your way. But that's the way the ball bounces. That's the way the cookie crumbles. That's the way the mop flops."

The Engineer jumped to his feet. He threw his clipboard to the floor. "No! No! No!" he shouted. "When will you learn, Calvin? You're hopeless, I say! Hopeless! There are no exceptions. You must control your life, Calvin. You are totally responsible for the results that you obtain. It's you, Calvin, you, not your mother, not your father, not your boss. It's not the breaks, Calvin, that control your life. It's you. Don't ever say, 'That's the way the ball bounces. That's the way the cookie crumbles. That's the way the mop flops.' Don't you understand, Calvin? You must bounce your own ball. Crumble your own cookies. Flop your own mop. It's totally up to you. I don't know what we're going to do with you, Calvin. I just don't know."

Were You Designed To Be Led?

We were not equipped with minds of our own so that we could abdicate control of our destiny to someone else.

It makes no sense to believe that we are in any way designed to be kept under the care and control of another. We were not designed to be led. We were not designed to follow. We were designed to achieve, to strive, to build.

We were never intended to act, for example, as does the pine caterpillar. Place a series of pine caterpillars end-to-end in a circle until the circle is closed, and each will follow the caterpillar in front of it around the circle indefinitely. Place food in the center of the circle, and the caterpillars will continue to follow each other around that food until they die from starvation. The pine caterpillar is an insect without imagination. It lacks the ability to seek any form of independent success on its own. It blindly adheres to a herd instinct, often to its detriment, and even to its demise.

We must control our lives. To do otherwise is to, quite literally, waste them. Papillon, the French prisoner who was condemned to life imprisonment on Devil's Island, was disturbed by a recurring nightmare. Repeatedly, he would dream that he stood before a harsh tribunal.

"You are charged," they would shout, "with a wasted life. How do you plead?"

"Guilty," he would say. "I plead guilty."

Papillon, the prisoner, knew the meaning of waste. For him, waste was to permit his life to be spent under the control of someone else. Yet, we too, each in his own way, are prisoners. We must break through the bars of conformity that we have constructed around ourselves. We must not permit our lives to be spent trudging in circles behind another, who follows another, who follows another, who might ultimately be following us.

We are equipped with the ability to lead our own lives. To do otherwise is, as Papillon might have attested, quite simply a waste.

Do You Prefer Mediocrity?

Too many of us try to right the world's wrongs from the outside-in. Rather than worrying about what is happening in our own back yard, we attempt to reform the entire world, or, at least, portions of it thousands of miles away.

The outside-in approach lends itself to what might be called *official mediocrity*. In the name of alleviating poverty, for example, we do not work on specifically equipping the person who is poor with the tools necessary to compete. Rather, we simply redistribute wealth, generally. It is an outside-in solution. Yet, most of us know at a gut level that the long-term solution to the type of poverty we most often encounter in our industrialized society cannot be found in the text of any book on macro-economics. The solution is micro in nature. It must begin inside the affected individual and work its way out. A Chinese proverb says, "Give a man a fish and you feed him for a day. Teach a man to fish and you feed him for life."

Communism is the clearest example mankind has of official mediocrity. It presumes that if the *system* is made right, the individuals living within it will ultimately benefit. All things, the system dictates, will be evenly shared. But that type of system consistently neglects the inside-out approach so necessary for positively motivating individuals to produce the items that the system needs. Consequently, the only things that are, in fact, evenly distributed by the system are scarcity and misery.

Man, generally, is not equipped for mediocrity. His imagination, for example, is merciful. Generally, we cannot imagine those things that we cannot accomplish. In the classic self-help volume *Think and Grow Rich,* by Napoleon Hill, it is written, "Whatever the mind of man can conceive and believe, he can achieve." We would not be equipped with the ability to imagine future accomplishment and conditions if we were not correspondingly equipped with the ability to turn those imaginings into reality.

But mediocrity may look comfortable. We all know those who have settled into a routine job at a routine salary, and who live in a routine home, in a routine neighborhood. They seem routinely comfortable and happy, at least from the outside. But on the inside they must contend daily with the rationalizations they have accepted, and the non-use of the abilities that they possess. The tension thus created is anything but comfortable.

As the great cartoon philosopher Ziggy has said: "Security is knowing what tomorrow will bring. Boredom is knowing what the day after tomorrow will bring."

Do You Accept Responsibility For You?

EST (Erhard Seminar Training) has survived attempts by many to characterize it as irresponsible, faddish, and as a typically Californian self-help gimmick.

The popularity of EST stems in part from the discipline it imposes upon the participants. Smoking is not permitted. Discussions between participants are not permitted. Restroom breaks are infrequent. Seating accommodations are spartan. Yet, most of the participants agree that the discipline (or, as it is called in EST, "the agreements") imposed upon them is necessary, for it helps each participant avoid the tendency to escape from himself.

When the dialogue becomes too real, or too hard-hitting, and when the participant feels that little man inside trying to sneak out, the tendency is natural to reach for a cigarette, to talk to another person, to get up and walk around, or to go to the restroom—anything to divert attention from that little man inside.

But EST, as well as many other responsible self-help philos-ophies, strips these diversions away from an individual and forces him to confront his innermost self directly and unabashed-ly. In short, EST forces participants to accept responsibility for themselves.

We frequently use diversion in our lives as a tool to avoid direct confrontation with our innermost feelings, and to avoid accepting total responsibility for who we are and what we do. Our approach is somewhat as we described above—outside-in. Instead of working on what is going on inside us, we try to rearrange things around us.

A familiar phenomenon among couples seeking divorce, for ex-ample, is that they will often have recently worked together at remodeling their home. They might even have recently added a child to the family. This is not to intimate that individuals who remodel their homes and have children are prime candidates for divorce. It is simply to say that in many instances such activities are utilized as a diversion by unhappy couples to keep them from confronting the essence of their problems.

It is always more convenient to assume the answer lies elsewhere, with others. But, of course, it does not. There is an old fable about the wise river barge captain who operated a ferry between two towns. Occasionally, an individual on one side would come to him and ask, "How are the people in the other town? I am thinking of moving there."

The captain, in his wisdom, would always ask, "How do you find the people in the town where you live now?" If the person would respond by saying that they were warm and kind and friendly, then the captain, in turn, would say that the people in the other town were warm and kind and friendly. But if the person would respond by saying that they were cruel and cold and un-friendly, then the captain would describe the people of the other town as being the same. The fable, of course, emphasizes that, while we're not responsible for every action and deed of another, we are responsible for how we react to others and, for that mat-ter, for how we react to ourselves.

The responsibility for us is ours.

Will You Prevent Your Own Success?

The Engineer had grown impatient. He tapped his pen against his clipboard and stared at Calvin.

"What are you now, Calvin," he asked, "and what will you become?"

Calvin shuddered at the question. How could he know what he should say? His very life on earth hung in the balance. "Humility," he thought. "I must be humble."

"I'm just a working stiff," Calvin said. "I'm just an average guy. I work hard, but of course I only have so much to work with. I try as best I can to get along with those around me. But I'm, you know, just me."

Again, The Engineer jumped from his chair. He began thrashing the air with his clipboard.

"No! No! No! A thousand times no!" he shouted. "Humility does not require mediocrity. By insisting that you are just this, or just that, or that you will never amount to much, in the name of humility you talk yourself down to a state of non-accomplishment. You program yourself for mediocrity. Humility requires no such sacrifice! It requires no such waste of life. Humility requires only that no matter what you do, you always recognize that it might have been done better. That you remain aware that your life on earth is temporary, and that those who occupy the planet with you have as much a right to be here as you do. I'm afraid there's very little hope, Calvin. This may be the end . . ."

Do You Feel That You Deserve Success?

Secretly, you may know you're a klutz.

"I'm the guy who can't even remember his car keys and wallet," you say. "I'm a stumble-bum, a schlock. My father said I was clumsy. My mother said I was accident-prone. My wife just laughs and says I'm cute. How can I deserve success?"

But how can you not deserve success? Your success is not measured relative to what others say or do or accomplish. It is merely the extent to which you utilize the potential that you possess. If part of your Personal Potential Package includes a tendency to be forgetful or clumsy, or whatever, that element makes you no less deserving of success. It is merely part of the total you. It is a characteristic that must, in its own way, be made to work for you when at all possible.

But others, you think, are obviously smarter, or younger, or harder working, or more educated, or better looking. "They deserve success more than I do," you think. But the characteristics of others remain irrelevant to your success. While the tendency to compare ourselves to others may be overwhelming, it is not against them we compete.

It is only our tendency not to utilize all the potential we possess against which we must constantly fight. Success is not something that must be deserved or earned. It is more an inherent right—an inherent responsiblity. The only qualification for success is that you *be you*, and that you utilize whatever combination of talent you possess to the fullest extent possible.

Do you deserve success? Of course. You deserve no less.

Will You Wait For The World To Come To You?

We all have a natural tendency to daydream. Perhaps among the most common of such dreams is the fantasy that in some way, and at some time, the world will beat a path to our door.

But the next time you catch yourself daydreaming about someone or something coming *to you*, stop yourself and resolve to do whatever is necessary to go to him or it. If, indeed, the world ever does beat a path to your door, it will do so only after it first discovers who you are and where you can be reached. You must supply the world with this information. You must let it know that you are here, that you are eager to do business, and that you offer to the world something of value to it.

We must resist our tendency to believe that the world will come to us, that things will happen to us. We must go to it. We must happen to things. There is nothing as sad as the man who spends his entire life waiting for his ship to come in, when he never sent one out. Don't spend your life waiting for that "big break." Don't rely upon luck. Make your own.

Your talent may be enormous. Your potential may be great. But talent and potential unannounced to the rest of the world is wasted.

Will You Act Now?

It is always easier to act tomorrow.

The world is filled with tomorrow people: those who will tell us in no uncertain terms that they're going to get started tomorrow, and tomorrow, and tomorrow.

The fact is, no matter what we do, where we do it, or when we start, we'll never do it perfectly. There will never be just that right combination of circumstances that will make each and every major undertaking of our lives come off without a hitch.

Before an author writes a book worth reading, he usually writes several that aren't. Before a speaker learns to bring audiences to their feet, he usually makes a complete jerk out of himself more than once. Before a salesman closes that big sale that puts him on top of the world for weeks, months, or even years, he suffers dozens of disappointments, rejections and refusals.

It will never be done perfectly no matter what it is, who you are, or what you're doing. All that we can ever do is our best, imperfect though it may be. But it is better to attempt to reach a goal and to reach an imperfect result than not to attempt at all. As has been said many times: *I would rather try to succeed and fail than try to do nothing and succeed.*

As we act now to reach our full potential, we must not permit ourselves to be deterred by the critics around us. There will always be that percentage of the population that takes pleasure, indeed delight, in pointing out to the rest of us the imperfection of what we do. Yet we need only remember that we are, by nature, imperfect. We claim to be nothing more. As such, the results that we obtain are bound to be imperfect as well. But most results, imperfect though they may be, are better than no results at all.

There are few who have the right to criticize. Only those who stand by our side on the firing line, and who suffer the same challenges as we do, possess the right; only those who, as Theodore Roosevelt said, are with us in the arena, with soiled hands and sweaty brows and a sense of purpose and daring and dedication, may critique us.

For now is the only time that we have. It is our only negotiable currency. Yesterday is a canceled check. Tomorrow is a promissory note. It is only today that we may spend in the noble effort of using all the gifts that God gave us.

"If none of this is sinking in, Calvin," The Engineer was saying, "then I'm afraid we'll . . .."

"But wait!" Calvin said. "But wait!"

Calvin was not looking at The Engineer. He was staring intensely into the hazy distance.

"I think I see," he said. "I think I see. The fact is I must have been put on earth to succeed. I don't have to apologize to anyone for being a success, or for trying to succeed, since I have an obligation, a responsibility, to use my abilities to the fullest. I can see, too, that wealth, honestly earned and well spent, is inherently good, not evil. I don't have to suffer now to prove my right to eternal happiness. If anything, I should use my experience on earth to practice being happy, to let my soul rejoice at the thrill and exaltation of life.

"Being here is all the permission I need to succeed! I must control my life, for I wasn't designed to be led. Not at all. I prefer excellence to mediocrity, and I accept total responsibility for me. I won't prevent my own success. I won't. I deserve success, for all success requires is that I am here, and that I use my talents to the fullest. I will bring my message and my talents to the world, and not wait for the world to come to me. And I'll act now, no matter how convenient waiting may seem, no matter how imperfect might be the results I obtain."

Tears welled in The Engineer's eyes. A smile creased his face.

"Yes, of course," he said. "Of course, Calvin. There is hope for you yet! You must return to the world from which you came, to make constructive use of the equipment with which you are blessed. Take with you all the love and energy and talent and hope that you have, and share it. Share it with all whom you meet, until it seems that you have no more to give. And when it seems that you have exhausted your supply of all the gifts you have been given, I promise there will always be more and more and more in reserve.

"For you are infinite, Calvin. Your potential extends beyond your wildest imaginings. And The Manufacturer wants you to know that the only limitations you will ever face will be those you place upon yourself."

XVII

To Build A Better You:
What To Do Now
To Get Started

*. . . by fine-tuning our existence in each of our
mini-environments, we may geometrically accelerate our rate of success.*

We mentioned in Chapter I that if advice is only as good as
that portion of it that can be used, then the vast majority of self-
help advice available today is worthless, because it has not been
reduced to manageable units.

Having devoted this entire book to a discussion of success
techniques in our four mini-environments, it seems entirely appropriate that we should spend this second-to-last chapter
reviewing the ideas that were discussed. In this way, we may insure that the advice contained herein has been reduced to the
manageable units so necessary for its application in our lives.

Throughout, we have focused upon those actions that we can
take *now* to increase our ratings in each of our four mini-
environments. Our assumption has been that by *fine-tuning* our
existence in each of our mini-environments, we may geometrically
accelerate our rate of success.

Let's take one last look at the Success Environment Formula to
perfect our understanding of how it works. By doing so, we can
insure that we will always have a useful context in which we may

place the self-help advice we receive, regardless of the language—Positive, Negative or Academic—in which it is written. Thereafter, we will review the principles and recommended actions we touched upon, relative to each mini-environment.

The Success Environment Formula

Please remember: our formula is a tool, a conceptual model, and nothing more. It is a handy method by which we can measure the extent to which we, as individuals, are utilizing our full potential. Using the formula, we may determine, first, the potential that we possess, and second, the extent to which we are utilizing that potential.

When working the formula, we do not compare our capabilities to those of another. Instead, we measure only the extent to which we are utilizing the capabilities we personally possess. Our goal in increasing our Success Environment Formula score is to burst through the Mediocrity Barrier—the resentment that others may feel toward us as we strive for, and actually achieve, our goals.

The equation is designed to be used and reused many times. A low score now does not indicate that you are now, always have been, and always will be, a failure. It means simply that you currently believe you have failed to utilize even an average amount of the abilities that you possess.

How It Works

The Success Environment Formula involves simple multiplication.

The formula is: $SE = (I \times O \times H \times W)Y$.

On the left side of the equation, SE represents our total Success Environment.

I, O, H, and W represent our Inside, Outside, Home and Work mini-environments, respectively.

Y equals the average extent to which we control our conduct in each of our four mini-environments.

As you may remember from the more detailed discussion contained in Chapter III, our first step in working the equation is to assign a value of from one to three to each of the four mini-environments (I, O, H, and W) on the right-hand side of the equation.

A rating of three in any mini-environment indicates that we find our existence there to be totally acceptable, with no substantial room for improvement. A rating of two in any mini-environment indicates that we find our existence there to be moderately acceptable, with moderate room for improvement. Finally, a rating of one in any mini-environment indicates that we find our existence there to be totally unacceptable, with substantial improvement needed.

I recommend that you use decimals to depict as exactly as possible the extent to which you are satisfied with your existence in each mini-environment. After we assign a value of no less than one, nor more than three, to each mini-environment, we then multiply them by each other. This gives us our Mini-Environment Product (that's the total number within the parentheses on the right-hand side of the equation.)

You may conduct the math and determine your Mini-Environment Product by reviewing the definitions, and conducting the exercises below.

The Success Environment Formula is:

$$SE = (I \times O \times H \times W)Y$$

SE = *Success Environment*—the total picture

I, O, H, and W are the four mini-environments that comprise our total Success Environment.

I = Inside: Our minds. The way we think. A function of our attitudes, emotions and logic.

O = Outside: Our bodies. The manner in which we care for and adorn ourselves. A function of health, grooming and attire.

H = Home: Our domestic existence. The extent to which we control the way outside pressures permeate our inner domestic sanctum.

W = Work: Where we pursue our livelihood. The efficiency with which we conduct ourselves, and the manner in which we relate to others while in pursuit of monetary and professional goals.

Evaluate I, O, H, and W as follows (Do not assign a value of more than 3.0, nor less than 1.0. Use decimals if desired.):

3 = Totally acceptable environment. No substantial room for improvement.

2 = Moderately acceptable environment. Moderate room for improvement.

1 = Totally unacceptable environment. Substantial improvement needed.

A. The current rating I give to my Inside (I) Mini-Envronment is: _____

B. The current rating I give to my Outside (O) Mini-Environment is: _____

C. The current rating I give to my Home (H) Mini-Environment is: _____

D. The current rating I give to my Work (W) Mini-Environment is: _____

Therefore, I may thus far express my Success Environment Formula as follows:

$$SE = (\_ \times \_ \times \_ \times \_)Y$$

Therefore:

$$SE = (_____)Y$$

Next, we must fix a value for Y. It is the average extent to which we control our conduct in each of our four mini-environments.

Remember, we are attempting to find an *Average Y Factor*. First, we will fix a Y-Rating for each mini-environment. Then we will add the ratings together and divide their total by the number of mini-environments (4) to obtain the Average Y Factor that we will utilize in the equation. Remember to utilize decimals whenever possible to obtain as exact an appraisal of the extent to which you control your conduct in each mini-environment as possible.

You may determine the value of Y by reviewing the definitions, and conducting the exercises below:

Y(the *Y Factor*) is the average extent to which we control our conduct in each of our mini-environments.

To determine the value of Y:

Enter either a 1, 2, or 3 opposite each mini-environment to express the extent to which you control your conduct in each mini-environment. (Use decimals if desired, but do not fix a value of less than 1.0, or more than 3.0.)

3 = I am totally in control of this environment, permitting others to substantially affect my behavior only upon my deliberate and express approval.

2 = I usually control this environment, but occasionally permit others to control my behavior without my deliberate and express approval.

1 = I do not control this environment, and always permit others to control my behavior without my deliberate and express approval.

A. The current Y-Rating I give to my Inside (I) Mini-Environment is: _____

B. The current Y-Rating I give to my Outside (O) Mini-Environment is: _____

C. The current Y-Rating I give to my Home (H) Mini-Environment is: _____

D. The current Y-Rating I give to my Work (W) Mini-Environment is: _____

TOTAL (The total of the figures in columns A, B, C, and D is): _____

Find your Average Y Factor by dividing the *Total* by four.

$$\frac{\rule{3cm}{0.4pt}}{\text{(TOTAL)}} \div 4 = Y$$

My Average Y Factor equals: _____.

Finally, we may determine our Success Environment Score by multiplying our Average Y Factor by our Mini-Environment Product. Complete the formula by performing the following exercises:

$$SE = (\rule{3cm}{0.4pt})\rule{2cm}{0.4pt}$$

Therefore:

$$SE = \rule{3cm}{0.4pt}$$

What The Scores Mean

Even if we used only whole numbers, the Success Environment Formula could produce 92 possible results. Nevertheless, these results can be lumped into three categories, called *Modes*. As our score within each mini-environment, or our Y-Rating, increases even slightly, the total result, or our Success Environment (SE) Score, increases geometrically. This result occurs because each of the four mini-environments positively or negatively reinforces the others. The highest, average, and lowest possible scores attainable with the Success Environment Formula are as follows:

A. Highest possible Success Environment (SE) = 243

B. Average Success Environment (SE) = 32

C. Lowest possible Success Environment (SE) = 1

The lowest possible mode extends mathematically from one through three. It is called the *Failure Mode*. The median mode extends mathematically from four through 48. It is called the *Mediocrity Mode*. Finally, the highest possible mode extends mathematically from 49 through 243. It is called the *Success Mode*. Each of the three modes can be divided into three levels. These levels are called *Levels of Potential*. There are nine levels of potential. Number 1 is the lowest level of potential. Number 243 is the highest level of potential.

Modes and Levels of Potential break down as depicted (Figure 3-2) on page 59. Remember: Most of us wallow in the Mediocrity Mode. We border on failure. The irony of this status is that, with slight additional effort, we can geometrically accelerate our rate of success.

Generally speaking, the extent to which we are satisfied with each of our four mini-environments will not change substantially until we change our Average Y Factor by personally seizing control of—and responsibility for—our conduct in each of the four mini-environments. This requires a critical evaluation of our Average Y Factor, and immediate efforts to seize control.

The Success Environment Monthly Progress Chart

Please examine the Success Environment Monthly Progress Chart (Figure 17-1) at the end of this chapter. Notice that it is very similar to the Success Environment Geometric Progression Chart (Figure 3-3) on page 60.

Whereas the Geometric Progression Chart depicts Levels of Potential along each vertical line, the Monthly Progress Chart depicts *months* along each vertical line. It gives us an opportunity to plot our progress on a monthly basis over a one-year period.

At the beginning of each month, work your Success Environment Formula. Then plot your score on the appropriate line in your Monthly Progress Chart. Connect the dots, and witness your own geometric rate of progress as you work to increase your rating by applying the principles we've discussed. You might also wish to enter your results on the Geometric Progression Chart (Figure 3-3), so that you can evaluate your progress relative to the various levels of potential listed.

By utilizing the formula and the chart monthly, you will become increasingly (sometimes painfully) aware of the extent to which you are utilizing your potential, and of the specific actions you can take to substantially increase your overall rating.

Inside

Our Inside Mini-Environment is our mind. It is a combination of mental processes comprised of our attitudes, emotions and logic. These are the principles we discussed, and actions we recommended, relative to this mini-environment:

Principle: As children, we are programmed to live up to (or, more specifically, down to) the expectations of others.

Recommended action: We must resist that tendency in our adult years by operating from an *I'm OK* status, thus quieting the little voice inside that says, "You're a big disappointment, Calvin, a big disappointment." Remember: the number of people who attend your funeral will be determined largely by the weather that day. Spend your life trying to please the only guy you know for sure is going to show up.

Principle: The negative expectations of others serve as self-fulfilling prophesies which limit the extent to which we utilize our potential.

Recommended action: Using the system of lists we discussed in Chapter Four, separate the qualities that you perceive in yourself from the qualities others may see in you, and develop your positive characteristics, regardless of what others have come to expect.

Principle: Our past will control our conduct and thoughts, unless we use all the current rational abilities we have to program ourselves in another direction.

Recommended action: Utilize responsible methods of prayer, contemplation and meditation to get in touch with that little guy inside. Utilize affirmations emphasizing your unconditional acceptance of yourself, and totally accept the guy in the mirror as your very best friend.

Principle: Consistency of purpose is the secret of success. Yet, the negative influence of other people (the NIOPs), if unchecked, will profoundly reduce the extent to which we utilize our full potential. Nevertheless, we are equipped with an automatic success mechanism which cannot work unless we relax and let it work.

Recommended action: Establish your goals and understand why their mere establishment, if maintained, will work. Adopt a conscious mental process by which you sustain the vivid image of your goals by consciously emphasizing your current abilities to succeed, rather than your past failures or disappointments. Do your worrying about today, and only today. Do one thing at a time. Keep a pad of paper and a pencil next to your bed, and permit your subconscious success mechanism to work on your problems while the rest of you gets a good night's sleep.

Principle: Our personal computer (our mind) can be programmed for success. Just as it is true that we are, physically, what we eat, so, too, is it true that we are, mentally, what we think. A clearly established goal, therefore, upon which we regularly concentrate, will tend to generate the qualities necessary for its accomplishment. Yet, the rest of the world is constantly programming us with negative information.

Recommended action: Adopt an attitude of Militant Positiveness and positively program your personal computer by utilizing the following techniques:

A. *Positive affirmations.* At least three times each day, repeat out loud affirmations that emphasize your ability to succeed.

B. *Avoid canned negativism.* Be sure to place the news in its proper context, and provide a buffer between it and your thoughts prior to going to bed.

C. *Beware of the two biggest threats.* Identify Wishy-Washy Positives as those individuals who mean well, but who subtly pull us down, and avoid them whenever possible. Also, identify Militant Mediocres and let them know, in no uncertain terms, that they have no right to resent your enthusiasm or success.

D. *Fly with the eagles.* Associate with those people whom you admire most, and unabashedly seek their advice.

E. *Read.* Acquire the habit of reading inspiring and uplifting literature.

F. *Listen.* Utilize cassette training on a regular basis.

Outside

Our Outside Mini-Environment is our body. Our success within it is measured by the manner in which we care for and adorn ourselves. It is a function of health, grooming and attire. These are the principles we discussed, and actions we recommended, relative to this mini-environment:

Principle: Sensory Man of millenniums ago has become Mental Man of today. Somehow, in the process, he has divorced his mental and physical existences, and fallen out of touch with that portion of him, which is most of him, that thinks and feels without conscious thought. Our cardiovascular system (the heart and blood vessels), our respiratory system (the lungs), and our nervous system have enough to do, without us recklessly contributing to their demise.

Recommended action: First, quit smoking. Second, our caloric intake from the three major food categories must be controlled as indicated in the tables at the end of Chapter VII. Third, we must, of course, maintain the highest possible level of personal hygiene. Finally, we must remember that our human machine demands use, and that we must therefore engage in strenuous, play-oriented, physical activity on a regular basis.

Principle: We must not be lulled into an early grave by accepting the three great American myths: *I'm just big boned, I can be back in shape in two weeks,* and *I can quit anytime I want.* We must take such action as is necessary to overcome what Viktor Frankl called the tragic triad of human existence: guilt for our past, pain in the present, and death in the future.

Recommended action: Honestly and carefully appraise your fitness at this time. Take specific height, weight and circumference measurements. Scrutinize your image in the mirror, and determine exactly where improvement is needed. Find your sport, and play at it. Select an activity that will cause you to work up a sweat within the first 15 minutes, and play at it *at least* five hours each week. If you have no other preference, try jogging, since its health effects are enormously beneficial. Obtain a physical examination before you start, but don't seek the advice of a fat doctor. Find someone who can geniunely empathize with your desire to be fit. Start slowly, and build gradually, to avoid the injuries that can set you back for months.

Principle: Clothes designers are, God bless them, in the business of selling clothes. Their ability to earn an income is based upon their ability to convince you that what you bought last year is already obsolete. We must not be swayed by the trendy fashion dictates of designers, or by the admonitions of sales clerks. Instead, we must wear those clothes and employ those grooming habits that convey the *E.S.P.* of business success: Enthusiasm, Sincerity and Professionalism.

Recommended action: As a general rule, within the business community, relatively short hair tests best on men. Women's hair should be worn no longer than shoulder length. Styles should not be too severe, frilly, or frizzy. A well-scrubbed, clean-cut appearance is imperative. Invest as much money as is necessary in precision haircuts and fresh razor blades. Seek to build the classic combination of a vital, healthy, athletic physique with subtle, conservative, well-tailored apparel. Do not attempt to utilize what are essentially sport clothes for business wear. Men should invest freely in quality accessories, such as belts and long socks, to complete their professional appearance. Women must seek accessories that minimize the prejudices they are bound to encounter in the business community. For example, they should replace a purse with a leather briefcase whenever possible. Men, in most instances, should utilize what has become their standard business uniform: the three-piece vested suit. Colors should be rich, subtle and conservative. Fancy patterns and designs should be avoided on suits and shirts. White shirts test best. Always wear long sleeves. Whenever possible, women should wear what is rapidly becoming their standard business uniform: the skirted suit, complemented by a man-tailored blouse, a contrasting scarf, an attaché case, natural color pantyhose, and simple pumps no more than two inches high.

Principle: Our demeanor, or *body language,* will profoundly affect the impression we make on others.

Recommended action: Remember to analyze gestures in terms of clusters, not single movements. Upon meeting clients for the first time, attempt to create an interpersonal triangle by touching the least enthusiastic member of the triad first. Make sure your "good old American hand shake" is warm, firm and dry. Seek the appraisal of your close associates to discover if you have developed any physical characteristics that interfere with the message you wish to present.

Home

Our Home-Mini-Environment is our domestic existence. Our success within it is measured by the extent to which we control the way outside pressures permeate our inner domestic sanctum. These are the principles we discussed, and actions we recommended, relative to this mini-environment:

Principle: Our overriding goal within the Home Mini-Environment is *the present enjoyment of love.* In marriage, our Home Mini-Environment involves three people: *you, me* and *us.* In the context of marriage, love is not a noun, but a verb. *You* and *me* must grow and flourish individually, if *us* is to survive and prosper.

Recommended action: We must remember that, since love is unconditional, what we earn from our partner each day is not their love, but their continued companionship. To retain that companionship, we must make and keep three promises: First, we must promise to make promises only because we want to, not because we have to. A relationship should involve the mutual sharing of promises, dynamic in nature, that are freely given because of what the relationship is, not because that relationship happens to be called a marriage. Second, we must promise to share. Regardless of how mundane or routine might seem our existence on any given day, we must share it with one another so that we may grow together. Third, we must promise to work at being happy. We must remember that happiness is not automatic, and that marriage is merely a license to work at acquiring the happiness that we seek. The only *happily-ever-after* is the one we make.

To maintain an enjoyable sex relationship after marriage, we must: First, recognize that men and women have varying biologic needs at different times of their lives; second, relax; third, use intercourse as a tool for expressing affection, and not just as a method of obtaining sexual release; and fourth, devote ourselves to the satisfaction of our partner. Finally, we must utilize the six separate qualities of warmth, respect, encouragement, sex, affection and caring to say, "I love you," without actually having to utter the words.

Principle: Next to poor communication, poor money management and immature financial expectations are the primary cause of marital discord in America. They are a contributing cause to a substantial number of suicides, and are frequently the cause of lifelong personal bitterness and disappointment. Yet, by exercising common sense and restraint, we can avoid financial difficulties. The most valuable commodity that money can buy is the freedom to choose how we spend our time. If, as our income increases, our expenditures continue to exceed our income, we will remain slaves to our money, rather than causing our money to be a slave to us.

Recommended action: Apply, without exception, the *seven cures for a lean purse*, first outlined by George S. Clason in his book, *The Richest Man in Babylon*. First, for every ten dollars you receive, save one. Second, budget your expenses so that you can actually live on that nine-tenths of your income. Third, put what you save to work for you, so that it will create a steady stream of new revenue. Fourth, invest what you have only where it may be reclaimed if desired, and where it will collect a fair return. Consult only with those experienced in the profitable handling of money. Fifth, own your own home. Sixth, provide in advance for the needs of old age, and for the protection of your family. And seventh, cultivate your own powers to become wiser and more skillful at what you do, since it is your primary source of income. Concentrate first upon getting rich slowly. Remember: money pushed too far, too fast, in pursuit of large short-term gain tends to evaporate. And utilize the *priority planning* system of priorizing those items you wish to purchase, in order to avoid wasteful impulse expenditures.

Principle: The ability of the family to survive stems primarily from its flexibility. Today, however, most of its traditional roles have been stripped away. But there is a bright side to the new role of the family. Now, for the first time, its members can devote themselves almost exclusively to *the present enjoyment of love*. Each family member possesses certain rights and obligations. Children retain the right to grow, the right to learn, and the right to be loved. Parents retain the right to grow as adults, to enjoy each other privately, and to pursue their own interests. To enable each member to enjoy these rights, the family must work at building quality time together.

Recommended action: Remember that togetherness is more of a mental process than a physical one. With prior planning, we can

involve the entire family in common projects, such as those mentioned in Chapter IX, that cause them to interrelate and grow
together. There are literally hundreds of projects that might be
undertaken. Each is appropriate, as long as it provides each family member with the opportunity to experience *the present enjoyment of love.*

Work

Our Work-Mini-Environment is where we pursue our livelihood.
Our success within it depends upon the efficiency with which we
conduct ourselves, and the manner in which we relate to others,
while in pursuit of monetary and professional goals. These are the
principles we discussed, and actions we recommended, relative
to this mini-environment:

Principle: Talent is a form of energy. We each possess a different combination of the stuff, and some of us possess more than
others. Yet, the quantity of talent that we possess is as irrelevant
in determining our success as is the weight of a steam-roller in
determining the damage it can do to an asphalt parking lot. What
matters is the manner in which we channel the talent that we do
possess. We must funnel our abilities through as small a space as
possible, so that their intensity may be increased 100 fold. It all
begins with deciding specifically upon the goals we wish to accomplish.

Recommended action: The mechanics of effective goal setting
are relatively simple. But we must be methodical in our approach.
Utilizing the forms contained at the end of Chapter XIII
establish goals that are written, realistic and affirmatively
specific. Conduct the *End is Near Test* by listing, first, the things
you would do with your remaining 12 months if you had just one
year to live, and second, the goals you would otherwise establish
while expecting a life of normal duration. Reconcile the difference. Be sure that you are not establishing goals simply
because you believe they are expected of you. Use this exercise as
a device to determine what you geniunely want to accomplish.
Next, conduct the *Goals Statements* exercise by listing your
lifetime, one-year and 30-day goals for each mini-environment.
Then select from among the goals listed the most important goal

you have established in each mini-environment, and write it out, in your own words, as your personal *Goals Statement*. Be sure that the 30-day goals you establish in each mini-environment will logically lead to the accomplishment of your one-year goals, and be sure that your one-year goals will logically lead to the accomplishment of your lifetime goals.

Principle: Goals alone are not enough. We must translate our desires into practical, affirmative conduct. The process of planning involves managing our time. The application of fundamental time management principles can free us to spend our energies on the more creative pursuits required for the accomplishment of our goals. Rather than concentrating on being *efficient*, we should concentrate on being *effective*. Time management helps us work smarter, not harder. There is nothing complicated about the process. It's as simple as A-B-C.

Recommended action: A. Always make a list of activities for accomplishing your goals. Using the form provided at the end of Chapter XIV, construct *Possibility Lists* for the accomplishment of the most important goal in each of your four mini-environments. After listing as many activities as you can imagine, use a system such as our three-star method to select the one activity that you consider to be most important for the coming week.

B. Be sure to schedule your activities into your weeks and your days. Using the technique known as horizontal planning, schedule the high-priority activities that you have listed on your *Possibility Lists* into your coming week. Spend a few minutes on, perhaps, Sunday afternoon to review the lists you have made thus far. To conduct your horizontal planning, invest in a *Week-At-A-Glance Professional Appointments Book*. Be sure not to schedule yourself too tightly. Treat the time you have set aside for the conduct of high-priority activities as sacred, and insist that those hours not be interferred with. Make use of a to-do list every day. Schedule the high-priority activities that you have already entered on your weekly calendar into your daily plan. Then, plan the rest of your daily activities around them. Be sure to complete your daily work plan before you arrive at the office. Utilize our form for now, but later, make your own preprinted to-do list. Be sure it provides you with space for the listing of goals, for daily scheduling, for the listing of miscellaneous items, and for the placement of messages and notes.

C. Constantly evaluate the most effective use of your time right now. Apply the *80-20 Rule* at work. Carefully analyze the 20 percent of what you do that produces 80 percent of your income, and strive to spend more of your time on those activities. Beware of the *Pal-Enemy Syndrome*, and refuse to permit those around you to burn up your time at work. Finally, avoid procrastination by using the following three techniques: First, confront directly your tendency to procrastinate, and take time to feel a bit guilty about your doing so. Second, chip away at your tendency to procrastinate by undertaking small portions of an overwhelming high-priority activity whenever possible. And third, do nothing for a few minutes, thus giving yourself an opportunity to recharge your mental batteries.

Principle: Three factors profoundly influence our effectiveness at work. They are: first, our ability to deal with others; second, the manner in which we manage and organize our immediate work area; and third, the extent to which we self-actualize on the job.

Recommended action: When dealing with others, we must remember the advice of Cavett Robert, that we are, at all times, in the *people* business. Rather than viewing our Work Mini-Environment as a cut-throat, win-at-all-costs arena, we should regard it simply as a series of opportunities to help other people, and to make a profit in the process. We must strive to be the type of person with whom others wish to do business, remembering that people don't care how much we know until they know how much we care. We should permit the more positive aspects of our existence in our other mini-environments to reflect themselves in our Work Mini-Environment. Also, we must remain on guard to maintain the highest level of enthusiasm possible, so that the rest of the world does not pull us down to its level of complacency.

In managing our work area, we must try to keep only one project at a time within our field of vision. Our desk-tops should be kept relatively clean, and our desk drawers should not be used as depositories for every unused item that we have accumulated over the years. Our desk equipment should be kept where we can best get to it. For example, if we are right-handed, our phone should be on our left side. We should invest, if necessary, in our own minor accessories, such as staplers, tape dispensers, and the like.

Whenever possible, handle paper once. Begin a *New Projects File,* so that your entire filing system does not have to be reorganized every time your business takes a new direction. Establish your own *File 22.* Place your low-priority projects in an out-of-the-way desk drawer. Periodically re-examine them, and dispose of those that have solved themselves. Concentrate exclusively upon utilizing your fullest potential at work, rather than worrying about what imagined competitors might be doing. Remember: the only person against whom you ultimately compete is the guy in the mirror. Develop a reputation as a *go-giver*—the type of person with whom others most wish to do business. And always remember that you, and you alone, may choose mediocrity or excellence at work.

There you have it: the principles and recommendations contained in this book, summarized for your convenience.

I recommend that from time to time you review this chapter. As you come upon ideas that seem particularly helpful, review again the chapters from which they came. Then fashion your own remedy in the form of action that you believe to be most appropriate.

But in the last analysis, the ideas contained, and the actions recommended, herein will only be as helpful to you as the extent to which you will devote your energy and enthusiasm to their realization or accomplishment.

For it is, as always, up to you, and it will never work, not any of it, not an ounce, unless you have the courage to chase rainbows.

Success Environment
Monthly Progress Chart

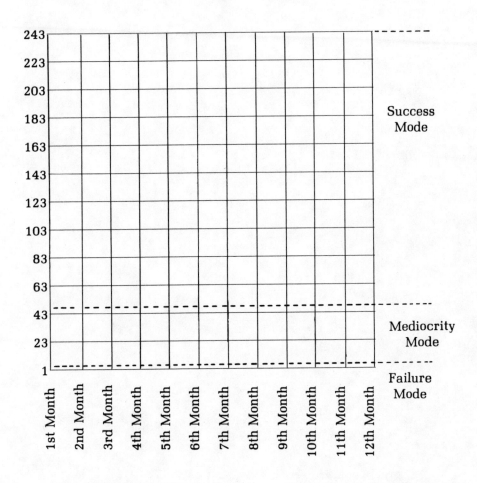

Figure 17-1

XVIII

"Y" Not Chase Rainbows?

A man's words are never the measure of his worth. Only his actions matter. Empty words are poor substitutes for actions filled with purpose. Action is the key. Conduct is the ultimate arbiter.

See the rainbow, my son.
Look lively.
See the colors so bright
And so true.
Keep trying, my son,
Keep striving.
Be all that you are.
Be you.

Tomorrow may never
Embrace us.
And the past has vanished
For us all.
'Tis today that's ever
The promise
Of our dreams, so handsome,
So tall.

It is for you, my son,
Not others,
For whom this rainbow shines.
Chase it now,
Forever and always,
For all time.
Chase rainbows, my son . . . Please . . .
Chase rainbows.

317

Chasing Rainbows

More than having a right to our dreams, we have the responsibility to pursue them.

In the last analysis, all of the self-help literature and all of the success formulas imaginable will not do us an iota of good if we do not dedicate ourselves, wholly and completely, at every level of our being, to the fullest realization of our potential.

But chasing rainbows is a tricky business. They are elusive things, and difficult to catch. Yet, what we must remember as we chase our personal rainbows, whatever they may be, is that their capture is not the thing that ultimately will have made the chase worthwhile. Rather, it will have been the chase itself that was its own reward. It is the process of pursuing our goals, not the mere final act of attaining them, that makes us all we can be, that calls upon us to use our every ounce of ability and talent.

It is the chase that counts, not the capture. For when all is said and done, we will remember not so much the goals that we attained, or the rainbows that we caught. We will remember, instead, the thrill, the excitement, the pleasure, the joy, the exaltation of the chase.

Here's To Those Who Chase Rainbows

Most great people were unusual people, and they faced more than their share of obstacles.

Thomas Edison was kicked out of school more than once. Lincoln was a perennial outcast. They laughed at the theories of Galileo. The Wright brothers were subjected to severe ridicule until that idiotic contraption they were building in the barn actually flew through the air. John Bunyon and O. Henry wrote literary masterpieces while in prison. Robert Burns was once an illiterate drunk. Beethoven was deaf. Milton was blind. And when Henry Marconi announced to his friends that he could send messages by invisible waves through the air, they tried to have him committed.

But each, in his own way, kept chasing rainbows. And so must we. History does not remember the names of those who scoffed at the Galileos, the Edisons, the Lincolns, the Wrights, or the Marconis. It does not remember the critics of their time. It remembers only those who pursued their dreams, those with the courage to proceed, and those who were undeterred by the critical voices around them. In the last analysis, only those who chased rainbows do we remember. Only they have earned a place in our hearts, and in our history.

Rocky Revisited

It was the original version of the movie *Rocky* that moved me most. I saw it at a time in my life when I needed to be reminded that just about anything we set our minds to was possible.

The movie *Rocky* involved a slightly punch-drunk heavyweight boxer. Rocky was a nice guy, and you loved him, but he was a bum. He was still fighting in the same gym in Philadelphia where he started; and it was obvious he never used the abilities he had. He lived in a dirty, one-room flat, and all the people he knew took him lightly, and with good reason.

But then one day opportunity fell in his lap. It was the Bicentennial, and the heavyweight champion of the world came to town and announced that, in the spirit of America's birthday, he would give an unknown challenger the opportunity to fight for the coveted championship of the world. They selected Rocky's name. Reluctantly, he accepted.

At first he didn't want the opportunity, but after he accepted, a change began to occur in Rocky. He started seeing himself as the champ.

So he started training. He got up at 4 a.m., drank five raw eggs, and went out to run. The first morning, as he ran up some steps at the end of his run, he almost died from the pain.

But he kept seeing himself as the champ. So he kept training, and for six weeks he trained like a man obsessed. He worked as hard as any man possibly could, and beyond; and a strange thing happened to the people around him. They started acting like winners, too. The whole city would cheer for him as he ran through the streets. The children would follow him, and the merchants would toss him fruit, and on the morning of the day before the fight, when again he ran up those steps, he took them four and five at a time. When he reached the top, he turned with his arms in the air, and as he faced the rising sun, he was ready—and mentally he was the champ.

But the night before the fight, he stood alone in the ring in the center of the huge, empty arena where the bout would be held. He thought about the real champion, and what an outstanding boxer he really was.

He went home and sat on the edge of the bed and woke his bride-to-be and said, "There's no way I can beat that guy."

She raised herself up on one elbow and said, "Well, what are we going to do about it?"

He said, "I want to go the distance. No one has ever gone 15 rounds with the champ. I want to go the whole distance, so the people here will know I'm not just another bum."

What followed was probably the greatest fight sequence ever filmed. For 15 rounds they stood there and nearly beat each other to death, for, if not very fancy, Rocky was a very strong man—and he had heart.

When the bell ended the 15th round, pure chaos reigned in that arena. Although you couldn't really hear what was going on over the shouts and confusion, it was evident that the bout had been scored a split decision in favor of the champ, not Rocky.

But Rocky's victory was won. He had reached his goal, and all he cared about in the post-fight confusion of that ring was finding his girl. He did, and she told him she loved him, and the movie ended. Everyone cheered and cried.

But there are two things that have always bothered me about that movie.

First was the way that the opportunity to fight the champ just fell in Rocky's lap. That kind of thing might happen in the movies, but not in real life. It's a funny thing about opportunity and luck in real life. The harder we work, the more opportunities just seem to fall in our laps. The harder we work, the luckier we get.

No one's going to drop opportunities in your lap or mine. We—you and I—have got to make them happen.

Second, it bothered me that Rocky sold himself short. For six weeks he was the champ in his mind. For six weeks he sustained that mental image. For six weeks he acted, thought, and worked like the champ. But on the night before the fight he sold himself short. Standing alone in that arena, he allowed the bigness of what he'd gotten himself into to intimidate him into lowering his goals.

We belong at center ring! In the largest arena imaginable! And we must *never, ever* let anyone or anything convince us that we don't!

But what bothered me most about the doubt he suffered was the opportunity his girl-friend had—and blew—to help him the night before the fight.

Her response to what he said as he sat on the edge of her bed, doubting himself, ought to go down in the *Guinness Book of World Records* as the worst possible response anyone could have given anybody at a time like that.

When he said, "I can't beat him," she said, "Well, what are we going to do about it?"

Although she meant well, she had the opportunity to help that man, and she blew it. A few kind words, a modicum, an iota, of sincere encouragement is all he would have needed to sustain his mental image as champ.

And the time to have told him she loved him was before—not after—the fight.

For in the last analysis, we have only two things of real value as we pass through this life: we have ourselves and each other.

So please don't let this, or any other, day pass without helping somebody you love.

GeeI'mgladIdids And DarnIwishIhads

It boils down to this: to chase rainbows, we must have faith in ourselves.

When we use the word *faith*, we usually refer to faith in God. But perhaps of equal importance (and perhaps, theologically, it is the same) is faith in ourselves.

We all appreciate the value of having faith in ourselves, because we all know that there are just two kinds of people in this world: the *GeeI'mgladIdids* and the *DarnIwishIhads*.

The *DarnIwishIhads* plod through life looking at challenges and opportunities, saying, "Nope, I can't do that. Nope, that can't be done." Then when someone comes along and does precisely what it is the *DarnIwishIhads* said couldn't be done, the *DarnIwishIhads* say, "Darn, I wish I had!"

Next are the *GeeI'mgladIdids*. These are the people who know the value of having faith in themselves. When they see challenges and opportunities, they seize them; and when they try and succeed—and they do succeed far more often than they fail—while others say, "Darn, I wish I had," they say, "Gee, I'm glad I did."

There are three periods in every person's life when the *GeeI'mgladIdids* and the *DarnIwishIhads* are separated.

The first period is best described as the *Love and Affection Period*.

Two young fellows, each about 16, are standing on the street corner next to the high school gym. They are loaded with problems. They're either too short or too tall, or too fat or too skinny, and, to make matters worse, in recent years they have both acquired a need for what we will politely call love and affection. To date, their need has gone unfulfilled. As they stand there, thinking about their problems, who drives by, in his shiny, red Triumph, but Vern Varsity.

Vern has everything. He's captain of the football team, has muscles on his muscles, a diamond smile—and the head cheerleader sitting in the car with him. Vern waves at our two friends, and our two friends wave back.

One of our friends is a *DarnIwishIhad*. He looks at Vern and thinks to himself, "Boy, I sure would like to be like Vern someday, but I guess I never will be." He sticks his hands in his pockets and trudges home.

Our other young hero is a *GeeI'mgladIdid*. He knows the value of having faith in himself. He looks at Vern and says, "If Vern can do it, *I* can do it!" He gets a job working nights to save money to buy a car, and runs laps around the gym to get his body into fighting condition.

A year later, *DarnIwishIhad* is standing on that same street corner thinking about the same problems, when who drives by— in his shiny, red Corvette—but *GeeI'mgladIdid*. An attractive young coed is sitting in the car with him.

The two friends see each other and wave. As *GeeI'mgladIdid* drives off in his Corvette, *DarnIwishIhad* watches his friend, thinks of all the great things his friend had done for himself during the past year, and says, "Darn, I wish I had!"

GeeI'mgladIdid looks in his rearview mirror at his friend, *DarnIwishIhad*. He looks at his shiny, red Corvette. He looks at the attractive young coed, and he says, "Gee, I'm glad I did!"

The second period in every person's life, when the *GeeI'mgladIdids* are separated from the *DarnIwishIhads*, is the *Rags to Riches Period*.

It's ten, maybe twenty years later now. *GeeI'mgladIdid* and *DarnIwishIhad* work together at the widget factory. On this particular evening, they're sitting together at a meeting of the local Elks Club.

Suddenly *GeeI'mgladIdid* turns to his friend and says, "Darn, (they're on a first-name basis now) I just had a great idea! If someone would bottle those widgets we manufacture at the widget manufacturing plant, he could make a fortune! Let's quit our jobs at the plant and go into the widget bottling business!"

But *DarnIwishIhad* says, "No, I can't do that! No, that can't be done!"

Yet, *GeeI'mgladIdid* knows the value of having faith in himself. He quits his job at the widget manufacturing plant and goes into the widget bottling business. For a long time the hours are long, money is short, and it looks like he might not make it. But he does make it.

A few years later, *DarnIwishIhad* is standing in front of the old widget plant, lunch pail in hand, waiting for a bus, when who drives by—in his shiny, red Cadillac—but *GeeI'mgladIdid*. His loving wife is sitting in the front seat with him. Two healthy children adorn the back seat. He's a wealthy man in more ways than one.

The two friends see each other and wave. As *GeeI'mgladIdid* drives off in his Cadillac, *DarnIwishIhad* looks out after him and thinks of all the great things his friend had done for himself during the past few years, and he says, "Darn, I wish I had!"

GeeI'mgladIdid looks in the rearview mirror at his old friend *DarnIwishIhad*. He looks at his beautiful car, at his happy wife, at his two beautiful children, and at his bank book.

He looks again at his bank book.

And he says, "Gee, I'm glad I did!"

But it is the third period in every person's life, when the *GeeI'mgladIdids* are separated from the *DarnIwishIhads*, that is the most important period of all—the *Looking Back Period*.

It's many, many years later. *Gee* and *Darn* are sitting together on a park bench. They're both very old. Each knows that his journey is almost over. Each, in his own way, reflects upon the life he has spent.

GeeI'mgladIdid remembers a life filled with challenge and with opportunity. When he thinks of all the risks he took, and all the faith it took, and all the success he had, for one last time he says, "Gee, I'm glad I did!"

But *DarnIwishIhad* remembers a life far different. He remembers a life of "no's and "maybe's," and "I can't do that's," and "that can't be done's." As he looks at *GeeI'mgladIdid*, he remembers all the great things his old friend had done for himself during his lifetime, and for one last time he says:

"Darn . . . I wish I had."

Faith in our God, yes; but always in ourselves as well. For, if each of us can find and develop that part of us which is a *GeeI'mgladIdid*, we will be the better for it, and this world will be the better for us all.

The Invincible Man: A Short Play[1]

The curtain rises. At center stage is a chair. Next to the chair is a small table with a phone. Nearby is a dresser and a large mirror. An alarm clock is on the dresser. The room belongs to The Invincible Man. He will pass through this room three times, in three acts: once at age 25, once at age 45, and again at age 75.

Act One: Age 25

VOICE FROM OFFSTAGE: Hey, wait up, you guys! I'll be out in a minute! Wait up!

Enter The Invincible Man, at age 25. He's wearing a white, three-piece suit. His shirt is open at the collar. His trousers are flared, with no pockets. His hair is disheveled. He runs toward the dresser, catches a glimpse of his torso as he passes the mirror, and gives himself an approving nod. He opens the top dresser drawer and shuffles through it.

THE INVINCIBLE MAN: Where's that brush, man? I got to get ready, or those guys are going to take off without me. I wish I had more time. I must be getting old. I'm slowing down. I got to relax. Where *is* that brush? Ow!

---

[1]CAUTION: Professionals and amateurs are hereby warned that *The Invincible Man*, being fully protected under the Copyright Laws of the United States of America, the British Commonwealth, including the Dominion of Canada, and all other countries of the Berne and Universal Copyright Conventions, is subject to royalty. All rights, including professional, amateur, recording, motion picture, recitation, lecturing, public reading, radio and television broadcasting, and the rights of translation into foreign languages, are strictly reserved, permission for which must be secured in writing from the author. All inquires for licenses and permissions for stock and amateur uses should be addressed to Keith DeGreen, c/o Summit Enterprises Inc., 3928 E. Corrine Drive, Phoenix, Arizona 85032.

He closes the dresser drawer on his finger. He backs away from the dresser and sits down on the chair.

To hell with it! Those guys can wait. Oh, great! It's starting to swell. I'm glad it's not bleeding. I'd never get a stain out of this suit. I'm getting too up-tight. I got to relax. Mainly, I'm in control, but this stuff can't last forever. Never thought I'd get tired of partying. But I guess I am. At least a little. Not entirely, mind you. But a little. It still beats not partying, but there's got to be something else.

Oh well, I've got plenty of time. No need to worry about it now. But these guys have got me worrying about all kinds of stuff that doesn't really matter. Chasing skirts all over town. And Smitty keeps coming up with these "can't lose" deals. Big money schemes, and they keep coming up zero—and I keep losing half my pay on 'em.

A horn beeps from offstage.

All right! All right! I'm coming (*shouting toward offstage*)! Hold your horses!

What's the hurry (*to himself*)? They're just going to go to another club and hang around. Smitty will tell some more lies, and Fred will tell us all how he's going to get rich. Then some of us will get lucky and the rest of us will get drunk. Then we'll get home too late, and get up too early tomorrow for work. Then, after work we'll come home, shower, and go out again.

It's not a bad life. (*He gets up and walks to the mirror.*) I'm still looking good. I'm fast on my feet, and strong. I might be getting a little soft from those beers, but I can get rid of that in no time. And I've got plenty of time to do it in. Yeah! (*admiring himself*) I'm looking good! No doubt about it. I can find all the women I want. But maybe Evelyn's right. God, I'd hate to think it, but maybe she's right. Maybe it is about time to settle down. If I did, I suppose it would be with her. Of course, she'll always be there. There's no rush. Can't blame her for loving me. (*He looks again in the mirror and smiles at himself.*) You dude, you! But I guess one of these days she and me better get down to it. But I'm not ready for that scene yet. Besides, I've got plenty of time. She'll be around.

What I really got to do is make some money. I mean, I've got to start thinking about my future. The boss wants me to go back to school. I told him not right now, I'm too busy, but I'd think about it for a few years from now. That seemed to satisfy him. He knows

I'm a good man. He's gonna stick by me, let me progress at my own rate. Man, I don't want to go back to school now. I just got out! Time to have some fun. There'll be plenty of time to buckle down. I've got an unlimited future in front of me at work. It won't be long now. I'll really put my nose to the grindstone and start making some *real* money.

Horn blares again. This time with more persistence.

All right! All right! Damn! Where is that brush?

He reaches into the bottom dresser drawer and pulls out a brush. Quickly, he brushes his hair and throws the brush on top of the dresser. He turns to run off stage, then stops himself.

Wait a minute! A minute ago I was thinking about not even going out with those guys. I'm like a trained seal. They honk their horn and I run. Maybe I ought to just stay home tonight, relax. Maybe I ought to call Evelyn and start getting serious. Maybe I ought to review those college catalogs. Maybe I ought to do all that stuff tonight.

He sits down on the chair, feet flat on the floor.

Yeah! Maybe that's what I'll do. I'll just stay here.

There is a long pause as The Invincible Man sits on the chair. He looks around. He begins to fidget. Suddenly, he jumps up.

Then again, maybe I'll stay home tomorrow night! There's plenty of time to do the rest of that stuff.

He gives the mirror a final check.

We are goin' schuckin' and jivin' *tonight!* Look out woman-kind, here I come! Man, I'm 25 years old, and I'm ready to roll! I'm invincible!

Black-out.

Act Two: Age 45

The phone rings. The Invincible Man runs on stage, toward the phone. He is heavier now, and fully 20 years older than he was in the preceding act. Breathless, he sits down in the chair and answers the phone.

THE INVINCIBLE MAN: Hello? Hello? Evelyn, is that you? Who? What? No, the lady of the house is not in. No, I don't want aluminum siding. No, I don't care if you have a special. No, we don't need storm doors either. (*He hangs up the phone.*)

The lady of the house sure isn't in! I can't imagine where she could have gone. Fifteen years of marriage out the window, just like that! And for no reason! Can you imagine? Just last month, I said, "Evelyn, let's take a romantic vacation. Just the two of us. We'll go fishing." Even that didn't satisfy her. Can you imagine not wanting to go fishing? I can't believe it. I just can't believe it.

And I just don't have the time to be worrying about this now, either. I've got so much on my mind. The world situation, for one thing. I work my fingers to the bone and I can hardly keep up with inflation. It's frustrating, I tell you. Frustrating. The politicians are ruining the system. No wonder I can't get ahead.

But look at me, will you? (*He rises to look in the mirror.*) I'm filling out! Strong as an ox, I tell you! Strong as an ox! I'm in the prime of my life. Why, most of that gut is muscle! Hell, I can compete with the *best* of 'em. I can be back in shape in no time! In the meantime, I better get these pants let out a bit.

I just can't believe she's gone. And what a time to choose—with all that's going on at work right now. The boss and I really had it out. Can you imagine? I finally took that course he's been begging me to take for years, and now he won't promote me. He says I don't move fast enough. Well I told *him* a thing or two! I told him he's not *motivating* me to move any faster. Hell, if he'd give me a raise I'd show him how motivated I could get! But it doesn't matter. I've got a good, safe job. The sky's the limit. No one in that company knows as much about our product as I do. Those young guys may have all the energy, but *I'm* the one who has the knowledge.

Yes sir, the sky's still the limit for me. There's still plenty of time. Yes sir, I've got as much going for me right now as I did 20 years ago. You bet! Why hell, I'm invincible!

I wonder if Evelyn's going to come back.

Black-out.

Act Three: Age 75

The alarm rings.

VOICE FROM OFFSTAGE SHOUTS: I'm coming! I'm coming!

The voice obviously belongs to an old man. Very slowly, The Invincible Man totters onto the stage. He makes his way toward the alarm clock. As he passes the mirror, he glances at himself, shrugs, and moves on. Finally he reaches the alarm clock and turns it off. He opens a dresser drawer and rummages through it.

THE INVINCIBLE MAN: All right! All right! It's time to take my pill. The little green one, I think. Or is it the little blue one? I forget which. It seems like, these days, there's a lot of little things I forget or confuse. I remember back in . . . or was it . . .? Well, whatever, it was a long time ago. I remember I . . . or was that me? I forget. Oh well.

He sits down and swallows his pill.

I'm still fit as a fiddle, though! Yes sir! What does that doctor know? Young buck! Tells me I don't have much time. Shows what *he* knows. Why, I'm as fit as I was back in . . . well . . . whatever. Yep! I can still compete with the best of 'em.

I finally got this old house fixed up the way I want it. I wonder where . . . what was her name? I wonder where she is now. I wonder if she's still alive. Still can't figure out why she left. It's a shame, though. She'd have been a lot happier here. You know, I guess I would have been happier, too, if she'd stayed. She might have helped me through that time at work. It would have helped to know someone cared.

The day they retired me, why . . . I thought they were going to promote me, and they retired me! They kicked me out of the company! The boss laughed and said they had to make room for the younger men. The younger men. Hell, I could compete with the best of 'em. Still can! There's still not a man there who knows as much about our product as I do. I just don't understand it, I tell you. I just don't understand. They just don't realize how much I know, how much I could have offered.

There is a long pause. The Invincible Man appears to be dozing.

You know, sometimes I wonder why. (*Very slowly he rises and walks to the mirror.*) Sometimes I wonder why this world just seemed to pass me by. I can remember as a younger man—much, much younger—why, I was more of a boy than a man, it all seemed so right and organized, and clear, and simple. And there was all the time in the world to do just anything I pleased, because there was always the next day, and the next, and the next. And I was a healthy young buck, and I enjoyed my play. And even though I knew the time would come for me to knuckle down, I never quite seemed to get around to it.

But even when I was older, I had so much to offer. I don't know why it didn't shine through. It must have been the things I did, or said. But maybe it was the things I didn't say, or do, that mattered.

Maybe it was the rest of the world that didn't give me my breaks. Maybe it wasn't me at all. An old man takes solace in that kind of reasoning. It's so much easier to blame someone else.

But I am *invincible*, I tell you! *Invincible!* My life is hardly over. And with what I've learned to date, I could conquer the world.

If only I knew then what I know now. I'm invincible, I tell you. I'm invincible.

The Invincible Man returns to the chair and sits down.

I will live forever. Forever.

At least until I run out of pills.

Black-out. Curtain closes.

The Parable Of The Precious Stones

In Nineveh, of Assyria, along the Tigris, which was the northeast border of the Fertile Crescent that extended from Eridu of Babylonia, near the Persian Gulf, to Thebes of Egypt, along the Nile, in the age of the Patriarchs, 2,000 years before the birth of Christ, there lived the greatest teacher of his time.

His name was Hazor. This is his story.

The Teacher And The Parable

As usual, they gathered at the teaching place on the east bank of the river, one hour after dawn. The three of them, Jashka, Gebal and Kaleb, arrived before Hazor. The young men were excited, for today they were to graduate! Hazor's three prized students would each be congratulated by the master himself, but only after the final lesson.

"What could he possibly say today that we have not already covered?" asked Gebal.

"We have little more to learn, save for what experience teaches," said Jashka. He turned to Kaleb. "Don't you agree, silent one?"

"Our need for knowledge is never ending," said Kaleb.

"Aha! So he speaks!" shouted Gebal.

"A miracle!" chuckled Jashka. "For three years barely a word. Yet today the makings of an orator! Assemble the masses at the Temple! Kaleb speaks!"

The laughter of Jashka and Gebal ended suddenly. The teacher, Hazor, had arrived. He stood on the river bank, facing them. Behind him, the morning sun glistened off the water so brightly that his face was but a shadow.

Silence fell upon them. The students sat and waited for Hazor to begin. Finally he spoke. Softly. Slowly.

"I will tell you now The Parable of the Precious Stones. It contains the most important lesson you will ever learn. Apply its moral, and you will live forever. Ignore its moral, and you will perish.

"Each day the master entered the square. Each day he brought with him a handful of precious stones. Sometimes he brought diamonds from the mountainous Kizzuwatna region near the Great Sea. Other times he brought rubies from Dedan near Midian, and occasionally he brought emeralds from the strange and unnamed land to the east, beyond the Caspian.

"Each day he sought, at random, someone in the square; whereupon he presented to the fortunate individual at least one half of the stones he had brought with him.

"Yet, despite the large number of stones given away by the master, his supply always replenished itself. Indeed, it is said that he was the most fabulously wealthy of all men.

"With his gifts, however, the master did impose a condition. To each recipient he would say, 'Tomorrow you must return to the square with at least one half of the stones you have received, and you must give those stones to another, as I have given these to you. You must repeat this process once each day for as long as you shall live, giving always at least one half of the precious stones you possess. Your supply will not diminish as you suspect. Obey my directive, accept this condition, and your wealth will multiply beyond your wildest imaginings.'

"But there were three at the marketplace to whom the master offered stones who did not comply. First was the doubter. He said, 'I will not take your stones, for if they are offered for free they must have no value. Besides, even if their value is immense, I would, by your plan, have given them all away within a few days.' And he walked away.

"Second was the thief. He said, 'Yes, I will do what you say without question,' but all along he had no intention of sharing the stones. He took the stones the master gave him and hoarded them to his own purpose. Within a fortnight he had spent the last of them on frivolous and temporal pleasures.

"Finally came the hypocrite. When he accepted the stones, he said, 'Yes, upon my sacred oath, I will share these with others.' True to his word, he shared for a time, and his wealth increased accordingly. But soon the pressures of business and luxury forced him to devote more and more of his wealth to selfish ends. He began not to share, but continued to profess compliance with the master's condition. Before long, he too, was without wealth.

"This, my students, ends The Parable of the Precious Stones. If its moral is not by now clear to you, then its discussion is pointless. For you have been trained by Hazor, the teacher; and if you cannot mold your own conclusion about what you have heard, and fashion your life accordingly, then there is nothing more I can say to save you.

"Go now and enter the world of commerce, and apply the principles you have learned."

"Hear! Hear!" shouted Jashka. "I shall apply this immortal teaching to my every transaction!"

"And so, too, shall I!" cheered Gebal. "The teachings of Hazor shall ring from my lips and guide my heart!"

Kaleb rose. He walked to where Hazor stood. Silently he touched the teacher's hand and walked away.

Jashka whispered to Gebal, "He says nothing, do you see? He is a doubter, I tell you. Mark my words. A doubter."

The Students' Lives

And it came to pass that each student grew to full manhood, and each took a wife and fathered children and entered commerce as a merchant, and each was initially well respected within the region, for they were known to have been students of Hazor, the greatest of all teachers.

Jashka utilized all of Hazor's teachings, except that he did not take the parable to heart. Nevertheless, soon he acquired great wealth. Yet, those around him came to know Jashka as an ungiving man, concerned only with the accumulation of property. Those who sought his advice and counsel, or a few coins for some worthy cause, were turned away. In time the three sons of Jashka turned away from their father, seeking careers of their own and wanting nothing to do with the business that Jashka had built.

Jashka died while still a relatively young man. Few mourned his passing.

Likewise, Gebal applied all of Hazor's teachings. Soon he, too, had acquired great wealth. But unlike Jashka, he professed from the outset compliance with the moral of the parable; and indeed, at first he gave freely from what he had to others.

But soon commerce within Assyria diminished because of the fighting in nearby Mitanni, and Gebal and Jashka competed harshly against one another for the available trade. Gebal found it necessary to devote more and more of his wealth to his own ends. Nevertheless, he continued to profess his compliance with the moral of the parable.

Not long after it had become apparent to most that Gebal's actions fell short of his words, he was found stabbed to death in the courtyard of his home. There were many suspects to the crime, but none were pursued.

For years, Kaleb worked quietly to build his reputation as a merchant. He spoke little of Hazor or of his teachings, but each day he found a way to give to another a substantial portion of whatever he had.

His business grew slowly at first, but then more and more rapidly, as each two new customers would bring four, and each four would bring eight, and each eight, sixteen, and so on, until finally Kaleb stood among the wealthiest men in Nineveh.

His family was happy too, and his sons worked hard for their father between their lessons, and spoke cheerfully of the day they would reach manhood and build upon what Kaleb had done.

This pleased Kaleb. Still, he continued giving from what he had. Still, his customers and his wealth increased.

The Teacher's Passing

Kaleb was in his courtyard breathing deeply the pre-dawn air when the messenger arrived.

"Come quickly," the messenger panted. "Hazor the teacher is ill. We think it is his time. You are honored among men. He requests your presence."

Together they ran to the teacher's cottage. Already the word had spread throughout Nineveh. Many had gathered by the great teacher's door. There was much wailing and grief in the air. Before he entered, Kaleb turned to the crowd.

"I know nothing of his death," he said. "But of the teacher's life I know much. He has not lived to spend his final moments here surrounded by grief. Silence your cries and rejoice out loud at his having shared life with us, or remove yourself from this house."

Kaleb entered the dark cottage and walked the few steps to the room wherein the teacher lay.

Hazor beckoned him closer.

"Sit by my side, my son."

Kaleb obeyed.

"What think you of Jashka's death?" asked Hazor.

"But what is there to think?" answered Kaleb. "He was the thief. He took what gifts you offered without ever intending to share with others."

"Yes! And how I rejoice that you understand," said Hazor. "But remember these things: A thief is to be pitied, for he steals mainly from himself. To him we must respond with compassion, and we must thank the Gods that we possess enough talent that we can earn our own way without having to steal from others."

"I shall remember," said Kaleb.

"And what think you of Gebal?" asked Hazor.

"The worst, I fear," said Kaleb. "He lied to all who would listen. He was a hypocrite."

"He deserved to die!" said Hazor. "I might have killed him myself, were it not that someone beat me to it! For he stole that which was of most value to others—their good will and good name. Beware the hypocrites, Kaleb! Beware the destruction they bring!"

"But does the teacher see this student as the doubter?" asked Kaleb.

"No! By the Gods, no!" Hazor replied. "You remained silent. But a man's words are never the measure of his worth. Only his actions matter. Empty words are poor substitutes for actions filled with purpose. No, Kaleb, you *lived* what you learned, and you gave what you had. You gave. Action is the key. Conduct is the ultimate arbiter.

"For, Kaleb—and this by now you must know—it was I who was the master in our parable. It was I who sought each day to give. It was I who gave from what precious stones were mine; and it was I who prospered greatly. I am, indeed, the wealthiest of all men. As you can see, I have little in the way of material things, but I possess the warmth and love and respect of those around me. What man of gold could ask for more?

"For these were the precious stones I had to give—my knowledge and the gift to teach it. And each of us possesses precious stones of his own, always different, but there nonetheless, always ready for another. And our supply is infinite; for the more of what we have we give, the more we shall receive.

"And it is because of this that I will never die. Now that you, Kaleb, have mastered the art of giving, my greatest guarantee of immortality is your quiet, burning ambition to give. For through you, another giver will be found, and he will find another, and so on, for eternity, and I will live in each of them.

"Therefore, watch me now as I close these eyes for the last time and begin my life forever."

Please chase rainbows.

Please.

Remember those who did, and won. Remember Rocky. Remember the *GeeI'mgladIdids* and the *DarnIwishIhads*. Remember The Invincible Man; and by all means live The Parable of the Precious Stones.

For the solutions to all the world's problems, large or small, begin—and end—with you.

An old story relates that a young father came home from work and wearily sat down in his easy chair. He picked up a magazine and started paging through it.

His 6-year-old boy walked up to the side of his father's chair and said, "Dad, let's play! Let's play!"

The father said, "No son, not now. I'm tired."

But the little boy persisted. He said, "Please Dad, let's play! Let's play!"

Then, an idea occurred to the father. In the magazine was a map of the world. He ripped the map out of the magazine and tore it into little pieces.

He handed the pieces to the boy and said, "Son, why don't you go up to your room and put this map of the world together like a puzzle. When you have it all pasted up, then we'll play."

The father thought he had bought himself at least an hour. But ten minutes later, his little 6-year-old was right back by the side of the chair. He had the map pasted up without an error.

The father looked at the map, and looked at his son, and said, "This is incredible. How did you manage to put it together so fast?"

With a look of pride, the little boy said, "It was easy, Dad. You see, on the back of the map was a picture of a man and a woman.

"And I just figured, if you put the man and woman together right, the world would take care of itself."

Please . . . chase rainbows.

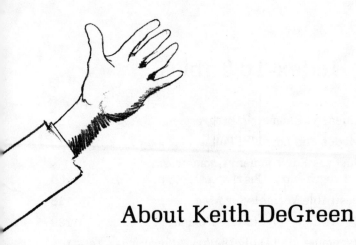

About Keith DeGreen

As exceptionally talented a speaker as he is a writer, Keith DeGreen spends much of his time addressing audiences around the globe.

A lawyer by training, Keith combines humor, wit and enthusiasm to produce enormously entertaining and informative keynote talks, banquet addresses, and seminars.

He is the author of the three-volume cassette training library, *Creating A Success Environment*, the cassette album, *Positive Living Through Goal Setting and Time Management*, and is the co-author of two other books: *Stand Up, Speak Out, and Win*, and *The Joy of Selling*, both published by Summit Enterprises Inc.

For additional information regarding either his availability as a speaker or his various cassette programs and books, contact Keith in care of:

Summit Enterprises Inc.
3928 East Corrine Drive
Phoenix, Arizona 85032
Telephone: (602) 992-5372

Index To Tables